Sullivan County, Tennessee

DEED BOOK 6

1809–1815

❧❧

Sallie Hayes

Heritage Books
2025

HERITAGE BOOKS

AN IMPRINT OF HERITAGE BOOKS, INC.

Books, CDs, and more—Worldwide

For our listing of thousands of titles see our website
at
www.HeritageBooks.com

A Facsimile Reprint
Published 2025 by
HERITAGE BOOKS, INC.
Publishing Division
5810 Ruatan Street
Berwyn Heights, MD 20740

— Publisher's Notice —
In reprints such as this, it is often not possible to remove
blemishes from the original. We feel the contents of this
book warrant its reissue despite these blemishes and
hope you will agree and read it with pleasure.

International Standard Book Number
Paperbound: 978-0-7884-8845-0

Before 1779, most of the lands in the area of what is presently considered Upper East Tennessee was referred to as Washington County, North Carolina. Many settlers from Virginia believed they were in Virginia's territory, when in actuality neither state gave the settlers help or protection.

Sullivan County, established in 1779, was named for Major General John Sullivan, a New Hampshire patriot who won acclaim during the early years of the American Revolution. Sullivan is the second oldest county in the state of Tennessee and possibly one of the richest sources for genealogical research.

In February, 1780, a commission composed of Justices of the Peace was selected to govern the new county of Sullivan. The commission consisted of Isaac Shelby, David Looney, William Christie, John Dunham, William Wallace, Samuel Smith, Gilbert Christian, Henry Clark, George Maxwell, Anthony Bledsoe, John Anderson, and Joseph Martin. John Rhea was appointed Clerk of the Court and Nathan Clark, was Sheriff.

The county was officially formed by the North Carolina General Assembly after the Virginia-North Carolina state line survey showed the area was in North Carolina, not Virginia.

These deeds were copied from WPA Records. Care has been taken to copy the records exactly, even when the name is spelled differently within one deed.

This book contains Sullivan County Deed Book Vol. 6, 1809-1815, consisting of approximately 585 deeds.

Some of the family names that can be found are: Booher, Cranberger, Longacre, and Spurgin, just to name a few.

Maybe the one door you haven't opened yet can be unlocked with these deeds.

Sallie Hayes
October, 1995

TENNESSEE

RECORDS OF SULLIVAN COUNTY

DEED BOOK NO. 6
1809 - 1815

COPYING HISTORICAL RECORDS PROJECT
Official Project No. 465-44-3-115

COPIED UNDER WORK'S PROGRESS ADMINISTRATION

MRS. JOHN TROTWOOD MOORE
STATE LIBRARIAN & ARCHIVIST, SPONSOR

MRS. ELIZABETH D. COPPEDGE
DIRECTOR OF WOMEN'S PROFESSIONAL PROJECTS

MRS. PENELOPE JOHNSON ALLEN
STATE SUPERVISOR

MRS. MARGARET HELMS RICHARDSON
PROJECT SUPERVISOR

COPIED BY
MISS HELEN CARTER

TYPED BY
MRS. BESSIE BRADSHAW
MISS JEAN PURKEY

OCTOBER 1, 1938

INDEX

(NOTE: Page numbers in this index refer to those of the original volume from which this copy is made. These numbers are carried in the left hand margin of this copy.)

Deed Book No. VI. 1809-1815. Pages 1 - 545.

GRANTEE			:	GRANTOR	
Blevins, John	434		:	Cox, Edward	19,20
Baughman, Nathan & Jonathan		444	:	Commissioners	38,63,306,307
Bragg, David	456		:	Capps, Thomas	23,318,364
Baskett, William	458,505		:	Catron, Peter	29,266,489
Britt, B. & John	459		:	Christian, Robt.	75,343,412,414
Barns, William	466		:	Cade, Hewes	79
Bowser, John	474,510		:	Cole, John	135
Booher, Martin	497		:	Crocket, Andw.	144,536
Barton & Riddle	512		:	Catron, Henry	176
Burkhart, George)	525		:	Christian, Patrick	188,194
Booher, Jacob)			:	Childres, William	190
Cole, Elisha	19,430		:	Clark, James	251
Catron, John	29		:	Copass, William	300
Curtain, John	58		:	Cawood, John	316
Cooke, Jacob	63		:	Coppinger, Higgins	400
Cox, Thomas	73		:	Carrier, Thomas	419
Carrier, Jonathan	115		:	Cranbarger, Michael	427
Cross, Z & Elijah	119,392		:	Cleveland, Larkin & Fanny	429
Crafford, Hugh	122		:	Cross, Aquilla	441
Chester, Jon	125		:	Clark, Joseph	442
Cole, Elisha	135		:	Chastain, (James)	456
Colpah, Henry	141		:	Cox, Joshua	470
Crocket, Andrew	149,365,371		:	Cox, Abraham	474,501
Carrier, Thomas	163		:	Cross, Elijah	493
Clark, Henry	168		:	Collins, John	531
Carson, Alex	172		:	Criggons, Patrick	188
Catron, Michael	176		:		
Crouch, John	184		:		
Christian, John	186		:		
Cowan, Robert	217,221		:		
Crawford, John	233		:		
Catron, Peter	239		:		
Cook, Jacob	276		:		
Copass, John	300		:		
Carothers, Saml.	305		:		
Capps, Thomas, Jr	318		:		
Clark, Joseph	324,366		:		
Christen, John	331		:		
Cox, Jesse	370		:		
Cross, Elijah	386,387,520		:		
Craft, Thomas	404		:		
Coppinger, Higgins	406		:		
Cranbarger, Michael	426		:		
Cox, Edward	470		:		
Cloud, Jeremiah	472		:		
Carter, William	487		:		
Carper, Joseph	539		:		
Cowan, William	541		:		
			:		
Dickson, Wm	2		:		
Dulaney, Elkanah	37		:	Dickson, John	2
Droke, Jacob	60,107,311		:	Davis, Nath'l.	24
			:		

GRANTEE		:	GRANTOR	
Delaney, Wm	179	:	Derting, John	79,189
Downs, Benjamin	307	:	Denton, James	169
Dever, John	319	:	Dickson, Wm	175
Dickson, William	332	:	Downa, Benj & Wm	307
Deery, William	355,356,379,502	:	Dulaney, William	426,432
Donalson, John	411	:	Deckard, George	462
Delaney,Elizabeth G &		:	Deery, William	493
Nancy R, Sarah G. &		:		
John R.	426	:		
Droke, Jacob	465	:		
Devalt, Daniel	489	:		
Duke, Jacob	531,532	:		
		:		
English, James	(No number given)	:	Edwards, Abel	68
Edwards, Joshua	160	:	Emmert, George	70
Everett, Joseph	202,363,413	:	Easley, Stephen	127
Easly, Peter	274	:	Ervin, William	164
Easley, Robert	317	:	Elder, Joseph	273
Easly, John	381	:	Emet, Jacob	279
Embrue, Elisha &		:	Easly, Peter	289
Elijah	403	:	English, James	363,463
Everitt, Benj	414	:	Ervin, james	517
Elder, Joseph	475,476	:		
		:		
Feltner, Henry	36,110	:	Fleenor, Jacob	34,39
Fleanor, Samuel	39	:	Fraime, Wm	41
Foust, John	30	:	Feltner, H.	104,108
Fream, Wm	73,374	:	Frazier, James	143
Ford, F.T.C.D.	161	:	Ford, John	161
Fain, Nicholas	327	:	Foust, Phillip	232
Foust, Phillip	339	:	Friend, Abraham	372
		:	Fain, Nicholas	534
		:		
Glover, Richd	20	:	Gilworth, John	26
Gale, W.N.	(No number given)	:	George, James	44
Gitgood, Alex	132,164	:	Gentry, Heirs	96
Grubb, Abrm	139,523	:	Goode, Thomas	15
George, James I	192,280,287	:	Greenway, George	156
Glover, Thomas	166	:	Gaines, James T.	202
Garland, John	180,181	:	Gamble, Samuel	244
Gammon, Richd	235	:	Garland,John & Hurly	280,282,287
Gross, George	329	:	Goad, Gabriel	342
Gifford, John	382,432,470,534	:	Gitt, Jacob	365,371
Geisler, Adam	447	:	Goruch, Edward	370
Good, Jacob	491	:	Gammon, Richard	393
Goddard, William	491	:	Gale, William N.	478
Gaisler, John	499	:	Goddard, Wm. Sr.	491
Grubb, Jacob	523	:	Gross, Jacob	513
Grubb, Abraham	523	:	Grubb, Jacob	523
Greenway, Elijah	530	:	Grubb, Abraham	523
Gibson, John	533	:	Greer, Andrew	541
Greenway, George	536	:	Greenway, George &	
Gregg, James	543	:	Joseph	439
		:		

GRANTEE		:	GRANTOR	
Hughes, David	22,116,259	:	Hazelrig, Richard	5
Hughes, Margaret	41	:	Howard, John	64
Haines, Jacob	54,144	:	Hammer, John	73
Harkleroad, Henry	70	:	Hugh, William	77,99
Hopkins, Thomas	71,267,283,427	:	Haines, Jacob	149
Hughs,S.W,Susanna	77,99	:	Harr, John	157
Hunt, John	83	:	Haggard, James	190
Hughes, James	92	:	Hughs, William	205
Hughes, William	100	:	Harkleroad, Henry	209
Hickman, Michael	114	:	Houser, Nicholas	234
Hershberger, John	137	:	Hopkins, Thomas	252,428,437,522
Housley, Robert	156	:	Hughs, James	259
Housley, Francis	159,294,433,536	:	Hall, James	274
Hartman, Jacob	167	:	Humphreys, Moses	281
Hedrick, Abrm	175,455	:	Hefleigh,Peter,Harry,David 347	
Hamilton, Timothy	182	:	Haggard, James	367
Hawkins, John	207	:	Hughes, John & Soffey, his wife 411	
Hawley, James	241	:	Hampton, Saml	430,448,509
Hicks, Stephen	281,314,472	:	Hart, Leonard	434,444
Hampton, Samuel	286	:	Hartman, Jacob	454
Hall, James	289	:	Hughes, William	464
Hart, Leonard	301,421	:	Hawkins, John	479
Hall, William	323	:	Hardin, Benj	510
Houser, George	372	:	Hite, John	527,528
Housley, John	375	:	Hughes, James	540,543
Hicks, Isaac	409	:		
Henderson, L.L.	423	:		
Hart, John	434	:		
Hobbang, Philip	441,479	:		
Hartman, Henry	443	:		
Hughes, James	450	:		
Hughes, Henry	461	:		
Hansher, William	463	:		
Harkelroad, Lawr.	487	:		
Hysinger, Henry	494	:		
Harkleroad, Martin	498	:	Isely, John	531
Hogard, James	521	:	Isley, Elizabeth	532
		:		
James,Walter	13,14,16,63,364,378,484,	:	Jennings, John	1
Johnson, Thos	33	:	Johnson, Jacob	31,178
Jones, Solomon	61,116	:	Johnson, Joshua	33
Johnson, Walter	76	:	James, Walter	61,67,84
Johnson,W.&R, &		:	Jones, Zach	171
D. Yearly	94	:	Jones, Charles	243,405
Jackson, Thomas	104	:	Jackson, Thomas	260
Jones, James	138,143	:	Jones, John	391
James, Elisha	315	:	Job, Samuel et al	449
Jackson, John	362	:	James, Elisha	497,521
Jones, William	391	:	Jones, Solomon	61
Jones, John	405	:		
Job, Jacob, Job Zachariah,		:		
Jon, James, Job, George,	449	:		
Jennings, Chris	522	:		

4

GRANTEE		:	GRANTOR	
Kaine, James	1	:	King, William	40
Key, Job	120	:	Key, Jobe	134
King, James	134,480	:	Kerr, Gilbert	136,177
King, David	173	:	King, Walter	246,407,459
Kingary, henry	197	:	Kerr, James	265,529
Kressell, Nicholas	214	:	Kain, James	275,317,503
King, Walter	222	:	King, James	286,473,474
Kenton, John	227	:	Kington, John	289
Keen, Jonas	239,243	:	Kelshaw, Sally &	
King, John	238	:	John Britton	340
Kerr, James	269	:	Key, Job &	
Kite, Phillip	282	:	Zacheus Jones	362
Kennedy, John	388	:	Kressell, Nicholas	379
King, John &		:	Kelly, Benj	533
Allison, John	453	:		
Kelly, Benj	472	:		
King, William	509	:		
		:		
Lane, William	6	:	Lee, Benj	50
Lindenberger,G.&C.	101	:	Latture, Harman	38,60,76,420
Looney, Abra	12,201	:	Little, George	106
Lille, Mathias	48	:	Little, George, Jr.	112
Little, George,Jr	106	:	Lewis, George	125
Ledick, George	140,504	:	Laughlin, John	139
Lature, Harman	186	:	Little, Mathias	141
Lots, Henry	248,249	:	Lewis, David	158
Looney, David	272	:	Laughlin, James	172,173
Lane, Richard	299	:	Lyons, John	222
David & George Lewis	327	:	Lauthlin, James	233
Lature, Harmon	330	:	Longacre, Ireson	241
Lynn, John	348,358,359	:	Looney, Abraham	272
Lane, Tidance	390	:	Lewis, Jonathan	327,398
Lewis, David,		:	Lewis, David	(No number given)
George & Jonathan	398	:	Lewis, George et al	346,351
Locke, William	409	:	Lewis, Molly	355
Looney, Moses & Sam	415	:	Lewis, Elizabeth &	
Lester, Lucinda	429	:	John Miller	356
Looney, Abraham	493	:	Lewis, Mary, David,	
Lady, John & Wm	539	:	William et al	356
		:	Looney Moses	386,387
		:	Lewis, Washington	395,396
		:	Lady, Jacob	407,539
		:		
Moore, Saml of R. Creek	7,464,467	:	Mingey, Peter	6
Munsey, Nathl	10	:	Massingale, H.	22
McCorkle, Saml & Joseph	25	:	Mahon, David	27,304
Miller, John	55	:	McCorkel, Saml	47
Moseley, John	74	:	Myers, Casper	51
Morgan, Peter	87	:	McCrabb, Alex	59
Morgan, Joshua	91	:	Maggert, Henry	80
Miller, Jacob	108	:	Morgan, Peter	91
Murphy, J	108	:	Moore, Saml	100,205,353
Morrell, Jesse & Isaac	111	:	Murphy, J.	110,332
Miller, Joshua	125	:	Morrell, Jonathan	111
Murrel, Richd Jr	145,148	:	Miller, Jacob	114
Moody, Valer,John		:	Merrick, James	123
Mary, William	150	:		

5

6

GRANTEE		:	GRANTOR	
Paxton, David	385	:	Roberts, James	3
Pemberton, Wm	417	:	Rhea, John	21
Powel, Joseph	437	:	Rockhold, Thos	55,112,328,485,505
Philips, Benj	448	:	Roller, Libby	113
Pickens, James	510	:	Rader, Peter	235
Roller, Martin	15	:	Rhinehart, Ludwick	238
Rhea, John	21,306,307	:	Rhea, Matthew	241
Rogan, Dan'l	75	:	Roller, Martin	248,249
Rhea, James	84,85,313,346,351,353,	:	Richards, Henry	269
	395,396,438,440,493	:	Roller, George	433
Rockett, Thos	112	:	Rhea,Matthew Capt	463
Roller, David	113,407,517	:	Roller, John	466
Richards, Rhode	136	:	Rhea, James	484,502
Rodaheffer,George	157	:	Rhea, Robert	543
Rhea, Wm	158	:		
Rhea, Matthew	164	:	Shirley, Saml	2
Richards, Henry	177	:	Snapp, Phillipp	4,37,85,95
Rutledge, Robert	219	:	Smith, David	10
Rhinehart,Ludwick	302	:	Shipley, Conrad	15
Rader, Peter	393	:	Snodgrass, Wm	21
Robbins, Isaac(Alesr)	422	:	Shipley, Conrad	39
Rhea, Marrhew Jr	455,543	:	Shoemaker,Judith & Jeremiah 52	
Russell, Joshua	469	:	Shell, Arnold	60
Rhea, Matthew Sent - Clk 485		:	Shrader, Jacob	62
Ryley, Andrew	505	:	Sheriff of Sullivan Co 35,45,52,65,101,334	
Rockhold, William	524	:	Spurgin, John Adm	73,154
		:	Smith, Ann	86
Snapp,Laurence Jr	4,210,257	:	State of TN	89,90,98,116,122,152,
~~Shrader, Jacob~~	515,516	:		196,197,199,200,201,205
Shrader, Jacob	9	:		208,209,210,211,265,271
Snodgrass, Wm	21	:		295,296,297,298,301,302
Snapp,Laurence Jr	39,468	:		325,326,339,373,374,381
Shrite, Henry	23	:		387,390,402,407,409,418
Stoffel, Jacob	27	:		421,431,434,451,464,465
Stephens, John	43,137	:		468,475,476,483,486,487
Shoemaker, Dan	52,79,444	:		495,507,508,525,532
Shell, Andrew	60	:	Smalling, Thomas	93
Snapp, Jacob	65	:	Shelby, Isaac	95,165,480
Sturm, Jacob	66,81,179,196,197,316	:	Sheretz, Conrad	103,128,130
Sams, Littleberry	68	:	Stevens, William	104
Shipler, Conrad	74	:	Stephens, John	105,129
Sinclair, John	82	:	Shelby, Catherine	132
Severs, George	88	:	Smith, Hugh	136
Smith, Adam	89,90	:	Shelby (Shelley?), Peter 137	
Stephens, J & F	(No page given)	:	Shell, John & A.	156
Smiley, Joseph	123	:		
Shiretz, Henry	128	:		
Sherretz, Henry	128	:		

GRANTEE		:	GRANTOR	
Sherritz, John	130	:	Smith, John	158
Sherritz, Conrad	130	:	Scott, William	160,298,380,496
Shelby, Isaac	132	:	Snapp, Jacob	179
Stephens, Samuel	154	:	Smith, Adam	180, 181
Smith, Solomon	171	:	Smith, James	189
Scott, William	184	:	Shipley,Sarah & Elenore	204
Shipley, Eli & Bery	(No page given)	:	Sharatz, Conrad	225
Snodgrass, John	215	:	Skillern, William	227
Sharetz, Conrad	223,225,229	:	Sheratz, John	229
Sharp, John	241,537	:	Stewart, John	245
Stoffle, Jacob	247	:	Steers, John	262
Shaver, David	266,271,298,418	:	Smith, Caleb	263
Snapp, Phillip	275,307	:	Sells, Henry	314
Smith, John	279	:	Scott, John & Joseph	328
Scott, John	334	:	Smith, Joseph	330
Smiley, John	342	:	Surgin, John	362,403
Soper, Alvin	353	:	Segler, Henry	394
Smith, John	444	:	Smith, Solomon	432,472 Bill of Sale
Slaughter, Jacob	507,508	:	Steadman, John	442,443
Smith, Henry	513	:	Shumaker, Henry	444
Strickler, Samuel	527,528	:	Stephens, Isaac & Felix	447
Simmermon, Daniel	538	:	Sharp, John	461,500
		:	Smith, Solomon & John	494
		:	Stephens, Samuel	499
		:		
Torbet, John Sr.	44	:	Taylor, Jeremiah	(No page given)
Torbet, Joseph	44	:	Tipton, John	13,66,81,132,137,164,
Troke, Peter	90	:		167,170,208,214,218,257
Thomas, Jacob Jr.	104,459	:		275,290,315,311,313,314
Talley, John	118	:		327,329,382,470,472,515
Tipton, Job	129,290,310	:		516,534
Trigg, William	194,343	:	Tipton, John	37,38,137
Thomson, John	202	:	Taylor, Arch	30,159,276
Tribbet, Robert	246,442	:	Thompson, John	42
Thompson, William	273	:	Torbet, John Jr	45,46
Thomas, John	368	:	Tipton, Isaac	116
Tribett, Robert	492,495	:	Tolard, Jacob	146,148
Taylor, Elijah	503	:	Thomas, George	189
Tipton, John	439	:	Tipton, John	438,Atty of Greenway,
		:		438,440,445,456,530,539
		:		543
		:	Torbet, Joseph	453
		:	Trower,Mary & Thomas	504
		:	Tribet, Robert	505
		:		
Vance, John	500	:	Vied, Harman C	40
		:	Vance, Sam'l	43,94
		:	Virginia	49,100,202,292,293
		:	Vance, D & John	57
		:		
Wassum, John	10	:	Waddle, Martin	7
White, Thomas	62	:	Whiteside, Jenkin	16
		:		
		:		

GRANTOR		:	GRANTEE		
Waddle, Jacob	78	:	Waddle, John	16	
Wirick, Wm	93	:	Wallace, Wm	82,460	
White, Jonah	95	:	Walling, Stephen	115,166	
Weishburn, B	100	:	Webb, David	119	
Wallingford, John	150	:	Woolfe, Lewis	121	
Weaver, Michael	191	:	Waddle, George	186	
Weaver, George	192	:	Weaver, Christian	191	
Willson, Benj	232	:	Weaver, John	192,433	
Webb, David	254,260	:	Waddle, Martin	193	
Wright, Patrick	275	:	Webb, Jonathan	254,260,392	
Willson, William	277	:	Weaver, John	294	
Witson, William	285	:	Willson, Benj, Amos, & Ann		311
Willoughby, Wallace	293	:	Waddle, Jacob	330	
Webb, George	297	:	Willoughby, Wallace	344	
White, George	311	:	White, Thomas	368	
Watson, John	339	:	Wicks, Zachariah	377	
Willett, Nathan	379	:	Webb, Benj	389	
Woolford, George	377,378,478,489	:	Wicks, John	463	
Webb, John	389	:	Webb, George &		
Wallingfor, John	402	:	David Looney	520	
Webb, Jonathan	431	:	Weaver, George	536	
Work, Jacob	452	:	White, Benjamin	544	
White, Thomas	457	:			
Ware, James	473,474	:			
Willyeard, George	528	:			
		:			
Yancey, Mary	59	:	Year, Loenard(sic)	239	

Volumn 6

Page	8	James Roberts, of Wayne County, KY
	5	Richard Hazelrig of Washington Co, VA
	10	David Smith, of Washington Co, VA
	14	John Adair, Esq, of Knox Co, TN
	24	Nathaniel Davis, of Washington Co, TN
	26	John Gilworth of Washington Co, TN
	27	Jacob Stoffel, of Washington Co, VA
	42	John Akard of Hawkins Co, TN
	54	Henry Pickett, of Carter Co, TN
	57	David Vance and John Vance of Jackson Co, TN
	59	Alexander McCrabb, of Montgomery Co, TN
	65	Jacob Snapp, of Shanando(sic), VA
	68	Abel Edwards, of Washington Co, TN
	70	George Emert, of Carter Co, TN
	73	John Hammer, of Washington Co, TN
	86	Ann Smith, of Grainger Co, TN
	87	John Page, of Smith Co, TN
	95	Josiah White, of Philadelphia City, PA
	96	Elizabeth Mayfield, George Gentry, Samuel Gentry, Nicholas Gentry, James Boyd, of Williamson Co, TN
	101	George Lindenberger & Christopher Lindenberger, merchants of Baltimore, in the state of MD
	104	Henry Feltner, of Hawkins Co, TN
	108	Henry Feltner, of Hawkins Co, TN
	110	Henry Feltner, of Hawkins Co, TN
	111	Jonathan Murrell, of Carter Co, TN
	114	Michael Hickman, of Washington Co, TN
	121	Isaac Newhouser, of Washington Co, VA

Volume 6

Page 150   George Moody of Hawkins Co, Tn, to Valen Moody, John Moody, Mary
Moody, William Moody of same

155   Elisha Adams, of Sevier Co, TN

162   Stanton Pemberton, of Washington Co, VA, Executor of James Offield, dec'd.

172   James laughlin, of Rutherford Co, TN

179   Jacob Snapp, of Shenandoah Co, VA

186   William Christian, of Bledsoe Co, TN, to John Christian of Cumberland Co, KY

193   Martin Waddle of Green Co, TN

194   William Trigg and Charles S. Carson, Merchants of Abington, VA

197   Jacob Miller, of Washington Co, VA

227   William Skillem, of Washington Co, VA

233   James Laughlin, Sr, of Washington Co, VA, to John Carson of same

234   Nicholas Houser of Hawkins Co, TN

237   William Priestly, late, of Washington Co, VA

251   James Clark, Sr, of Washington Co, TN

260   Thomas Jackson of Hawkins Co, TN

274   James Hall, of Washington Co, TN

281   Moses Humphreys of Washington Co and John McCall of Carter Co, (TN)

281   George Brooks, of Washington Co, VA

289   James Hall, of Washington Co, TN

290   Henry Borden, of Shenandoah Co, VA

292   James Monroe, Gov of Commonwealth of VA

293   James Monroe, Gov of Commonwealth of VA

310   William Armstrong, of Hawkins Co, TN

327   Jonathan Lewis of Franklin Co, Luisiana(sic) Territory, and Nancy, my wife,
to David and George Lewis of same

328   William Hall, of Green Co, TN

Volume 6

Page 342   Gabriel Good, of Lincoln Co, TN

343   William Trigg & Charles S. Carson, Merchants of Abingdon, VA

346   George Lewis, All of the Indiana for Jonathan Lewis Territory, Washington Lewis of Maddison Co, MS Territory

347   John Husluck, David Harry, Thomas C. Brent, Michael McKunnun, All of Washington Co, MD

        Executors: Henry Yorkman, heir of Henry Brockman, of KY

349   John Protzman, of Washington Co, MD

351   David Lewis, Atty in fact for George Lewis, Jonathan Lewis & Nancy Lewis, All of the Indiana Territory

372   Abraham Friend of Washington Co, Elizabeth Friend of TN

375   John Housley of Jefferson Co, TN

385   Benjamin Birdwell, of Washington Co, TN

394   Henry Singler, Jr, of Carter Co, Tn

395   Washington Lewis of Madison Co & MS Territory

396   Washington Lewis of Madison Co & MS Territory

411   John Hughs & Jaffey of Augusta Co, VA
                    To
    John Donaldson of Madison Co, KY

420   Benjamin Birdwell of Washington Co, Tn

422   Isaac Robbins of Alexander, VA

424   Peter Maye of Washington Co, VA

427   Michael Crowbarger & his wife, Eva Crowbarger, of Hawkins Co, TN

428   Michael Crowbarger of Hawkins Co, TN

429   Larkin Cleveland & wife, Fanny Cleveland, of Giles Co, TN
                    To
    Lucinda Lester, wife of German Lester

434   Leonard Hart of Carter Co, TN

12

Volume 6

Page		
435	John Brown of Granklin Co, KY	
443	Henry hartman of Washington Co, TN	
445	George Malock of Hawkins Co	
456	James Chastain of Greenville Co, SC	
459	Peter Brickhill of Sevier Co	
459	Benjamin Britt of Washington Co & John Britt & TN	
460	William Wallace of Washington Co, VA	
461	John Sharp of Roane Co, TN	
474	John Brown of Washington Co, TN	
480	Isaac Shelby, Executor of Evan Shelby, dec'd, of Lincoln Co; Now residing in the town of Frankfort, KY, & Susannah, his wife	
487	William Carter of Carter Co, Tn	
512	John Berland, Merchant of Baltimore, MD	
520	David Looney of Smith Co	
527	John Hite of Washington Co, TN	
528	John Hite of Washington Co, TN	
530	Elijah Greenway of Montgomery Co, VA	
534	Nicholas Fain of Hawkins Co, TN	
536	George Weaver of Wilson Co, TN	
537	Thomas McChesney of Washington Co, VA	
541	Andrew Greer of Smith Co, TN	
544	Benjamin White of Wythe Co, VA	

(Page)

(1)

JOHN JENNINGS   :
        TO   :   DEED OF WARRANTY
JAMES KAINE   :

Date: April 30, 1808
Consideration: $480.00
Amt of land: 120 acres
Location: Sullivan Co, TN
Description: A tract of land containing 120 acres, incl. the plantation
where John Jennings now lives, being a corner of William Bonds and
Patrick Wright
Wit: ? Sinclair, Abner Hughes
Acknowledged: Torn off this deed
Regst: Feb. 25, 1809

----

(2)

JOHN DICKSON   :
        TO   :   BILL OF SALE
WILLIAM DICKSON, Son   :

Date: Dec. 19, 1808
Consideration: Love and good will
Description: Given and granted unto my son, one gray horse, one brown
mare, 2 cows, and 9 sheep
Wit: Frances Hawley, George Roller, John Jennings
Acknowledged: By Frances hawley and George Roller, Sullivan Co, TN, Feb,
1809
Test: Mattw. Rhea, C.S.C.
Regst: Feb. 25, 1809

SAMUEL SHIRLEY   :
        TO   :   DEED OF TRUST
JOHN PUNCH   :

Date: Oct. 1, 1808
Consideration: $1.00 cash in hand and for the purpose of securing to
William King the payment of the sum of $21.96, and John Punch the sum
of $5.87
Condition: Provided always that it is understood that if Shirley should
within three months pay the above stated sum and interest (this instrument
to be revoked). This deed is torn at the bottom of page 2.
Land conveyed: All my right to a lot adj. the town of Blountville, now in
my occupancy
Wit: Jonathan McHenry, Jacob Gitt
Acknowledged: By Jacob Gitt and Jonathan McHenry, Sullivan Co, Feb.
1809
Test: Mattw. Rhea, C.S.C, by Robt. Rhea, D.C.
Regst: Feb. 25, 1809

14

JAMES ROBERTS of   :
Wayne Co, KY   :
     TO   :   DEED OF WARRANTY
THOMAS BRIGHT   :

Date: Oct. 30, 1805
Consideration: A valuable consideration
Amt of land: 100 acres
Location: Sullivan Co, TN
Description: A tract of land containing 100 acres on Reedy Creek
Wit: John Anderson, William Roberts, Graham Roberts
Proven: By oath of John Anderson
Test: Mattw. Rhea, C.S.C
Regst: Feb. 25, 1809

----

(4)   PHILLIP SNAPP   :
           TO   :   DEED OF WARRANTY
LAURENCA SNAPP   :

Date: April 24, 1800
Consideration: $1333.00
Amt of land: 200 acres
Location: Sullivan Co
Description: A plantation incl. the ferry on Holston River between land
formerly the property of James Smith and James Moore
Wit: Elkanah Dulaney, John Tipton
Proven: By Elkanah R. Dulaney, Sullivan Co, TN, Aug, 1807
Test: Mattw. Rhea, C.S.C, by Robt Rhea, D.C.
Regst: Feb. 27, 1807

----

(5)   RICHARD HAZELRIG of :
Washington Co, VA   :
      TO   :   DEED OF WARRANTY
HENRY PECTOL   :

Date: Feb. 20, 1809
Consideration: $1300.00
Amt of land: 285 acres
Location: Sullivan Co, Tn
Description: a tract of land on both sides of Reedy Creek, along with
Frederic Pectol's line
Wit: John Anderson
Proven: By Richard Hazelrig, Sullivan Co, TN, Feb, 1809
Test: Mattw. Rhea, C.S.C, by Robt P. Rhea, D.C.
Regst: Feb. 27, 1809

----

(6)   PETER MINGY   :
         TO   :   DEED OF WARRANTY
WILLIAM LAND &   :
ROBERT BROWN   :

Date: Aug. 20, 1808

(7)   MARTIN WADDLE   :

                  TO   :   DEED OF WARRANTY

       SAMUEL MOORE   :

Date: Sept 15, 1808
Consideration: $550.00
Amt of land: 145 acres
Location: Sullivan Co, TN
Description: A tract of land on the north side of Eaton's Ridge and south side of Reedy Creek, incl. the plantation where Waddle now lives on Blanton's line
Wit: Wm Hughes, Peter Branstetter
Proven: By William Hughes and peter Branstetter, Sullivan Co, TN, Feb, 1809
Test: Mattw Rhea, C.S.C, by Robt Rhea, D.C.
Regst: Feb. 28, 1809

----

(9)   SAMUEL PALMER   :

                  TO   :   DEED OF WARRANTY

       JACOB SHRADER   :

Date: Feb. 20, 1809
Consideration: 400 ___?___ to him in hand paid
Amt of land: 108 acres
Description: A tract of land containing 108 acres, beginning at a black oak on Robert Cowan's line
Wit: Washington Lewis, Ireson Longacre
Acknowledged: By Samuel Palmer, Sullivan Co, TN, Feb, 1809
Test: Mattw. Rhea, C.S.C, by Robt Rhea, D.C.
Regst: Feb. 28, 1809

----

(10)   TIMOTHY ACUFF   :

                  TO   :   BILL OF SALE

      NATHANIEL MUNSEY   :

Date: Feb. 21, 1809
Consideration: Sundry goods causes and for $1.00
Description: Six negro slaves namely, Sama abt 33 yrs old, Aggy abt 35 yrs old, and her four children Betsy, Ben, Sam and Charles and also increase of sd Aggy and her daughter Betsy, free from all and every claim and demand to Nathaniel Munsey and his heirs
Wit: Nathan Ashworth, Wm Pallet
Proven: By Nathan Ashworth and William Pallet, Sullivan Co, TN
Test: Mattw Rhea, C.S.C, by Robt Rhea, D.C.
Regst: Feb. 28, 1809

      DAVID SMITH of   :

      Washington Co, VA   :

                  TO   :   DEED OF LAND

      JOHN WASSOM   :

Date: Sept 6, 1808
Consideration: 700 ₺
Amt of land: 285 acres
Location: Sullivan Co, TN
Description: A tract of land on John Miller's line, corner to Berrup and Willoughby's
Wit: Thos Edmiston, W. Worsham, John Vance
Proven: By William Worsham and John Vance, Sullivan Co, TN, Feb, 1809
Test: Mattw. Rhea, C.S.C, by Robt Rhea, D.C.
Regst: Feb. 28, 1809

(Page)
(12)

JOSEPH BEELOR	:	
TO	:	DEED OF WARRANTY
JONAS NICELY	:	

Date: June 15, 1802
Consideration: $15.00
Amt of land: 9 acres
Location: Sullivan Co
Description: A tract of land containing 9 acres, beginning at a white oak near the head of a rocky spring
Wit: John Anderson, Ken Harkleroad
Proven: By John Anderson, Sullivan Co, Aug, 1802
Test: Mattw. Rhea, C.S.C.
Regst: March 4, 1809

JEREMIAH TAYLOR	:	
TO	:	DEED OF WARRANTY
ABRAHAM LOONEY	:	

Date: Feb. 17, 1809
Consideration: $500.00
Amt of land: 101 acres
Location: Sullivan Co, TN
Description: A tract of land containing 101 acres incl the plantation where Taylor now lives
Wit: John W. Nesbit, N. Lain
Acknowledged: By Jeremiah Taylor, Sullivan Co, TN, Feb, 1809
Test: Mattw. Rhea, C.S.C, by Robt. Rhea, D.C.
Regst: March, 1809

----

(13)

JOHN TIPTON	:	
TO	:	DEED OF WARRANTY
WALTER JAMES	:	

Date: Nov. 4, 1808
Consideration: A valuable consideration
Amt of land: 3/4 of an acre and 19 sq poles
Location: Sullivan Co, TN
Description: A parcel of land adj the town of Blountville, beginning at a stake corner of Elkanah R. Dulaney's, and joining William Deery's line
Wit: N. Lain, Richd. Gammon

17

Acknowledged: By John Tipton, Sullivan Co, TN, Nov, 1808
Test: Mattw. Rhea, C.S.C, by Robt Rhea, D.C.
Regst: March 6, 1809

(Page)
(14)

JOHN ADAIR, ESQ. of :
Knox Co   :
        TO   :   DEED OF WARRANTY
WALTER JAMES   :

Date: June 11, 1810
Consideration: $1600.00
Amt of land: 359 acres
Location: Sullivan Co, TN
Description: A tract of land beginning at a white oak corner of James Phagan's land
Proven: By John Phagan and James Phagan, Sullivan Co, TN, Nov, 1808
Test: Mattw. Rhea, C.S.C, by Robt Rhea, D.C.
Regst: March 7, 1809

----

(15)

CONRAD SHIPLEY   :
        TO   :   DEED OF WARRANTY
MARTIN ROLLER   :

Date: Aug. 15, 1808
Consideration: $1000.00
Amt of land: 96 acres
Location: Sullivan Co, TN
Description: A tract of land on the south side of Holston River
Wit: Robert Easley, John Jennings, Henry Lotts
Proven: By John jennings and Henry Lotts, Sullivan Co, TN, Feb. 1809
Test: Mattw. Rhea, C.S.C, by Robt. Rhea, D.C.
Regst: March 8, 1809

----

(16)

JENKIN WHITESIDE   :
        TO   :   DEED OF WARRANTY
WALTER JAMES   :

Date: March 7, 1807
Consideration: $1000.00
Amt of land: Two lots of land
Location: Sullivan Co, TN
Description: Two lots of land in the town of Blountville, being lot Nos. 3 and 4 in plan of town; Lot No. 3 was conveyed by Commissioner to Robert Work in his lifetime by deed bearing date Aug. 23, 1796, and Lot No. 4 was conveyed by Commissioners to Robert Work by deed dated Aug. 25, 1795, and both conveyed by Jacob Work and Joseph Work heris of Robert Work, dec'd, to Jenkin Whiteside by deed dated Oct. 9, 1805, being same lot now occupied by John Richardson, together with all and singular the houses, stables, gardens, office buildings and improvements of every description on or belonging to lots
Wit: Isaac Shelby
Acknowledged: Jenkins Whiteside personally appeared before me, David

Campbell, Esq, one of the judges of the Superior Court of Law for TN; he
signed, sealed, and delivered the above indenture to Walter James.
Regst: March 8, 1809

----

(18)

```
JENKINS MURPHY        :
        TO            :         DEED OF WARRANTY
DAVID ROLLER          :
```

Date: Jan 4, 1809
Consideration: $600.00
Amt of land: 97 acres
Location: Sullivan Co, TN
Description: A tract of land at a former corner of David Rollers
Wit: John Jennings, Elizabeth Andrew
Acknowledged: By Jenkins Murphy, Sullivan co, Tn, Feb, 1809
Test: Mattw. Rhea, C.S.C, by Robt Rhea, D.C.
Rest: March 13, 1809

----

19)

```
EDWARD COX            :
        TO            :         DEED OF WARRANTY
ELISHA COLE           :
```

Date: Feb. 17, 1807
Consideration: $500.00
Amt of land: 86 acres
Location: Sullivan Co
Description: A tract of land adj. Abraham Cross and Aquilla Cross and
containing 86 acres
Wit: Nathaniel Murphy, Isaac Stephens, John Punch
Acknowledged: By Edward Cox, Sullivan Co, Tn, Feb., 1807
Test: Mattw. Rhea, C.S.C, by Robt Rhea, D.C.
Regst: March 17, 1809

----

(20)

```
EDWARD COX            :
        TO            :         DEED OF WARRANTY
RICHARD GLOVER        :
```

Date: Aug. 16, 1808
Consideration: $33.300(sic)
Amt of land: 117 acres
Location: Sullivan Co, Tn
Description: The following tracts of land, one on the south side of Holston
River containing 67 acres, one other tract on the south side of Holston
River containing 50 acres beginning at Arnold Shall's corner
Acknowledged: By Edward Cox, Sullivan Co, TN, Aug, 1808
Test: Mattw. Rhea, C.S.C, by Robt Rhea, D.C.
Regst: March 22, 1809

----

(21)

```
JOHN RHEA             :
        TO            :         DEED OF DIVISION  (Partition Deed)
WILLIAM SNODGRASS     :
```

19

Date: Oct. 14, 1808
Object: To divide a certain tract of land
Amt of land: 629 acres
Location: Sullivan Co, TN
Description: Whereas John Rhea and William Snodgrass were purchasers in equal moieties of two tracts of land on the sides of Reedy Creek being part of a tract of land granted to Edmnd Pendleton, the same purchase having been made at a sheriff's sale and the same parties thereof became tenants in common and whereas the same two parties have agreed that they will divide the same two tracts of land containing supposedly 629 acres the same John Rhea and William Snodgrass do agree to divide the same land in the following manner:

That is to say by a line which shall run parallel with the line which runs across sd Reedy Creek dividing the same two tracts of land and which line shall be 38 poles south of the sd before mentioned lines and shall run parallel with the middle line from end to end thereof at the distance of 38 poles southwardly from the same from end to end and it is agreed that William Snodgrass shall possess all that part of the same two tract of land which is composed of the upper tract and that part of the lower tract which is contained between the lines divding the same two tracts originally and the same John Rhea shall have and possess all the rest and reside of the same lower tract of land containing the improvements which lay below this line
Wit: Thos Rockhold, Jr, John Punch
Proven, By John Punch and Thomas rockhold, Sullivan Co, TN, Nov. 1808
Test: Mattw. Rhea, C.S.C, by Robt Rhea, D.C.
Regst: April 5, 1809

(Page) 22)

HENRY MASSENGILL	:	
TO	:	QUIT CLAIM
DAVID HUGHES	:	

Date: Oct. 29, 1808
Consideration: A certain brown mare
Amt of land: 350 acres
Location: Sullivan Co, TN
Quit Claim: In consideration of a certain brown mare to me in hand paid by David Hughes (I) have forever quit claim unto the sd David Hughes -----all the right unto the land lying within the lines of or covered by David, the one for 200 acres granted to Hughes and the other for 150 acres granted to john Vertmiller
Wit: James Gregg
Acknowledged: By Henry Massengill, Sullivan Co, TN, Nov, 1808
Test: Mattw. Rhea, C.S.C, by Robt Rhea, D.C.
Regst: April 10, 1809

----

(23)

JAMES BLEVINS	:	
TO	:	BILL OF SALE
THOMAS SHELBY	:	

Date: June 27, 1808
Consideration: $450.00

Description: A negro slave named Anthony to Thomas Shelby, his heirs and assigns forever
Wit: Samuel Blackmore, Isaac Shelby
Acknowledged: By James Blevins, Sullivan Co, Tn, Nov. 1808
Test: Mattw. Rhea, C.S.C, by Robt Rhea, D.C.
Regst: May 18, 1809

THOMAS CAPPS, SR :
    TO   :   DEED OF WARRANTY
HENRY SHRITE :

Date: May 16, 1809
Consideration: $1200.00
Amt of land: 211 acres
Location: Sullivan Co, Tn
Description: A tract of land beginning at an ashe, a corner og John Wickes and also joining a corner of Isaac Jones
Wit: John Anderson
Acknowledged: By Thomas Capps, Sullivan Co, TN, May, 1809
Test: Mattw. Rhea, C.S.C, by Robt. Rhea, D.C.
Regst: June 8, 1809

----

(24)   NATHANIEL DAVIS of :
       Washington Co, TN :
           TO   :   BILL OF SALE
       FINLY ALISON :

Date: Jan. 13, 1809
Consideration: $500.00
Description: A certain negro man named Jack 22 yrs old last October, 1808, and in consideration of the sum of $500.00, Nathaniel do warrant and defend the negro man to Alison, his heirs and assigns forever from me and my heirs or any person
Wit: Frances Hodge, Thomas King, John King
Proven: By John King and Francis Hidge, Sullivan Co, TN, May, 1809
Test: Mattw. Rhea, C.S.C, by Robt Rhea, D.C.
Regst: June 8, 1809

----

(25)   STATE OF NORTH CAROLINA :
       ALEXANDER MARTIN, GOV. :   LAND GRANT
           TO   :   NO. 1056
       SAMUEL & JOSEPH McCORKLE :

Date: Nov. 27, 1792
Consideration: 50 shillings for every 100 acres of land
Amt of land: 52* acres
Location: Washington Co, NC
Description: A tract of land containing 320* acres on the south side of Holston River at a place known by Choats Ford, on Benjamin Webb's line
Granted: By his Excellys Comd. J. Glasgow, Sec.
Regst: June 10, 1809

(*Note: both amounts given)

JOHN GILWORTH of   :
Washington Co, TN   :
       TO   :   DEED OF WARRANTY
GEORGE BROWN   :

Date: Oct. 18, 1808
Consideration: $1000.00
Amt of land: 234 acres
Location: Sullivan Co, TN
Description: A tract of land on the waters of Reedy Creek, beginning at Alexander Lauglin's and joining Berry's corner and on William Worsham's line also joining Richard's Corner and on Shelby's line
Wit: John Vance, W. Willoughby
Proven: By Wallace Willoughby and John Vance, Sullivan Co, May, 1809
Test: Mattw. Rhea, C.S.C, by Robt Rhea, D.C.
Regst: June 12, 1809

----

(27)   DAVID MAHAN   :
           TO   :   DEED OF WARRANTY
    JACOB STOFFEL   :

Date: March 10, 1809
Consideration: $431.25
Amt of land: 86 1/4 acres
Location: Sullivan Co, TN
Description: A tract of land in Sullivan Co, TN, and a small part in VA, on the waters of Beaver Creek, being part of a tract of land granted by patent from NC to David Mahon, dated Oct. 23, 1782
Wit: Isaac Stoffel, Jacob Miller, Ephraim Smith
Acknowledged: By David Mahon, Sullivan Co, TN, May, 1809
Test: Mattw. Rhea, C.S.C, by Robt Rhea, D.C.
Regst: June 13, 1809

----

(29)   PETER CATRON   :
           TO   :   DEED OF WARRANTY
    JOHN CATRON   :

Date: Nov. 8, 1808
Consideration: A valuable consideration
Amt of land: 138 1/4 acres
Location: Sullivan Co, TN
Description: A tract of land containing 138 1/4 acres, beginning at a corner of James Igou's also near Lenard Yeast's line, also near John Britton's land
Wit: Henry Catron, Valentine Catron
Acknowledged: By Peter Catron, Sullivan Co, TN, May, 1809
Test: Mattw. Rhea, C.S.C, by Robt Rhea, D.C.
Regst: June 14, 1809

ARCHIBALD TAYLOR   :
      TO   :   DEED OF WARRANTY
JOHN FOUST   :

Date: March 25, 1809
Consideration: A valuable consideration
Amt of land: 42 acres
Location: Sullivan Co, TN
Description: A tract of land on Daniel Shoemaker's line and on Pendleton's patent line
Wit: Samuel Moore, Matthew Rhea, Ambrose Gaines
Proven: By Matthew Rhea and Ambrose Gaines, Sullivan Co, May 1809
Test: Mattw. Rhea, C.S.C, by Robt Rhea, D.C.
Regst: June 15, 1809

----

(31)   JACOB JOHNSON   :
             TO   :   DEED OF WARRANTY
JONATHAN BAUGHMAN :

Date: Jan. 12, 1809
Consideration: $400.00
Amt of land: 3 1/2 acres
Location: Sullivan Co, TN
Description: A tract of land containing 3 1/2 acres incl. all the house and improvements where Johnson now lives and incl. the following lots granted to Johnson; No. 1 granted by John Crum, No. 5 granted by John Crum, No. 7 granted by John Crum, No. 8 granted by Crum, No. 10 by Crum, No. 11 by Ely Shipley
Wit: George Vinsent, Thomas Titsworth, Thos. Dickson
Acknowledged: By Jacob Johnson, Sullivan Co, TN, May, 1809
Test: Mattw. Rhea, C.S.C, by Robt Rhea, D.C.
Regst: June 16, 1809

----

(32)   FREDERICK BRANSTETTER :
             TO   :   DEED OF WARRANTY
PETER BRANSTETTER   :

Date: Feb. 18, 1806
Consideration: $1200.00
Amt of land: 243 acres
Location: Sullivan Co, TN
Description: A tract of land on corner of Jacob Isley's
Wit: John Jennings, Thos Anderson, Josiah Whithal
Acknowledged: By Frederick Branstetter, Sullivan Co, TN, Feb, 1806
Test: Mattw. Rhea, C.S.C.
Regst: June 18, 1809

----

(33)   JOSHUA JOHNSON   :
             TO   :   DEED OF WARRANTY
THOMAS JOHNSON   :

Date: Oct. 23, 1809

Consideration: $500.00
Amt of land: 22 acres & 248 acres   (270)
Location: Sullivan Co
Description: A tract of land containing 22 acres beginning at William
Pallett's corner; one other tract containing 248 acres adj. the above
beginning at a forked chestnut thence on Anderson's line and also on
Fagan's line thence on Ann Pallett's line
Acknowledged: By Joshua Johnson, Sullivan Co, TN, May, 1809
Test: Mattw. Rhea, C.S.C
Regst: (No date given)

(Page)
(34)%   JACOB FLEANOR   :
                  TO   :   DEED OF WARRANTY
             ELIJAH WATSON   :

             Date: Nov. 21, 1808
             Consideration: A valuable consideration
             Amt of land: 172 acres
             Location: Sullivan Co, TN
             Description: A tract of land on the south side of Holston River
(%NOTE: Bottom of pages 35 & 36 if torn off)

----

(36)%   STATE OF TENNESSEE   :
             Henry Felton*, Surveyor :
                  TO   :   COMMISSIONER'S DEED
             JOHN REED   :

             Date: July 28, 1808
             Consideration: In Consideration of an entry made in the office of the
             Register of the Sixth District by Henry Feltner* of No. 70, July 28, 1808
             Amt of land: 530 acres
             Location: Sullivan Co, District of Wadhington(sic)
             Purpose: Founded on a warrant issued by the Commissioner of East TN by
             John Reed of No. 350 for 640 acres of land dated July 9, 1808, 630 of
             which are assigned by John Reed to Henry Fletner*, the enterer there is
             granted by state of TN unto Henry Fletner and his heirs
(*Note: Name spelled all three ways)

----

(37)   JOHN TIPTON   :
                  TO   :   DEED OF WARRANTY
             ELKANAH R. DULANEY :

             Date: May 24, 1805
             Consideration: $100.00
             Amt of land: 1/4 of an acre
             Location: In the town of Blountville
             Description: A lot known by Lot No. 2 with all buildings and improvements
             Acknowledged: By John Tipton, Sullivan Co, May, 1805
             Test: Mattw. Rhea, C.S.C.
             Regst: July 10, 1809

24

(38)

JOHN TIPTON   :
    TO   :   DEED OF WARRANTY
ELKANAH R. DULANEY   :

Date: May 24, 1805
Consideration: $100.00
Amt of land: 1/4 acre and 36 sq. poles
Location: In town of Blountville
Description: A lot known as lot conveyed by james Bigham to the
Commissioners of town
Acknowledged: By John Tipton, Sullivan Co, May, 1805
Test: Mattw. Rhea, C.S.C.
Regst: (No date given)

----

(37)(sic)

PHILLIP SNAPP   :
    to   :   DEED OF WARRANTY
ELKANAH DULANEY   :

Date: Nov. 16, 1802
Consideration: $50.00
Amt of land: 1/4 of acre
Location: In town of Blountville
Description: A lot known as Lot No. 4 with improvements
Acknowledged: By Phillip Snapp, Sullivan Co, TN, Nov, 1802
Test: Mattw. Rhea, C.S.C.
Regst: July 10, 1809

----

(38)(sic)

COMMISSIONERS   :
    TO   :   DEED OF WARRANTY
ELKANAH R. DULANEY   :

Date: Nov. 20, 1804
Consideration: For valuable consideration
Amt of land: 1/4 acre
Location: In town of Blountville
Description: A lot known as Lot No. 26
Wit: John Anderson, Rich'd Gammon, George Rutledge
Acknowledged: By John Anderson, Rich'd Gammon, George Rutledge,
Sullivan Co, TN, Nov, 1804
Test: Mattw. Rhea, C.S.C
Regst: July 10, 1809

----

(39)

MARTIN ROLLER   :
    TO   :   WARRANTY DEED
LAURENCE SNAPP   :

Date: March 13, 1809
Consideration: $1000.00
Amt of land: 96 acres
Location: Sullivan Co, TN
Description: A tract of land formerly owned by Conrad Shipley and
conveyed to Roller on the south side of Holston River

Wit: John Jennings, Sam'l Blackmore, George Rutledge
Proven: Sullivan Co, TN, May, 1809
Test: Mattw. Rhea, C.S.C, by Robt Rhea, D.C.
Regst: July 11, 1809

(Page)
(39)

JACOB FLEENER	:	
TO	:	DEED OF WARRANTY
SAMUEL FLEANOR	:	

Date: Nov. 25, 1808
Consideration: Natural love and affection
Amt of land: 88 acres
Location: Sullivan Co, TN
Description: A tract of land, corner of Elijah Watson's and on Matthias Little's line, also a corner of John Shell's line
Acknowledged: By Jacob Fleener, Sullivan Co, TN, Nov. 1808
Test: Mattw. Rhea, C.S.C, by Robt Rhea, D.C.
Regst: July 15, 1809
Regst: July 15, 1809

----

(40)

SAMUEL BLACKMORE	:	
TO	:	BILL OF SALE
HARMON C. VIEL*	:	

Date: Rec'd Blountville, Jan. 20, 1809
Consideration: $45.00
Description: 2 beds and bedding, his folding tables, 2 ovens, 6 Windsor chairs, 2 trunks, 2 bed steads, 1 black cow, and 1 set of curtains, 1 axe, I have this day sold to him
Wit: John Punch
Acknowledged: By Harmon C. Vied*, Sullivan Co, TN, May, 1809
Test: Robert Rhea, D.C.
Regst: July 25, 1809

(*Note: Name spelled both ways)

WILLIAM KING	:	
TO	:	DEED OF WARRANTY
JAMES ENGLISH	:	

Date: May 11, 1808
Consideration: $50.00
Amt of land: 1 acre more or less
Location: Sullivan Co, TN
Description: A lot No. 2, beginning at William King's of Abingdon's upper corner
Wit: James King, John O'Brien, James King, Jr.
Proven: By James King, Sullivan Co, May, 1808
Test: Mattw. Rhea, C.S.C.
Regst: July 25, 1807

WILLIAM FREAM   :
        TO   :   DEED OF WARRANTY
MARGRET HUGHES   :

Date: Aug. 22, 1809
Consideration: $100.00
Amt of land: By estimation 50 acres
Location: Sullivan Co, TN
Description: A tract of land originally granted to William Hughes
Wit: Lance Snapp, Wm N. Gale, John Rhea
Acknowledged: By William Fraimer, Sullivan Co, TN, May, 1809
Test: Mattw. Rhea, C.S.C.
Regst: Aug. 23, 1809

----

(42)   JOHN AKARD of   :
        Hawkins Co, TN   :
                TO   :   DEED OF WARRANTY
        JOHN THOMPSON   :

Date: April 13, 1809
Consideration: $500.00
Amt of land: 180 acres
Location: Sullivan Co, TN
Description: A tract of land on the waters of Reedy Creek
Wit: William Sherman, John McMinn, James Gaines
Acknowledged: By John Akard, Sullivan Co, TN, Aug. 1809
Test: Mattw. Rhea, C.S.C.
Regst: Sept. 1, 1809

----

(43)   SAMUEL VANCE   :
                TO   :   BILL OF SALE
        JOHN STEPHENS   :

Date: Dec. 7, 1805
Consideration: $252.00
Description: I acknowledge to have sold to John Stephens Dec. 7, 1805, by public sale, the sale was delivery upon the 4 head of horses, 1 black mare, and one rone, two bay colts, also 6 head of catele(sic), all my farming tools, 2 feather beds, all household and kitchen furniture for the sum of $250.00
Wit: William Snodgrass, Ezekiel Key
Acknowledged: By Samuel Vance, Sullivan Co, TN, Feb. 1806
Test: Mattw. Rhea, C.S.C.
Regst: Sept. 1, 1809

----

(44)   JAMES OFFILL   :
                TO   :   DEED OF WARRANTY
        JAMES GEORGE   :

Date: Aug. 21, 1809
Consideration: $100.00
Amt of land: 10 acres

Location: Sullivan Co, TN
Description: A tract of land on the waters of Holston River
Wit: Joseph Torbett, Henry Myers
Acknowledged: By Joseph Torbett and Henry Moyers, Sullivan Co, Tn, Aug, 1809
Test: Mattw. Rhea, C.S.C, by Robt Rhea, D.C.
Regst: Sept. 5, 1809

(Page)
(45)

JOHN TORBET, JR.   :
        TO   :   DEED OF WARRANTY
JOHN TORBET, SR.   :

Date: Dec. 9, 1808
Consideration: $259.00
Amt of land: 39 acres
Location: Sullivan Co, TN
Description: A tract of land containing 39 acres
Wit: Joseph Torbet, Henry Moyers
Test: Mattw. Rhea, C.S.C, by Robt Rhea, D.C.
Regst: Sept. 5, 1809

----

(46)

JOHN TORBET   :
        TO   :   DEED OF WARRANTY
JOSEPH TORBET   :

Date: Jan. 3, 1809
Consideration: $791.00
Amt of land: By estimation, 136 acres
Location: Sullivan Co, TN
Description: A tract of land where John Torbet now lives joining Moyers'* line
Wit: John Torbet, Henry Myers*
Proven: By John Tobet and Henry Myers, Sullivan Co, TN, Aug, 1809
Test: Mattw. Rhea, C.S.C, by Robt Rhea, D.C.
Regst: Sept 5, 1809

(*Note: name spelled both ways)

(47)

SAMUEL McCORKLE   :
        TO   :   DEED OF WARRANTY
JOHN BRADAN   :

Date: Feb. 16, 1809
Consideration: $40.00
Amt of land: 1/4 acre sq lot
Location: Sullivan Co, TN
Description: A tract of land where John Torbet now lives, Lot No. 6 in town of Middletown, being a corner lot adj. Robert Preston's
Wit: Thos Rockhold, Daniel Smith
Proven: By Thomas Rockhold, Sullivan Co, TN, Aug., 1808
Test: Mattw. Rhea, C.S.C, by Robt Rhea, D.C.
Regst: Sept. 5, 1809

28

JAMES WOOD, ESQUIRE, :
Gov. of Commonwealth of VA :
  TO : DEED OF WARRANTY
ROBERT PRESTON, Assignee of :
James Anderson :

Date: March 7, 1870(sic)
Consideration: By virtue of a preemption warrant No. 2389, issued March 7, 1780
Location: Washington Co
Description: A tract of land containing 203 acres by survey dated May 8, 1795, in the Rich Valley on the waters of Reedy Creek, a north branch of Holston River and known by Hickory Cabbin
Robert Preston hath title to the within
     Wm Price, Res. Off.
Regst: Oct. 25, 1809

----

(49)

JAMES MONROE, ESQUIRE, :
Gov. of Commonwealth of VA :
  TO :
ROBERT PRESTON, Assignee of :
William P. Skinner :

Date: May 17, 1783
Consideration: By virtue of a Land Office Treasurer Warrant, No. 16519, issued May 19, 1783
Amt of land: 80 acres
Location: Washington Co
Description: A tract of land on the waters of Reedy Creek, a north branch of main Holston River joining Meredith Archer's and William Goodert's land joining Sarah Robert's now John Foust's land
Robert Preston hath title to the within
     James Monroe
Regst: Oct. 26, 1809

----

(50)

BENJAMIN LEE :
  TO : DEED OF WARRANTY
WM N. GALE :

Date: May 2, 1809
Consideration: $700.00
Amt of land: 102 acres
Location: Sullivan Co, TN
Description: A tract of land containing 102 acres on the waters of Reedy Creek, joining William Elliott's line and also joining Peter Mingeas line
Wit: Henry Meiers, Henry Sprinkle, Henry Hawk
Acknowledged0 By Benjamin Lee, Sullivan Co, TN, May, 1809
Test: Mattw. Rhea, C.S.C.
Regst: Nov. 24, 1809

----

(51)   CASPER MAJORS   :

                 TO   :   DEED OF WARRANTY

JONATHAN BAUGHMAN &   :

NATHAN BAUGHMAN   :

Date: Aug. 19, 1808
Consideration: $10.00
Amt of land: 1/2 acre
Location: Sullivan Co, TN
Description: A tract of land in town of Manchester or Cum town, being a part of the tract John Crum purchasd of James and Thos Gaines at No. 2 on the north side of main road in sd town
Wit: Phillip Kite, Reuben Oler
Proven: By Phillip Kite and Reuben Oler, Sullivan Co, TN, Nov, 1809
Test: Mattw. Rhea, C.S.C.
Regst: Nov. 30, 1809

----

(52)   JUDITH SHOEMAKER & :

        JEREMIAH SHOEMAKER :

                TO   :   DEED OF WARRANTY

DANIEL SHOEMAKER   :

Date: Oct. 25, 1809
Consideration: $350.00
Amt of land: 72 acres and 118 poles
Location: Sullivan Co, Tn
Description: That tract of land on the north side of Holston River, beginning at William Thomas' corner and on a conditional line between John Shoemaker, dec'd, and Daniel Shoemaker
Wit: Robert Easley, William Dougherty*
Proven: By Robert Easley and William Daugherty*, Sullivan Co, Tn, Nov, 1809
Test: Mattw. Rhea, C.S.C, by Robt Rhea, D.C.
Regst: Nov. 30, 1809

(*Note: Name spelled both ways)

(54)   HENRY PICKETT of   :

        Carter Co, TN   :

               TO   :   DEED OF WARRANTY

JACOB HAINES   :

Date: Nov. 3, 1809
Consideration: $400.00
Amt of land: 61 acres
Location: Sullivan Co, Tn
Description: A tract of land on the north side of Holston River
Wit: Thomas Majors, Stephen Majors
Proven: By Stephen Majors and Thomas Majors
Test: Mattw. Rhea, C.S.C, by Robert Rhea, D.C.
Regst: Dec. 4, 1809

```
THOMAS ROCKHOLD       :
        TO            :      DEED OF WARRANTY
JOHN MILLER           :
```

Date: Oct. 16, 1809
Consideration: A valuable consideration
Amt of land: 105 acres
Location: Sullivan Co, TN
Description: A tract of land containing 105 acres
Wit: John Anderson, Zachariah Wicks
Acknowledged: By Thomas Rockhold, Sullivan Co, TN, Nov, 1809
Test: Mattw. Rhea, C.S.C, by Robt Rhea, D.C.
Regst: Dec. 5, 1809

----

(57)

```
DAVID VANCE & JOHN VANCE of   :
Jackson Co, TN                :
        TO                    :      DEED OF WARRANTY
JOHN PROFFITT                 :
```

Date: Aug. 22, 1808
Consideration: 200 ₺ current money of TN
Amt of land: 200 acres
Location: Sullivan Co, TN
Description: All that tract of land beginning at Garrett Fitzgerald's corner
Wit: John Billingsby, William Cox, George Sylvester
Proven: By John Billingsby, William Cox, Sullivan Co, Feb, 1809
Test: Mattw. Rhea, C.S.C.
Regst: Feb. 1, 1810

----

(58)

```
HARMAN LATTURE        :
        TO            :      DEED OF WARRANTY
JOHN CURTAIN          :
```

Date: (No date given)
Consideration: A valuable consideration
Amt of land: 35 acres
Location: Sullivan Co, TN
Description: a tract of land containing 35 acres more or less by virute of
a grant issued to me by TN, No. 675, which doth authorize me to
relinquish my claim, land joins a survey of Curtain's
Acknowledged: By Harman Latture, Sullivan Co, Feb, 1810
Test: Mattw. Rhea, C.S.C, by Robert Rhea, D.C.
Regst: Feb. 26, 1810

----

(59)

```
HARMAN LATTURE        :
        TO            :      DEED OF WARRANTY
JACOB DROKE           :
```

Date: Feb. 20, 1810
Consideration: A valuable consideration
Amt of land: 60 acres
Location: Sullivan Co, TN

Description: A tract of land on the waters of Reedy Creek
Wit: John Anderson
Acknowledged: By Harman Latture, Sullivan Co, Feb, 1810
Test: Mattw. Rhea, C.S.C, by Robt Rhea, D.C.
Regst: Feb. 28, 1810

(Page)
60)

ARNOLD SHELL	:	
TO	:	DEED OF WARRANTY
ANDREW SHELL	:	

Date: Aug. 15, 1809
Consideration: A valuable consideration
Amt of land: 75 acres
Location: Sullivan Co, TN
Description: A tract of land on the south side of Holston River
Wit: John Anderson, John Shell, Elijah Watson, John Miller
Proven: By John Anderson ' Elijah Watson, Sullivan Co, Feb, 1810
Test: Mattw Rhea, C.S.C, by Robt Rhea, D.C.
Regst: Feb. 28, 1810

----

(61)

WALTER JAMES	:	
TO	:	DEED OF WARRANTY
SOLOMON JONES	:	

Date: Oct. 10, 1809
Consideration: $40.00
Amt of land: 57 acres
Location: Sullivan Co, TN
Description: A tract of land containing 57 acres more or less
Wit: John Anderson, Samuel Jones, Peter Droke
Acknowledged: By Solomon Jones, Sullivan Co, TN, Feb, 1810
Test: Mattw. Rhea, C.S.C, by Robt Rhea, D.C.
Regst: Feb. 28, 1810

----

(62)

JACOB SHRODER	:	
TO	:	DEED OF WARRANTY
THOMAS WHITE	:	

Date: Jan. 1, 1810
Consideration: $265.00
Amt of land: 108 acres
Location: Sullivan Co, TN
Description: A tract of land containing 108 acres more or less
Wit: James Blevins, Jacob Miller, John Booher
Proven: By Jacob Miller, John Booher, Sullivan Co, TN, Feb, 1810
Test: Mattw. Rhea, C.S.C, by Robt Rhea, D.C.
Regst: March 2, 1810

----

(63)

COMMISSIONER OF BLOUNTVILLE	:	
TO	:	DEED OF WARRANTY
WALTER JAMES	:	

Date: Feb. 23, 1810
Consideration: $5.13
Amt of land: 792 sq ft
Location: Town of Blountville
Description: A tract of land joining Lot No. 4, and joining the alley before
the courthouse
Wit: (No names given)
Acknowledged: By George Rutledge and Jacob Sturm, Sullivan Co, TN, Feb,
1810
Test: Mattw. Rhea, C.S.C, by Robt Rhea, D.C.
Regst: March 3, 1810

(Page)
(64)   JOHN HOWARD   :
                    TO   :   DEED OF WARRANTY
              JACOB COOK   :

Date: Nov. 18, 1809
Consideration: 800 ? to him in hand paid
Amt of land: 127 acres
Location: Sullivan Co, TN
Description: A tract of land containing 127 acres running along Elish
Harbor's line
Wit: Thomas Morrison, Elisha Harbour, David Roller
Proven: By Elisha Harbour and David Roller, Sullivan Co, Feb, 1810
Test: Mattw Rhea, C.S.C, by Robt Rhea, D.C.
Regst: March 3, 1810

----

(65)   THOMAS SHELBY*, Sheriff   :
                    TO   :   SHERIFF'S DEED
              JACOB SNAPP of   :
              Shenandoah Co. VA   :

Date: Aug. 18, 1803
Judgment Obtained: Robert Preston and James preston obtained judgment
and execution against William Webb bearing date 1803. Execution was
returned to the court of Sullivan aforesaid levied on one lot in Blountville.
Issued from the court, directed to the sheriff commanding him to expose to
public sale the lot to satisfy the aforesaid execution by virture the lot
was exposed to sale to highest bidder
Description: Lot in Blountville adj. Jacob Sturm, containing 42 feet in front
upon the great road leading through the town and 264 feet back and
Jacob Snapp bid $20, being the highest
Wit: John Tipton, J. Gaines, Jon Carithers
Acknowledged: By Thomas Shelley*, Sheriff
Test: Mattw. Rhea, C.S.C, by Robt Rhea, D.C.
Regst: March 22, 1810

(*Note: Name spelled both ways)

(66)   JOHN TIPTON   :
                    TO   :   DEED OF WARRANTY
              JOHN STURM   :

33

Date: Sept 14, 1809
Consideration: $250.00
Amt of land: 2 1/2 acres
Location: Sullivan Co, TN
Description: A tract of land near the town of Blountville
Wit: John Anderson, Lawrence Snapp, J. Robert Blackmore
Acknowledged: By John Tipton, Sullivan Co, TN, Feb, 1810
Test: Mattw. Rhea, C.S.C, by Robt Rhea, D.C.
Regst: March 29, 1810

----

(67)　　WALTER JAMES　　　　　:
　　　　　　　TO　　　　　　　:　　DEED OF WARRANTY
　　　　RICHARD BASKET &　　　:
　　　　JOHN BASKET　　　　　 :

Date: Feb. 19, 1810
Consideration: $1168.00
Amt of land: 200 acres
Location and Description: A tract of land on the south side of Holston
River on Kendrick's Creek incl. a grist mill and saw mill, and between
Henry Hughes and William Fitzgerrald's land and on a dividing land between
Henry Hughes and John Bailey and joining Isaac Agee's line
Acknowledged: By Walter James, Sullivan Co, Tn, Feb, 1810
Test: Mattw. Rhea, C.S.C, by Robt. Rhea, D.C.
Regst: March 29, 1810

----

(68)　　ABEL EDWARDS of　　　 :
　　　　Washington Co, TN　　　:
　　　　　　　TO　　　　　　　:　　DEED OF WARRANTY
　　　　LITTLEBURY SAMS　　　 :

Date: Dec. 29, 1807
Consideration: $1000.00
Amt of land: 160 acres
Location: Sullivan Co, TN
Description: A tract of land on the south side of Holston River
Wit: Joshua Edwards, Obediah Sams, William Erwin
Proven: By Joshua Edwards and Obediah Sams, Sullivan Co, TN, Feb, 1807
Test: Mattw. Rhea, C.S.C, by Robt. Rhea, D.C.
Regst: March 30, 1810

　　　　GEORGE EMMERT of　　　:
　　　　Carter Co, TN　　　　　:
　　　　　　　TO　　　　　　　:　　DEED OF WARRANTY
　　　　HENRY HARKELROAD　　　:

Date: Feb. 21, 1810
Consideration: $5000.00
Amt of land: 43 acres
Location: Sullivan Co, Tn
Description: A tract of land on Beaver Creek, branch of Holston River on
a corner of John Beeler's land
Wit: Martin Harkleroad, John Hickman

Acknowledged: By George Emmert, Sullivan Co, TN, Feb, 1810
Test: Mattw. Rhea, C.S.C, by Robt Rhea, D.C.
Regst: March 31, 1810

(Page)
(71)

PHILLIP KING, Attorney :
         TO   :   ATTORNEY'S DEED OF WARRANTY
THOMAS HOPKINS   :

Date: Dec. 7, 1808
Consideration: $80.00
Amt of land: 200 acres
Location: Sullivan Co, TN
Description: A tract of land on the waters of Reedy Creek on Pendleton's
old patent line also on Thomas White's line
Wit: John Lynn, John H. Rader, Robert christian
Acknowledged: By Phillip King, Sullivan Co, TN, Nov, 1809
Test: Mattw. Rhea, C.S.C, by Robt Rhea, D.C.
Regst: April 7, 1810

----

(72)   STATE OF NORTH CAROLINA :
ALEXANDER MARTIN, GOV.   :   LAND GRANT
         TO   :   NO. 213
JOSEPH BRAGG   :

Date: Oct. 10, 1782
Consideration: 50 shillings for every 100 acres of land
Amt of land: 200 acres
Location: Sullivan Co, TN
Description: A tract of land containing 200 acres on the south side of
Walker's fork a branch of Horse Creek betwen John Christian and the big
ridge incl. the Big Clay Lick
Alexander Martin, Gov. By his Excellys. Comd. J. Glasgow, Sec.
Regst: May 1, 1810

----

(73)   JOHN HAMMER of   :
Washington Co, TN   :
         TO   :   BILL OF SALE
WILLIAM FREAM   :

Date: June 29, 1808
Consideration: $275.00
Negro sold: One negro girl named Poll, whose right and title I do by these
presents from me and my heirs, executors or any other persons whatsoever
comes claiming or to claim I will forever warrant and defend
Wit: Henry King, Jonathan Hammer
Proven: By Henry King and Jonathan Hammer, Sullivan Co, TN, May, 1810
Test: Mattw. Rhea, C.S.C,
Regst: May 21, 1810

```
ELIZABETH SPIRGEN,      :
ADMINISTRATOR           :
        TO              :       DEED OF WARRANTY
THOMAS COX              :
```

Date: Feb. 20, 1809
Consideration: $500.00
Amt of land: 194 acres
Location: Sullivan Co, TN
Description: A parcel of land beginning at Jennings corner
Wit: Jacob Slaughter, Alexander Moore
Proven: By Jacob Slaughter, Sullivan Co, TN, Nov, 1809
Test: Mattw. Rhea, C.S.C.
Regst: May 28, 1810

----

(74)
```
CONRAD SHIPLEY          :
        TO              :       DEED OF WARRANTY
JOHN MOSELY             :
```

Date: Nov. 5, 1801
Consideration: $900.00
Amt of land: 3 acres
Location: Sullivan Co, TN
Description: All that parcel of land on the south side of Holston River
beginning on Alexander Cavitt's corner
Wit: Jacob Slaughter, Alexander Moore
Proven: By Jacob Slaughter, Sullivan Co, TN, Nov, 1801
Test: Mattw. Rhea, C.S.C
Regst: May 28, 1810

----

(75)
```
ROBERT CHRISTIAN        :
        TO              :       DEED OF WARRANTY
DANIEL ROGAN            :
```

Date: May 21, 1810
Consideration: $43.00
Amt of land: 1 acre
Location: Sullivan Co, TN
Description: A lot of land in the town of Christianville, commonly called
Boatyard
Wit: William Smithers, John Lynn
Proven: By William Smithers and John Lynn, Sullivan Co, TN, May, 1810
Test: Mattw. Rhea, C.S.C, by Robt. Rhea, D.C.
Regst: May 29, 1810

----

(76)
```
HARMAN LATTURE          :
        TO              :       QUIT CLAIM DEED
WALTER JOHNSON          :
```

Date: (No date given)
Consideration: A valuable consideration
Amt of land: 50 acres

Location: Sullivan Co, TN
Description: A tract of land containing 50 acres by virtue of a grant
issued to me by TN, No. 674, which is on a line of former survey of
Walter Johnson
Acknowledged: Sullivan Co, Feb, 1810
Test: Mattw. Rhea, C.S.C, by Robt Rhea, D.C.
Regst: May 29, 1810

(Page)
(77)

```
WILLIAM HUGHES              :
       TO                   :        BILL OF SALE
SAMUEL MOORE HUGHES &       :
SUSANNAH HUGHES             :
```

Date: Feb. 19, 1810
Consideration: Natural love and affection and for divers other good causes
and considerations
Sold: I, William Hughes, do give grant and confirm unto Samuel and
Susannah and their heirs and assigns the following negro slaves Queean,
Fan, Elisha, and Lucinda and their increase to have sd slaves to Samuel
and Susannah from the day on which my son, Samuel Hughes, shall attain
his age of 21 years without lawful issue his or her moiety of slaves and
their increase to be held by my children, their heirs and assigns forever
Proven: By William Hughes, Sullivan Co, Tn, Feb, 1810
Test: Mattw. Rhea, C.S.C, by Robt. Rhea, D.C.
Regst: May 20, 1810

----

(78)
```
JOHN WADDLE       :
     TO           :        DEED OF WARRANTY
JACOB WADDLE      :
```

Date: May 12, 1810
Consideration: A valuable consideration
Amt of land: 1 acre
Location: Sullivan Co, Tn
Description: A tract of land on the waters of Reedy Creek
Wit: John Anderson, Margaret Maggil, Henry Maggart, Joseph Cox
Acknowledged: By John Waddle, Sullivan Co, Tn, May, 1810
Test: Mattw. Rhea, C.S.C, by Robt Rhea, D.C.
Regst: (No date given)

----

(79)
```
HEWES CADE        :
     TO           :        BILL OF SALE
REUBEN OHLER      :
```

Date: Jan. 25, 1810
Consideration: $400.00
Articles sold: One studd horse namde Rockingham, with three stills and all
the vessels pertaining to the stilling business for and in consideration of
$400.00
Wit: John Lynn
Proven: By John Lynn, Sullivan Co, TN, May, 1810

Test: Mattw. Rhea, C.S.C, by Robt Rhea, D.C.
Regst: June 6, 1810

(Page)
(79)   JOHN DERTING   :
            TO   :   DEED OF WARRANTY
       DANIEL SHOEMAKER   :

       Date: March 19, 1810
       Consideration: $15.00
       Amt of land: 5 acres, 132 poles
       Location: Sullivan Co, Tn
       Description: A tract of land beginning at Shoemaker's line and joining
       Weaver's line
       Wit: Peter Branstetter, Robert Easley
       Proven: By robert Easley and Peter Branstetter, Sullivan Co, Tn, May, 1810
       Test: Mattw. Rhea, C.S.C, by Robt Rhea, D.C.
       Regst: June 14, 1810

----

(80)   HENRY MAGGERT, SR.   :
            TO   :   DEED OF WARRANTY
       HENRY PECTAL   :

       Date: Feb. 20, 1810
       Consideration: A valuable consideration
       Amt of land: 118 acres
       Location: Sullivan Co, TN
       Description: a tract of land on the waters of Reedy Creek
       Wit: Ambrose Gaines, John Carithers
       Acknowledged: By Henry Magart, Sullivan Co, Tn, Feb, 1810
       Test: Mattw. Rhea, C.S.C, by Robt Rhea, D.C.
       Regst: June 18, 1810

----

(81)   JOHN TIPTON   :
            TO   :   DEED OF WARRANTY
       JACOB STURM   :

       Date: March 6, 1810
       Consideration: $40.00
       Amt of land: 1/2 acre
       Location: Sullivan Co, TN
       Description: A tract of land on the north side of Blountville on the road
       leading to Samuel Carrithers'
       Wit: George Rutledge, Phillip Snapp
       Acknowledged: By John Tipton, Sullivan Co, Tn, May, 1810
       Test: Mattw. Rhea, C.S.C, by Robt Rhea, D.C.
       Regst: June 19, 1810

----

(82)   WILLIAM WALLACE   :
            TO   :   DEED OF WARRANTY
       JOHN SINCLAIR   :

       Date: Aug. 31, 1809

                        38

Consideration: $100.00
Amt of land: 23 acres
Location: Sullivan Co, TN
Description: All that parcel of land on Kendrick Creek, being a part of
the tract the state of NC granted to David Perry*
Wit: George Vincent, Lot O'Gott, Hugh Martin
Proven: By Lot O'Gott, Hugh Martin, May, 1810
Test: Mattw. Rhea, C.S.C, by Robt Rhea, D.C.
Regst: June 19, 1810

(*Note: Name spelled both ways)

(Page)
(84)

WALTER JAMES	:	
TO	:	DEED OF WARRANTY
JAMES RHEA	:	

Date: Sept. 7, 1809
Consideration: $70.00
Amt of land: 76 poles and 6 sq feet
Location: Sullivan Co, TN
Description: A piece of land adj. the town of Blountville on the north side
Acknowledged: By Walter James, Sullivan Co, TN, May, 1810
Test: Mattw. Rhea, C.S.C, by Robt. Rhea, D.C.
Regst: June 19, 1810

----

(85)

PHILIP SNAPP	:	
TO	:	DEED OF WARRANTY
JAMES RHEA	:	

Date: Aug. 2, 1809
Consideration: $110.00
Amt of land: 1/2 acre
Location: Sullivan Co, TN
Description: Two lots of land in Blountville containing 1/2 acre, known by
Lot Nos. 31 and 31
Wit: John Punch, Jonathan M. Henry
Acknowledged: By Philip Snapp, Sullivan Co, TN, May, 1810
Test: Mattw. Rhea, C.S.C, by Robt Rhea, D.C.
Regst: June 19, 1810

----

(86)

ANN SMITH of	:	
Grainger Co	:	
TO	:	DEED OF WARRANTY
JACOB BOY	:	

Date: Aug. 9, 1810
Consideration: A valuable consideration
Amt of land: 470 acres
Location: Sullivan Co
Description: A tract of land on the north side of Holston River
Wit: Thos Rockhold, Andrew Crockett

Proven: By Thomas Rockhold and Andrew Crockett, Sullivan Co, Tn, May, 1810
Test: Mattw. Rhea, C.S.C, by Robt Rhea, D.C.
Regst: June 19, 1810

(Page)
(87) JOHN PAYE(Page ?) of :
    Smith Co, TN   :
      TO   : DEED OF WARRANTY
    PETER MORGAN :

Date: Nov. 1, 1809
Consideration: $1104.00
Amt of land: 276 acres
Location: Sullivan Co, TN
Description: A tract of land on the waters of Horse Creek
Wit: Hugh Martin, John McBride, Jacob Toland, Joshua Morgan
Proven: By Jacob Toland and Joshua Morgan, Sullivan Co, TN, 1810
Test: Mattw. Rhea, C.S.C, by Robt Rhea, D.C.
Regst: June 20, 1810

----

(88) STATE OF NORTH CAROLINA :
    RICHARD DOBBS SPAIGHT, GOV. : LAND GRANT
      TO   : NO. 580
    GEORGE SEVERS   :

Date: June 27, 1793
Consideration: 50 shillings for every 100 acres
Amt of land: 200 acres
Location: Sullivan Co
Description: A tract on the north side of Holston River
Proven: Rich'd Dobbs Spaight, By his Excelly, Com. J. Glasgow, Sec. No. 765
Regst: (No date given)

----

(89) GEORGE LEWIS   :
            : SURVEY

Date: Aug. 14, 1792
Entered: March 28, 1781
Order for Survey: By virtue of a warrant to me directed containing 200 acres, No. 765. I have survey for George Lewis the following land
Description: 200 acres more or less in the territory south of the River Ohio on the north side of Holston River
Wit: James McClair, Isaac Taylor, C.B.
Regst: Aug. 22, 1810   George Vincent, C.S.

----

(90) STATE OF TENNESSEE
    ARCHIBALD ROANE : LAND GRANT
      TO   : NO. 710
    BENJAMIN KEY   :

46

Date: May 23, 1809
Consideration: Of an entry made in the office of the Surveyor of the
Sixth District of No. 271, dated May 23, 1809, founded on a warrant of
No. 542 issued by Archibald Roane to Benjamin Key for 300 acres of land
dated Oct. 8, 1808, 64 acres of which are assigned to Adam Smith the
enterer.
Description: There is granted by the state of TN unto Adam Smith and his
heirs a tract of land containing 30 acres in the District of Washington on
the south side of Holston River
The great seal of the state to be affixed at Knoxville, Feb. 3, 1810, and
of American Independence the thirty-fourth
By the Governor: Willis Blount
Certified: E.W. Scott, Feb. 3, 1810, land office for E. TN
Regst: Aug. 23, 1810

(Page)
(90)

STATE OF TENNESSEE   :
ARCHIBALD ROANE   :   LAND GRANT
        TO   :   NO. 711
BENJAMIN KEY   :

Date: May 23, 1809
Consideration: An entry made in the office of the surveyor of the Sixth
District of No. 270, dated May 23, 1809, founded on warrant of No. 542,
issued by Archibald Roane to Benjamin Key for 300 acres, dated Oct. 8,
1808. 64 acres of which are assigned to Adam Smith the enterer.
Description: There is granted by the state ot TN to Adam Smith and his
heirs, a tract of land containing 34 acres in the District of Washington on
the south side of Holston River
The great seal to be affixed at Knoxville, Feb. 3, 1810. By the Gov.
Willie Blount, R. Houston, Sec.
Certified: E.W. Scott, Feb. 3, 1810, Land Office for E. TN
Regst: Aug. 23, 1810

----

(91)

PETER MORGAN   :
        TO   :   DEED OF WARRANTY
JOSHUA MORGAN   :

Date: March 14, 1810
Consideration: Love, good will and affection.
Amt of land: 100 acres
Location: Sullivan Co, TN
Description: All that tract of land on Horse Creek being part of a tract
purchased from John Page, beginning on Walkers Fork at the mouth of
Lynches Branch
Wit: Richard Murrell, Frederick Titsworth, Vansandt Morgan
Proven: By Frederick Titsworth and Vansandt Morgan, Sullivan Co, TN, Aug,
1810
Test: Mattw. Rhea, C.S.C, by Robt Rhea, D.C.
Regst: Aug. 21, 1810

----

(92)

ISRAEL W. BONHAM :
          TO   :   QUIT CLAIM
JAMES HUGHES :

Date: Aug. 13, 1810
Purpose: David Hughes, dec'd, made his last will and testament dated July 29, 1806. Among other legacies therein contained give and bequeath unto Israel W. Bonham of Sullivan Co, 50 acres, made James Hughes sole executor authorizing Hughes to make I.W. Bonham a deed for the land for a valuable consideration paid by James Hughes sd I.W. Bonham, executes this deed of quit claim to the sd 50 acres of land
Wit: (No names given)
Regst: (No date given)

----

(93)

THOMAS SMALLING, JR. :
          TO   :   DEED OF WARRANTY
WILLIAM WIRICK :

Date: Aug. 17, 1810
Consideration: $200.00
Amt of land: 40 acres
Location: Sullivan Co, TN
Description: A tract of land, being the same where Thomas Smalling, Sr, now lives
Wit: Isaac McKinley, Nicholas Mattorn, Christian Weaver
Proven: By Nicholas Martin and Isaac McKinley, Sullivan Co, TN, Aug, 1810
Test: Mattw. Rhea, C.S.C, by Robt Rhea, D.C.
Regst: Aug. 29, 1810

----

(94)

SAMUEL VANCE :
          TO   :   BILL OF SALE
WALTER JOHNSON :

Date: Jan. 11, 1801
Consideration: $400.00
Description: Samuel Vance has sold unto Walter Johnson and David* Yearsley, 3 negro slaves for life; one woman named Pol, one man named Jas, and one boy named Ed, for the sum of $400.00 to me in hand paid to have the following negroes for the following times: Pol to serve them one year after my decease, Jas to serve them five yrs after my decease, and Ed to serve them 12 years after my decease as their servants, then at the expiration of the servant tenus aforesaid as they shall expire, Walter Johnson and Daniel* Yearsley. If the sd negroes are in their possession or if they are to freely discharge them from their service by legal means.
Proven: By Samuel Evans, Sullivan Co, TN, Aug, 1805
Exhibited in court a bill of sale from Samuel Vance, late dec'd, to David Yearsley and Walter Johnson for three negro slaves to prove by the oath of Samuel Evans to the sd bill of sale and also provide that John Taylor has attested the same by his proper mark thereto subscribed and therefore ordered the same to be registered.
Test: Mattw. Rhea, C.S.C, by Robt. Rhea, D.C.
(Regst): Aug. 30, 1810

PHILLIP SNAPP   :
      TO   :   MORTGAGE OF LAND
JOSIAH WHITE of   :
City of Phila.   :

Date: Aug. 13, 1808
Consideration: $456.00 lawful money
Amt of land: Two lots with all improvements where Snapp now lives; 3/4
and 1/2 of 1/4 an acre and 929 sq ft and one other lot in the town of
Blountville, Lot No. 13, containing 1/4 acre
Terms of mortgage: Subject to the conditions that Snapp has this day given
his bond obligatory commonly called a bill single to White for $465.00
payable 15 months after date. If Phillip shall not pay White sd sum with
interest then this deed to be poid(sic), otherwise to remain in full force.
Snapp to have full possession of these presents until default be made
Wit: D. Yearsley, John Snapp
Acknowledged: By Phillip Snapp, Sullivan Co, TN, Feb, 1809
Test: Mattw. Rhea, C.S.C, by Robt Rhea, D.C.
Regst: Sept. 20, 1810

ELIZABETH MAYFIELD, GEORGE GENTRY :
SAMUEL & NICHOLAS GENTRY, and   :
JAMES BOYD of Williamson Co, TN   :   QUIT CLAIM DEED
      TO   :
PETER DROKE   :

Date: June 3, 1808
Consideration: A valuable consideration
Amt of land: 240 acres
Location: Sullivan Co, TN
Description: A tract of land on the waters of Fall Creek
Acknowledged: By Elizabeth Mayfield, George Gentry, Nicholas Gentry, Jas.
Boyd.
Test: N.P. Hardihan, Clk of Williamson Co Court
(Regst): Sept. 21, 1810

ISAAC SHELBY   :
      TO   :   DEED OF WARRANTY
JOHN ACREE   :

Date: Nov. 10, 1809
Consideration: $800.00
Amt of land: 200 acres
Location: Sullivan Co, TN
Description: All that tract of land on the north side of Holston River
known as Sugar Hollow, beginning on John Bolden's line, formerly the lines
of Laurence Heatsin and joining John Shelby's corner
Acknowledged: By Isaac Shelby, Sullivan Co, TN, Feb, 1810
Test: Mattw Rhea, C.S.C, by Robt Rhea, D.C.
Regst: Oct. 5, 1810

STATE OF TENNESSEE   :
JOHN CARTER   :   L A N D   G R A N T
     TO   :   NO. 714
JAMES OFFIELD   :

Date: Sept. 8, 1808
Consideration: Of an entry made in the office of the Sixth District of No. 124, dated Sept. 8, 1808, and founded on a warranty of No. 1604 issued by John Carter to James Offield for 400 acres dated Sept. 12, 1779.
Amt of land: 400 acres
Location: Sullivan Co, TN
Description: There is granted by the state of TN to James Offield for 400 acres of land dated Sept. 12, 1779
Amt of land: 400 acres
Location: Sullivan Co, TN
Description: There is granted by the state of TN to James Offield a tract of land containing 100 acres in Sullivan Co, in the District of Washington. (Warrant reads 400 acres, Amt granted 100 acres)
Wit: By the Gov. Willie Blount, R. Houghton, Sec.
E.W. Scott, Register of the land office for East TN
I do certify that this grant is recorded in my office. Given under my hand, Feb. 3, 1810
Regst: Oct. 5, 1810

----

(99)

WILLIAM HUGHES   :
     TO   :
SAMUEL MOORE HUGHES and :   DEED OF GIFT
SUSANNAH, THEIR HEIRS AND :
ASSIGNS   :

Date: Feb. 19, 1810
Consideration: Natural love and affection
Amt of land: 200 acres
Location: Sullivan Co, TN
Description: A tract of land on the north side of Reedy Creek, joining Ambrose Gaines' line
Wit: (No name given)
Acknowledged: By William Hughes, Sullivan Co, TN, Feb, 1810
(Regst): Oct. 30, 1810

----

(100)

SAMUEL MOORE   :
     TO   :   DEED OF WARRANTY
WILLIAM HUGHES   :

Date: Jan. 26, 1810
Consideration: $800.00
Amt of land: 242 acres
Location: Sullivan Co, TN
Description: A tract of land on both sides of Reedy Creek
Acknowledged: By Samuel Moore, Sullivan Co, TN, Feb, 1810
Test: Mattw. Rhea, C.S.C, by Robt Rhea,D.C.
Regst: Nov. 1, 1810

----

(100)   JAMES WOOD, ESQUIRE   :
          GOV. OF COMMONWEALTH OF VA   :
                      TO   :   LAND GRANT
          BENJAMIN WASHBURN   :

Date: April 5, 1782
Reason for Grant: By virtue of presumption Warrant No. 2091, issued april 5, 1782
Amt of land: 186 acres, No. 291
Location: Washington Co,TN
Description: A tract of land containing 186 acres by survey, dated May 5, 1795, on the north fork of Reedy Creek, north branch of Holston River, in Washington Co
Wit: James Wood
Benjamin Washburn hath title to the within
Regst: Nov. 23, 1810

----

(101)   JAMES PHAGAN, SHERIFF   :
                  TO   :
          GEORGE & CHRISTOPHER   :   SHERIFF'S DEED
          LINDENBERGER, Merchants of   :
          Baltimore, MD   :

Date: Aug. 18, 1808
Consideration: $2,002.28
G. & C. Lindenberger recovered judgment in the court of Pleas and Qtr Sessions for Sullivan Co, TN, May, 1802, for the sum of $2,002.28. In virtue of same judgment a writ of execution ws issued returnable to the Aug Session and directed to Sheriff Frances H. Gaines, commanding him to make of the goods of Jacob Emmert cause to be made the same sum of $2,028.28 and fees endorsed and to have the same moneis ready to render to same George and Christopher Lindenberger at the court of pleas and qtr sessions to be held in and for the same county in Aug, 1802. In pursuance of the command of the sd writ execution was levied on a tract of land on the drains of the Watauga River containing 149 acres. Sd land sold by Francis H. Gaines, Sheriff, Aug. 13, 1802, at public sale at the courthouse in the county aforesaid, and Laurence Snapp, Sr, agent for the aforesaid Lindenbergers did bid the sum of $23.00 for the same tract of land. They being the highest bidders became the purchasers of the same tract of land and whereas the same Francis Gaines removed from the county before he made a deed for the land as he was authorized by law. I, James Phagan, Sheriff, of the sd county aforesaid have signed my name and affixed my seal this 18th day of Aug, 1808
Acknowledged: By James Phagan, Sullivan Co, TN, Aug, 1808
Test: Mattw. Rhea, C.S.C, by Robt Rhea, D.C.
Regst: Nov. 26, 1810

----

(103)   CONRAD SHERITZ   :
                  TO   :   DEED OF WARRANTY
          JACOB MILLER   :

Date: Nov. 19, 1810
Consideration: $18.00

Amt of land: 40 poles
Location: Sullivan Co, TN
Description: A lot of land laid off by Wallace Willoughby and number 5th on the west bank of Sinking Creek
Acknowledged: By Conrad Sheritz, Sullivan Co, TN, Nov, 1810
Test: Mattw. Rhea, C.S.C, by Robt Rhea, D.C.
Regst: Nov. 27, 1810

(Page)
(104)

WILLIAM STEPHENS   :
         TO   :   DEED OF WARRANTY
JACOB THOMAS, JR.   :

Date: Nov. 19, 1810
Consideration: Not stated
Amt of land: 100 acres
Location: Sullivan Co, TN
Description: One tract of land on the south side of Holston River, being part of a tract of land devised to William Stephens by the last will and testament of Thomas Stephens, dec'd.
Wit: Robert Rhea
Acknowledged: By William Stephens, Sullivan Co, Tn, Nov, 1810
Test: Mattw. Rhea, C.S.C, by Robert Rhea, D.C.
Regst: Nov. 28, 1810

HENRY FELTNER of   :
Hawkins Co   :
         TO   :   DEED OF WARRANTY
THOMAS JACKSON   :

Date: Aug. 29, 1810
Consideration: $330.00
Amt of land: 110 acres
Location: Sullivan Co, TN
Description: All that tract of land joining the land of George Roller, Jenkins Murphy place formerly the widow Bailey's now in possession of John Richardson and Eatons Ridge and on Pendleton's line
Wit: Jacob Welelrood, Aaron Brown, John Westmoreland
Proven: By Jacob Rultner and Aaron Brown, Sullivan Co, TN, Nov, 1810
Test: Mattw. Rhea, C.S.C, by Robt Rhea, D.C.
Regst: Nov. 29, 1810

----

(105)   JOHN STEPHENS   :
         TO   :   DEED OF WARRANTY
ISAAC STEPHENS &   :
FELIX STEPHENS   :

Date: Aug. 29, 1810
Consideration: $100.00
Amt of land: 228 acres
Location: Sullivan Co,TN

Description: A tract of land on the north bank of the Holston River incl.
the plantation where John Stephens now lives, being the tracts of land
granted to John Crisman, dec'd.
Wit: Joyn(sic) Tipton, E.R. Dulaney, Laurence Snapp
Proven: By John Tipton and Elkahan R. Dulaney, Sullivan Co, TN, Nov.
1810
Test: Mattw. Rhea, C.S.C, by Robt Rhea, D.C.
Regst: Dec. 1, 1810

(Page)
(106) GEORGE LITTLE, SR.   :
              TO   :   DEED OF WARRANTY
       GEORGE LITTLE, JR.   :

       Date: Nov. 13, 1808
       Consideration: A valuable consideration
       Amt of land: 60 acres
       Location: Sullivan Co, TN
       Description: A tract of land on the north branch of the Holston River,
       joining Charles Newton's line
       Wit: Isaac Brownlow, John Anderson, Henry Sigler, John McCorkle
       Proven: By John Anderson and John McCorkle, Sullivan Co, TN, Feb, 1809
       Test: Mattw. Rhea, C.S.C, by Robt Rhea, D.C.
       Regst: Dec. 4, 1810

----

(107) HENRY PECTOL   :
              TO   :   DEED OF WARRANTY
       JACOB DROKE   :

       Date: Nov. 1, 1810
       Consideration: A valuable consideration
       Amt of land: 118 acres
       Location: Sullivan Co, TN
       Description: A tract of land joining James Bright's line and a conditional
       line between Henry Maggert and John Carithers
       Wit: John Anderson, Henry Maggert
       Acknowledged: By Henry Pectal, Sullivan Co, TN, Nov, 1810
       Test: Mattw. Rhea, C.S.C, by Robt Rhea, D.C.
       Regst: Dec. 4, 1810

----

(108) HENRY FELTNER of   :
       Hawkins Co   :
              TO   :   DEED OF WARRANTY
       JENKIN MURPHY   :

       Date: Aug. 29, 1810
       Consideration: $1260.00
       Amt of land: 420 acres
       Location: Sullivan Co, TN
       Description: A tract of land at the foot of Eaton's Ridge and joining land
       of George Roller, David Ross and others near Pendleton(s patent line

Wit: Jacob Deliland, Thos Jackson, Aaron Brown
Proven: By Thomas Jackson and Jacob Fultner, Sullivan Co, TN, Nov, 1810
Test: Mattw. Rhea, C.S.C, by Robt Rhea, D.C.
Regst: Dec. 6, 1810

(Page)
(110)

```
JENKINS MURPHY          :
        TO              :        MORTGAGE
HENRY FELTNER of        :
Hawkins Co              :
```

Date: Nov. 19, 1810
Consideration: $1260.00
Amt of land: Not stated
Location: Sullivan Co, TN
Description: All that tract of land joining the land of George Roller, David
Ross and others. Henry Feltner is to have the sd tract of land unless
Jenkins Murphy do fully perform his covenant with Henry Fultner, that is
to pay unto Feltner $100 per year besides the first payment until the full
sum of $1260.00 be paid for the above tract of land and this mortgage
shall cease and be entirely void upon the full payment of sum at the
expiration of ten years or any time hereafter. When the sd sum is fully
paid should there be any defalcation this deed or mortgage is to be
considered as binding the tract of land, should Jenkins fail to pay the sum
according to the agreement then Henry shall have good right and full title
to the described premises and may take possession thereof
Acknowledged: By Jenkin Murphy, Sullivan Co, Tn Nov, 1810
Test: Mattw. Rhea, C.S.C, by Robt Rhea, D.C.
Regst: Dec. 8, 1810

----

(111)

```
JONATHAN MORRELL of:
Carter Co               :
        TO              :        DEED OF WARRANTY
JESSE & ISAAC           :
MORRELL, Minors         :
```

Date: March 25, 1810
Consideration: Love, good will and affection for my two friends, Jesse and
Isaac Morrell, both legatees and minors.
Amt of land: Not stated
Location: Sullivan Co, TN
Description: All the interest in the tract of land that fell to me by
heirship in the death of my father, Jonathan Morrell, and further give in
like manner the one half of John Blevins share, one of the legatees by
marriage unto the sd jesse and Isaac, sd land situate as follows where the
widow Morrell now lives in Sullivan Co on the south side of Holston River
Wit: William Rockhold, William Morrell, Samual Millard
Proven: By William Morrell and Samuel Millard, Sullivan Co, TN, Nov, 1810
Test: Mattw. Rhea, C.S.C, by Robt Rhea, D.C.
Regst: Dec. 20, 1810

----

(112)

GEORGE LITTLE, JR.   :
    TO   :   DEED OF WARRANTY
THOMAS ROCKHOLD   :

Date: April 11, 1810
Consideration: A valuable consideration, of which receipt is acknowledged
Amt of land: 60 acres
Location: Sullivan Co, TN
Description: A tract of land on the north side of the Holston River and on Charles Newton's line
Wit: Robert Blackmore, George Little, Sr.
Proven: By Robert Blackmore and George Little, Sr, Sullivan Co, Nov, 1810
Test: Mattw. Rhea, C.S.C, by Robt Rhea, D.C.
Regst: Dec. 22, 1810

----

(113)

LIBBY ROLLER   :
    TO   :   BILL OF SALE
DAVID ROLLER   :

Date: May 5, 1810
Consideration: Love, good will and affection I have to my son, David Roller
Property sold: One negro woman named Jude abt 40 yrs old, one negro girl named Becky abt 6 yrs old, one negro boy named Isaac abt 4 yrs old and boy named Abram abt 2 yrs old and all children of Jude
Wit: John Jennings, Richard Blaylock
Proven: By John Jennings and Richard Blaylock, Sullivan Co, TN, May, 1810
Test: Mattw. Rhea, C.S.C, by Robt Rhea, D.C.
Regst: Dec. 29, 1810

----

(114)

JACOB MILLER   :
    TO   :   DEED OF WARRANTY
MICHAEL HICKMAN of   :
Washington Co, TN   :

Date: Nov. 18, 1810
Consideration: $600.00
Amt of land: 7 acres
Location: Washington Co, VA
Description: A tract of land containing 7 acres in Washington Co, VA, joining Peter Hickman's
Wit: Isaac Newhouse, Abraham Stoffel
Acknowledged: By Jacob Miller, Sullivan Co, TN, Nov, 1810
Test: Mattw. Rhea, C.S.C, by Robt Rhea, D.C
Regst: Jan. 9, 1811

----

(115)

UNITED STATES OF AMERICA :
STEPHEN WALLING   :
    TO   :   DEED OF WARRANTY
JONATHAN CARRIER   :

Date: Oct. 2, 1810

Consideration: $266.66
Amt of land: 100 acres
Location: Sullivan Co, TN
Description: A tract of land on Frederick Kealler's line
Wit: Jonathan Combs, Thomas Glover, John Delock
Acknowledged: By Stephen Walling, Sullivan Co, TN, Nov. 1810
Test: Mattw. Rhea, C.S.C, by Robt Rhea, D.C.
Regst: Jan. 11, 1811

(Page)
(116)

```
ISAAC TIPTON          :
     TO               :     DEED OF WARRANTY
SOLOMON JONES         :
```

Date: May 15, 1809
Consideration: A valuable consideration
Amt of land: 1/2 acre
Description: A tract of land adjacent to the town of Blountville known by
Lot No. 7
Wit: D. Yearsley, John Gifford
Proven: By David Yearsley and John Gifford, Sullivan Co, Tn, May 1809
Test: Mattw. Rhea, C.S.C, by Robt Rhea, D.C
Regst: (No date given)

```
STATE OF TENNESSEE    :
DAVID HUGHES          :     LAND GRANT
     TO               :     NO. 671
NATHANIEL TAYLOR      :
```

Date: Feb. 27, 1809
Consideration: An entry made in the office of the surveyor of the Sixth
District of No. 240, dated Feb. 27, 1809, founded on a warrant of No.
2448 issued from Carter's office to David Hughes for 200 acres of land
dated Feb. 28, 1780, and adjuged(sic) valid for the board of Commissioners
for East TN on Jan. 30, 1809, and assigned by David Hughes to Nathaniel
Taylor, 50 acres of which is assigned by Taylor to Peter Harrington, the
enterer.
Description: There granted by the state of TN to Peter Harington and his
heirs a tract of land containing 50 acres in the district of Washington,
Watauga River, beginning on Finley Alison's line, also joining John Alison's
line, surveyed March 30, 1809
Wit: (No name given)
Granted: By the Gov. Willie Blount, R. Houghton, Sec.
Certified: I do certify that this grant is recorded in my office. Given
under my hand Sept. 27, 1809,
                         Edw. Scott, Register for E. TN
Regst: Jan. 25, 1811

----

(119)

```
DAVID WEBB            :
     TO               :     DEED OF WARRANTY
ZACHARIAH CROSS &     :
ELIJAH CROSS, JR.     :
```

56

Date: Sept. 25, 1810
Consideration: A valuable consideration
Amt of land: 190 acres
Location: Sullivan Co, TN
Description: A tract of land beginning on Weaver's line and joining Thomas Smalling's line
Wit: John Anderson, Akl. Key, John Jennings
Proven: By John Anderson and John Jennings, Sullivan Co, TN, Feb. 1811
Test: Mattw. Rhea, C.S.C.
Regst: April 12, 1811

(Page)
(120)

BENJAMIN PHILLIPS   :
      TO   :   BILL OF SALE
JOB KEY   :

Date: Nov. 27, 1810
Consideration: $300.00
Sale: Benjamin Phillips hath bargained to Job, one negro slave named Loose abt 10 yrs old, healthy, sound and sensible to have forever
Wit: Washington Lewis, Ekl. Key, Elisha Cole
Proven: By Elisha Cole and Philip Hobeck, Sullivan Co, TN, Feb, 1811
Regst: (No date given)

----

(121)

LEWIS WOLFE   :
      TO   :   DEED OF WARRANTY
ISAAC NEWHOUSE of   :
Washington Co, VA   :

Date: Nov. ?, 1810
Consideration: $500.00
Amt of land: 100 acres
Location: Sullivan Co, TN
Description: A tract of land beginning at James Steel's line crossing steels Creek near William Snodgrass' old line
Wit: Ephraim Smith, Jno Keys, Jacob Olinger
Proven: By Jacob Olinger, John Keys, Sullivan Co, TN, Feb, 1811
Test: Mattw. Rhea, C.S.C.
Regst: April 12, 1811

----

(122)

STATE OF TENNESSEE   :
JAMES GAINES   :
      TO   :   LAND GRANT
HUGH CRAWFORD   :

Date: Aug. 26, 1809
Consideration: An entry made in the surveyor's office 6th District No. 306, Aug. 26, 1809. Founded on warrant No. 69, dated Feb. 8, 1780. Issued by James Gaines to Hugh Crawford for 100 acres
Description: A tract of land in Washington District joining John Hamilton's corner, also Thomas King's line, and joining former survey of Crasford

51

Granted: By Gov. Willie Blount, R. Houston, Sec.
Certified: By Edward Scott, Register of E. TN, May 4, 1810
Regst: April 12, 1811

(Page)
(123)   JAMES MERRICK   :
              TO   :
       JOSEPH SMILEY   :

Date: Aug. 29, 1810
Consideration: $400.00
Amt of land: 100 acres
Location: Sullivan Co, TN
Description: All that tract of land on the waters of Horse Creek incl. the
plantation where Merrick lives and all his improvements, beginning at
Thomas McClain's corner and joining Daniel Duff's line and a conditional
line between Greenbery Dixon and Henry Allison
Wit: John Chester, Nathan Brockman
Proven: By John Chester and Nathan Brockman, Sullivan Co, TN, Feb, 1811
Test: Mattw. Rhea, C.S.C
Regt: April 18, 1811

----

(124)   ROBERT BIRDWELL   :
              TO   :   BILL OF SALE
       JOHN CHESTER   :

Date: Nov. 5, 1810
Consideration: 50 ₤
Sold: Robert Birdwell has granted to John Chester and his heirs forever,
one negro girl, Cloe, aged 3 yrs old with the toes off one foot caused by
a burn, I, Robert Birdwell, will warrant and forever defend the negro girl
against all persons
Wit: Richard Daniel, Hugh Martin, Joseph Smiley, Jacob Keen
Proven: By Hugh Martin and Jacob Keen, Sullivan Co, TN, Feb, 1811
Test: Mattw. Rhea, C.S.C
Regst: April 19, 1811

----

(125)   GEORGE LEWIS   :
              TO   :   DEED OF WARRANTY
       JOSHUA MILLER   :

Date: Sept 19, 1809
Consideration: $430.00
Amt of land: 94 acres, 10 poles
Location: Sullivan Co, TN
Description: A tract of land beginning at a hickory corner of John
Hacking's land, joining Joshua Miller's land
Wit: Elijah Cross, Job Key
Proven: By John Key and Elijah Cross, Sullivan Co, Tn, Feb, 1811
Test: Mattw. Rhea, C.S.C
Regst: April 24, 1811

----

(127)   STEPHEN EASLEY   :

                TO   :   DEED OF WARRANTY

CALEB SMITH and   :

WILLIAM PIERCE   :

Date: Jan. 25, 1811
Consideration: $600.00
Amt of land: 220 acres
Location: Sullivan Co, TN
Description: a tract of land on both sides of Horse Creek beginning on Easley's old patent line, being part of two tracts of land granted by the state of NC to Easley containing 500 acres No. 41, dated Oct. 23, 1783
Wit: Robert Easley, Peter Easley
Proven: By Robert Easley and Peter Easley, Sullivan Co, TN, Feb, 1811
Test: Mattw. Rhea, C.S.C
Regst: April 24, 1811

----

(128)   CONRAD SHARRITZ   :

                TO   :   DEED OF WARRANTY

HENRY SHARRITZ   :

Date: Aug. 18, 1810
Consideration: $1400.00
Amt of land: 90 acres
Location: Sullivan Co, TN
Description: A tract of land where Henry Sharritz now lives containing 90 acres more or less
Wit: Ben Harkleroad, George Birkhart, Martin Harkleroad
Acknowledged: By Conrad Sharritz, Sullivan Co, TN, Nov, 1810
Test: Mattw. Rhea, C.S.C, by Robt Rhea, D.C.
Regst: April 24, 1811

----

(129)   JOHN STEPHEN   :

                TO   :   BILL OF SALE

JOHN TIPTON   :

Date: Aug. 1, 1810
Consideration: $1000.00
Sold: To John Tipton the following negroes: one fellow named Joshua, one boy named Edmund, which negroes purchased on April 22, 1807, of John Brabston, also included is one woman named Pol, Deputy Marshall for East TN at public sale in Blountville; all which was sold as the property of Samuel Vance which sd negroes John Stephens will warrant and defent unto John Tipton
Wit: Felix Stephens, Isaac Stephens, E.R. Dulaney, Lan Snapp
Proven: By Elkanah R. Dulaney and Isaac Stephen, Sullivan Co, TN, Nov, 1810
Test: Mattw. Rhea, C.S.C
Regst: May 8, 1811

CONRAD SHARRITZ   :
             TO   :   DEED OF WARRANTY
JOHN SHARRITZ   :

Date: Aug. 18, 1810
Consideration: $225.00
Amt of land: 225 acres
Location: Sullivan Co, TN
Description: A tract or part of the plantation where John Sharritz now lives, beginning at a white oak on Thomas Shelby's corner and on Jacob Bealer's line and joining Martin Builher's(sic) line
Wit: Henry Harkelroad, George Burkhart, Mart Harkelroad
Acknowledged: By Conrad Sharritz, Sullivan Co, TN, Nov, 1810
Test: Mattw. Rhea, C.S.C, by Robt Rhea, D.C.
Regst: May 9, 1811

CONRAD SHARRITZ, SR.:
             TO   :   DEED OF WARRANTY
CONRAD SHARRITZ, JR.:

Date: Aug. 18, 1810
Consideration: $2,920.00
Amt of land: 330 acres
Location: Sullivan Co, TN
Description: a part of a tract of land estimated 330 acres more or less on John Sharritz's line and joining George Bealer's line and a corner of John Peters' land
Wit: Henry Harkelroad, George Burkhart, Martin Harkleroad
Acknowledged: By Conrad Sharritz, Sullivan Co, TN, Nov, 1810
Test: Mattw. Rhea, C.S.C, by Robt Rhea, D.C.
Regst: May 10, 1811

----

(132)   JOHN TIPTON   :
             TO   :   DEED OF WARRANTY
ALEXANDER GITGOOD   :

Date: April 12, 1808
Consideration: $100.00
Amt of land: 1/4 acre
Location: Town of Blountville, Sullivan Co
Description: A lot known by No. 23
Wit: John Tipton
Acknowledged: By John Tipton, Sullivan Co, TN, Aug, 1808
Test: Mattw. Rhea, C.S.C, by Robt Rhea, D.C.
Regst: May 10, 1811

CATHERINE SHELBY   :
             TO   :   DEED OF WARRANTY
ISAAC SHELBY   :

Date: Jan. 5, 1810
Consideration: $2000.00

Amt of land: 520 acres
Location: Sullivan Co, TN
Description: A tract of land on both sides of Reedy Creek, beginning on a line of Thomas Johnson's land
Wit: thomas Shelby, Matilda May, Sam'l May, Henry Shelby
Proven: By Thomas Shelby, Sullivan Co, TN, Nov, 1810
Regst: May 10, 1811

(Page)
(134)

JOB KEY	:	
TO	:	DEED OF WARANTY
JAMES KING	:	

Date: Jan. 23, 1811
Consideration: $1000.00
Amt of land: 250 acres
Location: Sullivan Co, TN
Description: A tract of land on Beaver Creek which was granted by the state of NC to Thomas Wallace for 250 acres by patent No. 358, dated Nov. 10, 1784, running along a former survey of Wallace and joining a suppose line of John Malone's and joining John Rhea's land
Wit: James Ware, Elk. Key, William King
Acknowledged: By Job key, Sullivan Co, TN, Feb. 1811
Test: Mattw. Rhea, C.S.C, by Robt. Rhea, D.C.
Regst: May 11, 1811

----

(135)

JOHN COLE	:	
TO	:	DEED OF WARRANTY
ELISHA COLE	:	

Date: July 20, 1810
Consideration: 500 Spanish milled dollars
Amt of land: 100 acres
Location: Sullivan Co, TN
Description: A tract of land south of Holston River and being taken out of Leonard Hart's survey for the benefit of Walter Cunningham, joining George Malone's corner
Acknowledged: By John Cole, Sullivan Co, TN, Feb, 1811
Test: Mattw. Rhea, C.S.C
Regst: May 13, 1811

----

(136)

HUGH SMITH	:	
TO	:	BILL OF SALE
SAMUEL & ROBERT BLACKMORE	:	

Date: April 26, 1810
Consideration: $40.25
Sale: Received the sum of $40.25 in full for 21 head of sheep with the fleeces of wool on, 12 lamb, one this year, part red cow with a white heifer calf with a red head and a small star in its forehead which I have this day sold to Blackmore and which I hereby warrant to the Blackmores. The property to be delivered May 10, next
Wit: J. Punch, John Gifford

Proven: By John Punch and John Gifford, Sullivan Co, TN, Feb, 1811
Test: Mattw. Rhea, C.S.C, by Robt Rhea, D.C.
Regst: May 18, 1811

(Page)

GILBERT KARR   :
        TO   :   BILL OF SALE
RODE RICHARDS   :

Date: May 20, 1811
Consideration: Natural love and affection which I have and bear toward
Rode Richards and also for divers good causes and considerations
The above mentioned cause and consideration hereunto moving the sd
Gilbert, have given unto Rode Richards all and singular three heads of
horse creature and three heads of chattle(sic) to have
Wit: William Snodgrass, George White
Proven: By William Snodgrass and George White, Sullivan Co, TN, May, 1811
Test: Mattw. Rhea, C.S.C.
Regst: May 28, 1811

----

(137)   JOHN TIPTON   :
        TO   :   BILL OF SALE
JOHN STEPHENS   :

Date: Aug. 1, 1810
Consideration: $300.00
Description: For and in consideration of $300.00 to me in hand paid have
sold to John Stephens, one negro boy named Bob
Wit: Felix Stepahensm(sic), Isaac Stephens, E.R. Dulaney, Law. Snapp
Test: Mattw. Rhea, C.S.C.
Regst: May 28, 1811

PETER SHELLEY   :
        TO   :   DEED OF WARRANTY
JOHN HERSHBERGER   :

Date: Oct. 10, 1810
Consideration: $1700.00 the receipt of $1200.00 is hereby acknowledged
Amt of land: 293 acres
Location: Sullivan Co, TN
Description: All that tract of land in Sullivan Co, TN, containing 293 acres
Wit: George Houser, George Wilhelms
Proven: By George Houser and George Wilhelm, Sullivan Co, Tn, May, 1811
Test: Mattw. Rhea, C.S.C.
Regst: May 28, 1811

----

(138)   MARTIN BOOHER   :
        TO   :   DEED OF WARRANTY
GEORGE BURKHART   :

Date: May 20, 1811
Consideration: $1700.00

Amt of land: 40 poles
Location: Sullivan Co
Description: A lot containing 40 poles on the west bank of Sinking Creek,
the 25th number layed off by Wallace Willoughby to George Burkhart
Acknowledged: By Martin Booher, Sullivan Co, TN, May, 1811
Test: Mattw. Rhea, C.S.C
Regst: May 28, 1811

(Page)
(138)   RICHARD BASKET   :
                  TO   :   DEED OF WARRANTY
         JAMES JONES   :

         Date: Jan. 27, 1810
         Consideration: $200.00
         Amt of land: 26 acres
         Location: Sullivan Co, TN
         Description: All that tract of land on both sides of Garret's Branch
         Wit: John Wallingsford, Isaac Wallingsford, Horton, James Frazier
         Proven: By John Wallingsford and James Frazier, Sullivan Co, TN, May,
         1811
         Test: Mattw. Rhea, C.S.C.
         Regst: (No date given)

----

(139)   JOHN LAUGHLIN   :
                  TO   :   DEED OF WARRANTY
         ABRAM GRUBB   :

         Date: May 18, 1811
         Consideration: $70.00 current money of the U.S.
         Amt of land: 24 acres
         Location: Sullivan Co, TN
         Description: One tract of land in Sullivan Co containing 24 acres
         Proven: By William King and Martin Booher, Sullivan Co, TN, May, 1811
         Test: Mattw. Rhea, C.S.C.
         Regst: May 28, 1811

----

(140)   PETE PECTOL   :
                  TO   :   DEED OF WARRANTY
         GEORGE LYDICHER   :

         Date: May 20, 1811
         Consideration: $480.00
         Amt of land: 134 acres
         Location: Sullivan Co, TN
         Description: A tract of land on the waters of Fall Creek, on a conditional
         line of John McDonald and James Anderson
         Wit: John Jennings, George Roller
         Acknowledged: By Peter Pectol, Sullivan Co, TN, May, 1811
         Test: Mattw. Rhea, C.S.C
         Regst: (No date given)

----

(141)   MATHIAS LITTLE   :

             TO   :   DEED OF WARRANTY

      HENRY COLPAH   :

Date: Feb. 15, 1811
Consideration: A valuable consideration
Amt of land: 54 acres
Location: Sullivan Co, TN
Description: A tract of land containing 54 acres on Indian Creek
Wit: Elijah Watson, Nicholas Martin
Test: Mattw. Rhea, C.S.C.
Regst: May 29, 1811

----

(142)   HUGH McKINGHAM   :

             TO   :   DEED OF WARRANTY

      DANIEL PAYNE   :

Date: Feb. 9, 1811
Consideration: $100.00
Amt of land: 32 acres
Location: Sullivan Co, TN
Description: (Land) Beginning at John Adwell's corner and joining Nathan Jobe's and Samuel Jobe's line
Wit: James P. Hulse, Charles Jones, James Frazier
Proven: By James P. Hulse and James Frazier, Sullivan Co, TN, May, 1811
Test: Mattw. Rhea, C.S.C.
Regst: May 29, 1811

----

(143)   JAMES FRAZIER   :

             TO   :   DEED OF WARRANTY

      JAMES JONES   :

Date: March 22, 1809
Consideration: $333.00
Amt of land: 97 acres
Location: Sullivan Co, TN
Description: All that parcel of land on both sides of a stream known by Jarrott's branch, beginning on James Frazier's line
Wit: James Frazier, Jr, Isaac Wallingsford, Horton, John Wallingsford
Acknowledged: By James Frazier, Sullivan Co, TN, May, 1811
Test: Mattw. Rhea, C.S.C.
Regst: (No date given) From the minutes of the court

----

(144)   ANDREW CROCKET   :

             TO   :   DEED OF WARRANTY

      JACOB HAINES   :

Date: April 10, 1811
Consideration: $366.66
Amt of land: 150 acres
Location: Sullivan Co, TN

Description: A tract of land on the south side of Holston River on a branch called Callers Fork, formerly belonging to Patrick Caler
Acknowledged: By Henry Crocket, Sullivan Co, TN, May, 1811
Test: Mattw. Rhea, C.S.C.
Regst: (No date given) From the minutes of the court

(Page)
(145)

```
HUGH McKEIGHAN        :
       TO             :      DEED OF WARRANTY
DANIEL PAYNE          :
```

Date: Feb. 9, 1811
Consideration: $300.00
Amt of land: 42 acres
Location: Sullivan Co, TN
Description: All tract of land on Kendricks Creek incl. the plantation where Hugh McKeighan now lives
Wit: James P. Hulse, Charles Jones, James Frazier
Proven: By James P. Hulse, James Frazier, Sullivan Co, TN, May, 1811
Test: Mattw. Rhea, C.S.C.
Regst: May 30, 1811

----

(147)

```
PETER AND JAMES MORGAN :
       TO              :      DEED OF WARRANTY
DAVID BRAGG            :
```

Date: April 30, 1811
Consideration: $1000.00
Amt of land: 276 acres
Location: Sullivan Co, TN
Description: A tract of land on the waters of Horse Creek; beginning at a corner line formerly John Mullens corner; on a dividing line between this tract and Thomas Titsworth and crossing Horse Creek the several courses which fork is a bounded line between this tract and one Thomas Bragg, Sr, purchased of Larkin Pairpoint; along Thomas Bragg's line which was formerly James Holland's containing all that tract of land which the state of NC granted to Bragg by deed, Nov. 10, 1784, excepting the part that Mullens granted to Bragg by a deed of conveyance and also it containing all that tract which Garrett Fitzgerald made to Moses Calvert by a deed of conveyance which joins the old survey that was formerly Mullens' and also all that land containing 60 acres granted to Calvert by the stae of NC which joins the old survey which was Mullens'
Wit: thomas Pairce, William Pickens, Joseph Bragg
Proven: By Thomas Pairce and William Pickins, Sullivan Co, TN, May, 1811
Test: Mattw. Rhea, C.S.C.
Regst: May 30, 1811

----

(148)

```
JACOB TOLAND          :
       TO             :      DEED OF WARRANTY
RICHARD MURRELL, JR   :
```

Date: Aug. 25, 1810
Consideration: $300.00

59

Amt of land: 125 acres
Location: Sullivan Co, TN
Description: A tract of land on the waters of Horse Creek; beginning at
Lesters corner and on a dividing line between Bennett and Lester and
along a conditional line made between Thomas McClain and Daniel Duff
(Wit): Thomas McBride, Frederick Titsworth, Amen Hail
Proven: By Frederick Titsworth and Amen Hail, Sullivan Co, TN, May, 1811
Test: Mattw. Rhea, C.S.C.
Regst: May 30, 1811

(Page)
(149)

JACOB HAINES   :
        TO   :   DEED OF WARRANTY
ANDREW CROCKETT   :

Date: Dec. 13, 1810
Consideration: $160.00
Amt of land: 61 acres
Location: Sullivan Co, TN
Description: A tract of land on the north side of Holston River
Wit: William Carr and John Weaver
Acknowledged: By Robert Haines, Sullivan Co, TN, May, 1811
Test: Mattw. Rhea, C.S.C.
Regst: (No date given)

----

(150)   RICHARD BASKET   :
                 TO   :   DEED OF WARRANTY
           JOHN WALLINGSFORD   :

Date: Jan. 20, 1810
Consideration: $165.00
Amt of land: 47 acres
Location: Sullivan Co, Tn
Description: All that tract of land on both sides of Jarrott's branch on a
conditional line between Richard Basket and William Jones, Sr, on a
conditional line between John Wallingsford and James Jones containing 47
acres
Wit: James Jones, isaac Wallingsford, James Frazier
Proven: By James Jones and James Frazier, Sullivan Co, TN, May, 1811
Regst: (No date given) From the minutes of the court

GEORGE MOODY of Hawkins Co   :
        TO   :   DEED OF WARRANTY
VALENTINE, JOHN, MARY AND   :
WILLIAM MOODY, My Children and :
their heirs severally of Hawkins Co :

Date: Jan. 15, 1810
Consideration: Love and natural affection to my children, Valentine, John,
Mary and William Moody
Amt of land: 500 acres
Location: Sullivan Co, TN

Description: A tract beginning on James Hollin's line, joining Dever's corner and on Roller's line
Wit: Robert Easley, Joseph Bishop
Proven: By Robert Easley and Joseph Bishop, Hawkins Co, TN, May, 1811
Test: Given under my hand and seal - Richard Mitchell, Clk
Regst: June 14, ????

```
STATE OF TENNESSEE     :                        STATE OF TENNESSEE
ARCHIBALD ROANE        :      LAND GRANT               TO
      TO               :      NO. 1932          JOHN McCORKLE
JOHN NAVE              :
```

Date: Oct. 13, 1809
Consideration: In condsideration of an entrymade in the office of the surveyor of the 6th District of No. 349, Oct. 13, 1809, funded on a warrant of No. 149, issued by Archibald Roan to John Nave for 200 acres of land dated July 6, 1808, which warrant is assigned to John McCorkle the enterer
Granted: There is granted by the state of TN to John McCorkle and his heirs a tract of land containing 123 acres in the Washington District, beginning on the south bank of the Holston River and along a line of Samuel McCorkle, dec'd, joining Benjamin Webb's line and Elijah Watson's line
Surveyed: Dec. 4, 1809
By order of: Willie Blount, Gov. R. Houston, Sec.
The within named John McCorkle hath title to the within described tract of land.
I do certify that this grant is recorded in my office, April 25, 1811
                    Edw. Scott, Register of Land, E. TN
Regst: Aug. 19, 1811

```
STATE OF NORTH CAROLINA      :
SAMUEL ASHE, GOV.            :      LAND GRANT
      TO                     :      NO. 725
ELISHA ADAMS of Sevier Co, TN :
```

Date: Dec. 20, 1796
Consideration: 50 shillings for every 100 acres of land
Amt of land: 50 acres of land incl. where he lives and survey of which is described below
Granted by Samuel Ashe, Gov, By Commd. J. Glasgow, Sec.
Survey: Nov. 27, 1795   SURVEY
By virtue of a warrant to me directed of No. 538 containing 50 acres entered April 29, 1781, I have surveyed for Elisha Adams, 50 acres of land in the territory south of the Ohio River, incl. where he lives; beginning at John Sigler's corner on or near John Funkhouser's line, then with the same straight to the beginning. Plated by a scale of a 100 equal parts to an inch
                    Per George Vincent, C.S.
(Wit): Jacob Weaver
(Test): Arnold Ramsey, Clk
(Regst): Aug. 19, 1811

ELIZABETH SPURGIN, GEORGE WEBB, JOHN   :
HAMILTON, DAVID LOONEY, WILLIAM CRAWFORD:
WILLIAM SPURGIN, JAMES WALLACE, & HEIRS   :   DEED OF WARRANTY
OF JOHN SPURGIN, dec'd.   :
       TO   :
JOHN SPURGIN, dec'd, BY JOSEPH COOK   :

Date: Sept 10, 1810
Consideration: $300.00
Amt of land: By estimation, 400 acres
Location: Sullivan Co, TN
Description: a tract of land on the south side of Holston River being part
of a 300 acre tract granted to Robert Sellars
Wit: James Gregg, John Stephens
Regst: (No date given)

THOMAS GOODE   :
     TO   :   EXCHANGE OF SLAVES
FINLEY ALLISON   :

Date: Jan. 23, 1811
Exchange: Received of Mr. Finley Allison, a negro woman called Polly abt
17 yrs old, in exchange for a negro girl named Leah, the right and title
of which negro Leah I do warrant and do fend from my heirs and all
severy(sic) other persons whatsoever
Wit: Henry Massengill, John Alison
Proven: By Henry Massengill and John Allison, Sullivan Co, Tn, Aug, 1811
Test: Mattw. Rhea, C.S.C.
(Regst): Aug. 20, 1811

----

(155)   ELISHA ADAMS of   :
            Sevier Co   :
               TO   :   DEED OF WARRANTY
            SAMUEL McCORKLE   :

Date: Jan. 25, 1811
Consideration: 50 ₤
Amt of land: 50 acres
Location: Sullivan Co, TN
Description: A tract of land on the north side of Holston River; beginning
at John Sigler's corner and on or near John Funkhouser's line
Wit: John McCorkle, Simon Adams
Acknowledged: By Elisha Adams, Sullivan Co, TN, Aug, 1811
Test: Mattw Rhea, C.S.C
Regst: Aug. 21, 1811

----

(156)   GEORGE GREENWAY   :
               TO   :   DEED OF WARRANTY
            NICHOLAS MARTIN   :

Date: Aug. 19, 1811
Consideration: $36.75

Amt of land: 12 1/4 acres
Location: Sullivan Co
Description: A tract of land; beginning near the land of Solomon Smith
Wit: John Anderson, Joseph Greenway
Acknowledged: By George Greenway, Sullivan Co, Tn, Aug, 1811
Test: Mattw. Rhea, C.S.C
Regst: Aug. 21, 1811

(Page)

```
JOHN & ANDREW SHELL :
      TO             :      DEED OF WARRANTY
ROBERT HENSLEY       :
```

Date: Nov. 17, 1810
Consideration: $500.00
Amt of land: 100 acres
Location: Sullivan Co, TN
Description: A tract of land on the south bank of Holston River adj. the
land of Jacob Fleenor
Wit: Thomas Rockhold, Andrew Crockett
Proven: By Thomas Rockhold and Andrew Crockett, Sullivan Co, Tn, Nov,
1811
Test: Mattw. Rhea, C.S.C.
Regst: Aug. 21, 1811

----

(157)
```
JOHN SMITH           :
      TO             :      DEED OF WARRANTY
WILLIAM RHEA         :
```

Date: July 25, 1811
Consideration: $40.87
Amt of land: 100 acres
Location: Sullivan Co, TN
Description: A tract of land on the waters of Beaver Creek; beginning on
Abraham McClellen's line
Wit: Joseph Rhea, Thomas Cawood
Proven: By Joseph Rhea, Thomas Cawood, Sullivan Co,Tn, Aug, 1811
Test: Mattw. Rhea, C.S.C.
Regst: Sept. 2, 1811

----

(158)
```
DAVID LEWIS &        :
JOSEPH MALONE        :
      TO             :      DEED OF WARRANTY
WILLIAM SMITH        :
```

Date: Aug. 22, 1811
Consideration: $500.00
Amt of land: 100 acres
Location: Sullivan Co, TN
Description: A tract of land on the waters of Beaver Creek
Wit: John Anderson
Acknowledged: By David Lewis, Sullivan Co, TN, Aug, 1811

Test: Mattw. Rhea, C.S.C
Regst: Sept. 2, 1811

(Page)
(163)(sic)   THOMAS MORRELL   :
                        TO   :   DEED OF WARRANTY
              THOMAS CARRIER   :

              Date: Nov. 20, 1809
              Consideration: $300.00
              Amt of land: 25 acres
              Location: Sullivan Co, Tn
              Description: A tract of land on the south side of Holston River beginning
              on a conditional line of Jonathan Morrell and Thomas Morrell
              Wit: Nathan Morrell, Edmond Morrell, Obediah Pigmond
              Acknowledged: By Thomas Morrell, Sullivan Co, Tn, Nov, 1809
              Test: Mattw. Rhea, C.S.C.
              Regst: Nov. 4, 1811

              ----

(159)   ARCHIBALD TAYLOR   :
                        TO   :   DEED OF WARRANTY
              FRANCIS HAWLEY   :

              Date: Aug. 9, 1811
              Consideration: A valuable consideration
              Amt of land: 382* acres
              Location: Sullivan Co, TN
              Description: A tract of land containing 282* acres more or less, except
              these acres of land that were willed to James Patterson, Jr, by his father,
              on the waters of Fall Creek
              Acknowledged: By Archibald Taylor, Sullivan Co, TN, Aug. 1811
              Test: Mattw. Rhea, C.S.C.
              Regst: Sept 14, 1811

(*Note: both amounts given)

(160)   WILLIAM SCOTT   :
                        TO   :   DEED OF WARRANTY
              JOSHUA EDWARDS   :

              Date: Nov. 26, 1809
              Consideration: $93.00
              Amt of land: 15 1/2 acres
              Location: Sullivan Co, TN
              Description: A tract of land containing 15 1/2 acres more or less;
              beginning at the corner of Scott's original deed
              Acknowledged: By William Scott, Sullivan Co, TN, Aug, 1811
              Test: Mattw. Rhea, C.S.C
              Regst: Sept 5, 1811

              ----

(161)   JOHN FORD, SR.   :
                        TO   :   DEED OF WARRANTY
              FREDERICK S.C. FORD :

Date: May 18, 1811
Consideration: $400.00
Amt of land: 102 acres
Location: Sullivan Co, TN
Description: 102 acres of land being in two small tracts, it being abt 20 poles from each other, one containing 82 acres and beginning at a corner of a continaul(sic) line made between John Ford and Alexander hail; the other tract containing 20 acres and beginning at Aquilla Lane's corner and joining John Gillihan's and along a dividing line made between John Ford and Alexander Hail and joining Robertson's line; the two tracts being on the south side of Holston River and joining the land of Frederick S.C. Ford
Wit: Benjamin Strickler, Samuel Strickler, John C.D. Ford, William Cox
Proven: By Benjamin Strickler, William Cox, Sullivan Co, TN, May, 1811
Test: Mattw. Rhea, C.S.C.
Regst: Nov. 2, 1811

(Page)
(162)

STANTON PEMBERTON of Washington Co, VA,	:	
Executor of James Offield, dec'd	:	EXECUTOR'S
TO	:	DEED OF WARRANTY
JAMES L GEORGE	:	

Date: Aug. 18, 1810
Consideration: $500.00
Amt of land: 100 acres
Location: Sullivan Co, TN
Description: A tract of land, the plantation where Walter Blevins now lives on the north bank of the Holston River
Acknowledged: By Stanton Pemberton, Sullivan Co, TN, May, 1811
Test: Mattw. Rhea, C.S.C.
Regst: Nov. 4, 1811

----

(164)

WILLIAM ERWIN	:	
TO	:	DEED OF WARRANTY
MATTHEW RHEA	:	

Date: Nov. 19, 1810
Consideration: A valuable considertion
Amt of land: Amt not stated
Location: Sullivan Co, TN
Description: a tract or undivided part of land devised to him by the last will and testament of his father, David Erwin, dec'd, on the waters of Fall Creek; being the tract where the heirs of David Erwin, dec'd, now live and the tract where James Holt now lives
Acknowledged: By William Erwin, Sullivan Co, TN, Nov, 1810
Test: Mattw. Rhea, C.S.C, by Robert Rhea, D.C.
Regst: Nov. 4, 1811

ALEXANDER GITGOOD	:	
TO	:	DEED OF WARRANTY
JOHN TIPTON	:	

65

Date: March 2, 1811
Consideration: $500.00
Amt of land: 1/4 acre
Location: Sullivan Co, TN
Description: A lot of land containing 1/4 acre and 18 feet from the land and the lane back in width in addition be the lane more or less and a corner of William King's lot in the town of Blountville, No. 24
Acknowledged: By John Tipton, Sullivan Co,TN, Aug, 1811
Test: Mattw. Rhea, C.S.C.
Regst: Nov. 4, 1811

(Page)
(165)

```
ISAAC SHELBY            :
        TO             :      DEED OF WARRANTY
RACHEL BLACKMORE        :
```

Date: March 28, 1810
Consideration: A valuable consideration
Amt of land: 840 acres
Location: Sullivan Co, TN
Description: A tract of land on the waters of Reedy Creek, near Sharps Branch and on the wagon road and then along Varner's line
Wit: Christopher Latture, Wm Owen, Wm N. Gale
Proven: By Wm Owen and William N. Gale, Sullivan Co, TN, May, 1811
Test: Mattw. Rhea, C.S.C
Regst: (No date given) From the minutes of the court

----

(166)

```
UNITED STATES OF AMERICA :
STEPHEN WALLING         :
        TO             :      DEED OF WARRANTY
THOMAS GLOVER           :
```

Date: Oct. 2, 1810
Consideration: $150.00
Amt of land: 22 1/2 acres (Also in one place in deed 32 1/2 A)
Location: Sullivan Co, TN
Description: A tract of land on the south side of Holston River; beginning on Thomas Vandenvanter's on the river
Wit: Jonathan Combs, Jonathan Coner, John Deder
Acknowledged: By Stephen Walling, Sullivan Co, TN, Nov, 1810
Test: Mattw. Rhea, C.S.C.
Regst: Oct. 8, 1811

```
JOHN TIPTON             :
        TO             :      DEED OF WARRANTY
JACOB HARTMAN           :
```

Date: July 29, 1811
Consideration: A valuable consideration
Amt of land: Two lots of land in the town of Blountville
Location: Blountville, Sullivan Co, TN
Description: Two lots of land in Blountville, Nos. 46 and 47, near the east end of town

Wit: D. Yearsley, William Rockhold
Proven: By David Yearsley and William Rockhold, Sullivan Co, TN, Aug, 1811
Test: Mattw. Rhea, C.S.C.
Regst: (No date given)

(Page)
(168)   STATE OF NORTH CAROLINA :
          ALEXANDER MARTIN, GOV.   :   LAND GRANT
               TO   :   NO. 291
          HENRY CLARK   :

          Date: Oct. 24, 1782
          Consideration: 50 shillings for every 100 acres of land
          Amt of land: 300 acres
          Location: Washington Co
          Description: A tract of land containing 300 acres on both sides of Kendrick's Creek
          By his Excellys Comd. J. Glasgow, Sec.

----

(169)   JAMES DENTON   :
               TO   :   DEED OF WARRANTY
          WILLIAM MILLBOURN*   :

          Date: July 19, 1810
          Consideration: 25 ₺ 50 shillings current money of VA
          Amt of land: 21 1/4 acres
          Location: Sullivan Co, TN
          Description: One tract of land being part of a tract conveyed to Denton April 8, 1802, by Milbourn*
          Proven: By William Owen, William King, Sullivan Co, Nov, 1811
          Test: Mattw. Rhea, C.S.C
          Regst: (No date given)

(*Note: name spelled both ways)

(170)   JOHN TIPTON   :
               TO   :   DEED OF WARRANTY
          JAMES ANGLEA   :

          Date: Nov. 9, 1810
          Consideration: $150.00
          Amt of land: 1 acre
          Location: Sullivan Co, TN
          Description: A lot at the west end of the town of Blountville, being the lot on which Isaac Bonham built a shop
          Wit: Robert Blackmore, William Smith
          Acknowledged: By John Tipton, Sullivan Co, TN, May, 1810
          Test: Mattw. Rhea, C.S.C.
          Regst: Feb. 25, 1812

ZACHUS JONES　　　　　:
　　　　TO　　　　　　　　:　　　DEED OF WARRANTY
JAMES ANGLEA　　　　　:

Date: Nov. 9, 1810
Consideration: $40.00
Amt of land: 1/2 acre
Location: Sullivan Co, TN
Description: A lot of land adj. the west end of Blountville on the north side of the street or main road
Wit: John Tipton, Isaac Jones
Acknowledged: By Zachus Jones, Sullivan Co, TN, Nov. 1811
Test: Mattw. Rhea, C.S.C
Regst: Feb. 25, 1812

SAM McCORKLE　　　　　:
　　　　TO　　　　　　　　:　　　DEED OF WARRANTY
SOLOMON SMITH　　　　　:

Date: June 29, 1798
Consideration: $20.00
Amt of land: 2 lots containing 1/4 acre each
Location: Middletown, TN
Description: Two lots in Middletown containing 1/4 acre each and being lots Nos. 8 7 9 containing 1/2 acres as aforesaid
Wit: Leonard Hart, Richard Sampson
Proven: By Richard Sampson, Sullivan Co, TN, Aug, 1810
Test: Mattw. Rhea, C.S.C.
Regst: Feb. 25, 1812

JAMES LAUGHLIN of　　　:
Rutherford Co, TN　　　 :
　　　　TO　　　　　　　　:　　　DEED OF WARRANTY
ALEXANDER CARSON　　　:

Date: Feb. 17, 1812
Consideration: 330 £ lawful money
Amt of land: 93 acres 2 rood(sic),38 poles
Location: Sullivan Co, TN
Description: a tract of land containing 93 acres, 2 rood(sic), 38 poles; beginning on the bank of Holston River, on Wm King's line
Wit: David King, William King
Proven: By David and William King, Sullivan Co, TN, Feb, 1812
Regst: (No date given)

----

(173)　　　DAVID KING　　　　　:
　　　　　　　　TO　　　　　　　:　　　(No Deed Given)
　　　　　　JAMES LAUGHLIN　　:

Date: Feb. 10, 1812
Consideration: $225.00
Amt of land: 45 acres and 42 poles

68

Location: Sullivan Co, TN
Description: A tract of land containing 45 acres and 42 poles; beginning at a stake on King's line
Wit: John Sharp, William King, Alexander Carson
Proven: By John Sharp and William King, Sullivan Co, TN, Feb, 1812
Test: Mattw. Rhea, C.S.C.
Regst: Feb. 25, 1812

(Page)
(174)   HENRY SHARITZ   :
              TO   :   DEED OF WARRANTY
         JACOB BRUHER   :

Date: Aug. 19, 1810
Consideration: $196.00
Amt of land: 39 acres and 32 poles
Location: Sullivan Co, TN
Description: A tract of land where Henry Sharritz now lives; being part of a tract of land made over by the will of Richard Shipley, Sr, a corner of Hedrick's
Wit: John Jennings, Martin Roller, W.P. Shipley
Proven: By John Jennings, Martin Roller, Sullivan Co, TN, Aug, 1811
Test: Mattw. Rhea, C.S.C.
Regst: Feb. 26, 1812

----

(176)   HENRY CATRON   :
              TO   :   DEED OF WARRANTY
         MICHAEL CATRON   :

Date: Aug. 1, 1810
Consideration: $900.00
Amt of land: 145 acres
Location: Sullivan Co, TN
Description: A tract of land on the waters of Reedy Creek; beginning at a corner of Samuel Brashears and crossing the wagon road
Wit: Peter, Valentine, John Catron, and David Shaver
Test: Mattw. Rhea, C.S.C
Regst: March 9, 1812

----

(177)   GILBERT FARR (CARR?)* :
              TO   :   ARTICLES OF AN AGREEMENT
         HENRY RICHARDS   :

Date: Sept. 25, 1811
Consideration: $3.00 per acre
Amt of land: 202 acres
Location: Sullivan Co, TN
Agreement: Gilbert Carr hath bargained and sold a piece of land joining the lands of James Stite and Robert Cowan containing 202 acres; in consideration of $3.00 per acre and paid by Henry Richards in manner following all my just debts to be paid first and the residue to be paid to William Fritts, when he come to be of age of 21 and it is further understood that Gilbert Karr* is to have his maintenance of the land

during his life the title is to be made on the tax payment to the true
performance of every of the above covenants & agreements. We bind
ourselves our heirs, administrators and assigns in the final sum of $1212.00
Wit: William Snodgrass, G. Keys
Proven: By William Snodgrass and G. Keys, Sullivan Co, TN, Feb, 1812
Test: Mattw. Rhea, C.S.C, Samuel Lowery, D.C.
Regst: (No date given)

(*Note: Name spelled all three ways)

(Page)

(178)   JACOB JOHNSTON   :
                    TO   :   BILL OF SALE
          JONATHAN BACHMAN &   :
          NATHAN BACHMAN   :

          Date: Jan. 24, 1811
          Consideration: $140.00
          Articles sold: I, Jacob Johnston, do sell to Jonathan Bachman and Nathan
          Bachman all the bedding and household furniture and all the horses and
          cattle and hogs incl. all the property Jacob Johnston now owns. All
          singular which sd property are now remaining standing and being in the
          county and state aforesaid now in the occupation of Jacob Johnston.
          Wit: Jas Gains, Joseph Smiley, Samuel Owens
          Acknowledged: By Jacob Johnston, Sullivan Co, TN, Aug, 1811
          Test: Mattw. Rhea, C.s.c.
          Regst: (No date given)

----

(179)   SAMUEL BLACKMORE   :
                    TO   :   BILL OF SALE WITH SECURITY
          WM DULANEY   :

          Date: May 23, 1811
          Consideration: $118.25
          Bill of Sale: May 23, 1811. Received of Wm Dulaney, $118.25 in full, for a
          negro boy named Rich'd 3 yrs old, which I warrant forever for value
          received of Wm Dulaney. If I do not pay a certain note to James L.
          George for the sum above mentioned in witness whereof I have hereunto
          set my hand and seal the date above mentioned
          Wit: James L. George, Charles N. George
          Proven: By James L George, Sullivan Co, TN, Feb, 1812
          Test: Mattw. Rhea, C.S.C, by Samuel Lowery, D.C.
          Regst: March 15, 1812

          JACOB SNAPP of   :
          Shenandoah Co, VA   :
                    TO   :   DEED OF WARRANTY
          JACOB STURM   :

          Date: March 20, 1809
          Consideration: $12.00
          Amt of land: A lot of ground
          Location: Sullivan Co, TN

Description: A lot of ground adj. the town of Blountville, which was formerly sold by John Tipton to Wm Webb of VA and became vested in Snapp by virtue of a public sale under an execution against Webb, bounded and the east and west by lots now the property of Sturm
Wit: Jacob Snapp, Elknr. R. Dulaney
Proven: By John Snapp and Elkanah R. Dulaney, Sullivan Co, TN, May, 1809
Test: Mattw Rhea, C.S.C.
Regst: March 15, 1812

(Page)
(180)

ADAM SMITH	:	
TO	:	DEED OF WARANTY
JOHN GARLAND	:	

Date: Aug. 31, 1810
Consideration: $100.00
Amt of land: 30 acres
Location: Sullivan Co, TN
Description: A tract of land on the south side of Holston River and containing 30 acres
Proven: By Thomas Moyers, John Buher, Sullivan Co, TN, Feb, 1812
Test: Mattw. Rhea, C.S.C, by Samuel Lowery, D.C.
Regst: March 16, 1812

----

(181)

ADAM SMITH	:	
TO	:	DEED OF WARRANTY
JOHN GARLAND	:	

Date: Aug. 31, 1810
Consideration: $100.00
Amt of land: 34 acres
Location: Sullivan Co, TN
Description: A tract of land on the south side of Holston River and containing 34 acres of land founded on a warrant No. 542, issued by Archibald Roan to Benjamin Key for 300 acres dated Oct. 18, 1808
Wit: Thomas Moyers, John Booher
Proven: By Thomas Moyers and John Booher, Sullivan Co, TN, Feb, 1812
Test: Mattw. Rhea, C.S.C, by Samuel Lowery, D.C.
Regst: March 16, 1812

NATHANIEL MUNSEY	:	
TO	:	DEED OF WARRANTY
TIMOTHY HAMILTON	:	

Date: March 1, 1811
Consideration: $500.00
Amt of land: 67 acres
Location: Sullivan Co, TN
Description: A tract of land containing by survey 67 acres, joining Jacob Hartman's line, joining John Phagan's land, and William Pallett's line, and along a dividing line between Munsey and Timothy Acuff
Wit: James Phagan, John Acuff, William Zateet

Proven: By James Phagan, John Acuff
Test: Mattw. Rhea, C.S.C
Regst: March 17, 1812

(Page)
(184)

WILLIAM L. BROWNLOW :
Attorney in Fact for :
Isaac Brownlow : DEED OF WARRANTY
    TO :
WILLIAM SCOTT :

Date: Feb. 18, 1812
Consideration: $100.00
Amt of land: 25 acres
Location: Sullivan Co, TN
Description: Land to which he claims by virtue of a grant from TN, No. 1912, issued April 12, 1807; beginning at Matthias Little's corner and crossing Indian Creek
Acknowledged: By William Brownlow, Atty for Isaac Brownlow, Sullivan Co, TN, Feb, 1812
Test: Mattw. RHea, C.S.C, by Sam'l Lowery, D.C.
Regst: March 18, 1812

PETER MORGAN :
    TO : DEED OF WARRANTY
JOHN CROUCH :

Date: Feb. 18, 1811
Consideration: Amt omitted
Amt of land: 230 acres
Location: Sullivan Co, TN
Description: A tract on the waters of Horse Creek incl. house where George Crouch now lives; on cond'l line between Titsworth and Vincent
Wit: John Vincent, Samuel Edgeman, Thomas White
Test: Mattw. Rhea, C.S.C, by Samuel Lowery, D.C.
Regst: (No date given)

----

(186) GEORGE WADDLE :
    TO : BILL OF SALE
HERMAN LATTURE :

Date: Jan. 27, 1812
Consideration: $150.00
Articles sold: George Waddle sold unto Harman Latture: 1 mare, 2 cows, 5 head of sheep, and sow and 5 pigs, 2 beds and furniture, 1 large pot, 2 ovens, 1 table and chest, 1 cupboard, and all the dish ware, 1 man's saddle, barshear plow, 1 shovel, 1 axe, 1 still, 1 crib of corn, upwards of 100 stacks of hemp, 1 stack of fodder, and abt 50 doz oats, 7 head rye
Wit: John Jennings, John Waddle
Proven: By John Jennings, Sullivan Co, TN, Feb, 1812
Test: Mattw. Rhea, C.S.C
Regst: March 19, 1812

----

(186) ROBERT CHRISTIAN & :
     WILLIAM CHRISTIAN of :
     Bledsoe Co   :
        TO   : DEED OF WARRANTY
     JOHN CHRISTIAN of :
     Cumberland Co, KY :

Date: Oct. ?, 1811
Consideration: $1470.00
Amt of land: 1280 acres
Location: Overton Co, TN
Description: A tract of land in Overton Co on the waters of Roaming
(Roaring?) River, being part of a 1280 acre tract of land originally
granted to Gilbert Christian, dec'd, and joining a survey made for James
McNair, and with a line of a survey of 300 acres belonging to the heirs
of john Williams, dec'd
Wit: Thos Milligan, Jacil P. Gosher, Stephen Hicks
Test: Mattw. Rhea, C.S.C, by Samuel Lowery, D.C.
Regst: March 19, 1812

----

(188) PATRICK CREGGER   :
        TO   : DEED OF WARRANTY
     CHARLES BARNETT :

Date: Feb. 9, 1812
Consideration: A valuable consideration
Amt of land: 164 acres
Location: Sullivan Co, TN
Description: A tract of land on Indian Creek; beginning on Solomon Smith's
line and on line between Cregger and Felty Little
Acknowledged: By Patrick Cregger, Sullivan Co, TN, Feb, 1812
Test: Mattw. Rhea, C.S.C, by Samuel Lowery, D.C.
Regst: March 19, 1812

----

(189) JOHN DERTING   :
        TO   : DEED OF WARRANTY
     JOHN SMITH   :

Date: Feb. 27, 1811
Consideration: $108.00
Amt of land: 35 1/4 acres
Location: Sullivan Co, TN
Description: A tract of land; beginning on James Hollin's old patent line
and on John Shoemaker's old line
Wit: Alex Gitgood, John Jennings, James Wright
Acknowledged: By John Derting, Sullivan Co, TN, Aug, 1811
Test: Mattw. Rhea, C.S.C.
Regst: March 19, 1812

```
GEORGE THOMAS          :
        TO             :    DEED OF WARRANTY
GABRIEL MORGAN         :
```

Date: May 9, 1807
Consideration: $325.00
Amt of land: 120 acres
Location: Sullivan Co, TN
Description: A tract of land on the waters of Horse Creek; beginning at Thomas Titsworth's corner thence south with several courses of a deed given by John Hedrick
Wit: Samuel Edgeman, George Crouch, John W. Bride
Proven: By George Crouch and John W. Bride, Sullivan Co, TNM, Feb, 1812
Test: Mattw. Rhea, C.S.C, by Samuel Lowery, D.C.
Regst: March 19, 1812

```
(190)   WILLIAM CHILDRESS      :
             TO                :    DEED OF WARRANTY
        GEORGE HAZZARD         :
```

Date: Feb. 15, 1812
Consideration: 150 ₤
Amt of land: 100 acres
Location: Sullivan Co, TN
Description: A tract of land on the south side of Holston River
Wit: A. Fain, Robert Easley
Acknowledged: By William Childress, Sullivan Co, TN, Feb, 1812
Test: Mattw. Rhea, C.S.C, by Samuel Lowery, D.C.
Regst: March 20, 1812

```
CHRISTIAN WEAVER       :
        TO             :    DEED OF WARRANTY
MICHAEL WEAVER         :
```

Date: Feb. 17, 1812
Consideration: $1000.00
Amt of land: 300 acres
Location: Sullivan Co, TN
Description: A tract of land; beginning at a corner to John Scott's, joining Jonathan Willis
Acknowledged: By Christian Weaver, Sullivan Co, TN, Feb, 1812
Test: Mattw Rhea, C.S.C, by Samuel Lowery, D.C.
Regst: March 20, 1812

```
(192)   JOHN WEAVER            :
             TO                :    DEED OF WARRANTY
        GEORGE WEAVER          :
```

Date: Nov. 10, 1811
Consideration: $500.00
Amt of land: 83 acres
Location: Sullivan Co, TN

Description: A tract of land containing 83 acres
Wit: John Jennings, Daniel Shoemaker, John Dertin
Proven: By John Jennings, Daniel Shoemaker, Sullivan Co, TN, Feb, 1812
Test: Mattw. Rhea, C.S.C, by Samuel Lowery, D.C.
Regst: March 28, 1812

(Page)
(193)

MARTIN WADDLE of	:	
Greene Co, TN	:	
TO	:	DEED OF WARRANTY
JACOB PEAVLER	:	

Date: Oct. 19, 1811
Consideration: $300.00
Amt of land: 144 acres
Location: Sullivan Co, TN
Description: A tract of land supposing to be 144 acres excepting 1 acre
that I have laid off for a meeting house that is now on the top of
Eaton's Ridge and adj. Samuel Moore's conditional corner
Wit: David Peavler, William Smith, Washington Hanshaw
Proven: By David Peavler, William Smith, Sullivan Co, TN, Feb, 1812
Test: Mattw. Rhea, C.S.C, by Samuel Lowery, D.C.
Regst: March 20, 1812

ROBERT CHRISTIAN	:	
TO	:	
WILLIAM TRIGG, CHARLES S. CARSON,	:	DEED OF WARRANTY
JOHN LYNN of the Firm Lynn, Trigg,	:	
& Carson - Merchants of Abingdon, VA	:	

Date: Feb. 15, 1812
Consideration: $100.00
Amt of land: 2 acres, 12 sq. poles
Location: Christianville Boat Yard (Kingsport)
(Note: William Trigg and Charles S. Carson, merchants of the town of
Abington, VA. Robert Christian of Sullivan Co, TN. John Lynn, merchant of
Christiansville)
Description: A (tract) containing 2 acres and 12 sq poles in Christiansville
(Boatyard)
Acknowledged: By robert Christian, Sullivan Co, TN, Feb, 1812
Test: Mattw. Rhea, C.S.C, by Samuel Lowery, D.C.
Regst: March 20, 1812

---

(196)

STATE OF TENNESSEE	:	
WILLIE BLOUNT, GOV.	:	LAND GRANT
TO	:	NO. 2015
JACOB STURM	:	

Date: Oct. 8, 1808
Consideration: An entry made in the office of the sruveyor of the 6th
District of No. 566, founded on a warrant of No. 542 issued by the
Commissioners of E. TN to Benjamin Key for 300 acres of land dated Oct.
8, 1808, entry dated Nov. 24, 1810, 115 acres of which sd warrant is

vested in Jacob Sturm the enterer
Land granted: By assignment there is granted by state of TN to jacob
Sturm and his hiers a tract of land containing 82 acres in the District of
Washington; beginning on Henry Sheet's line and joining Samuel Carrither's
line and also joining Walter James' line and John Parker's, surveyed Dec.
15, 1810
Granted by Gov. Willie Blount, R. Houston, Sec.
Jacob Sturm is entitled to the within described tract of land. Recorded
Oct. 3, 1811
        Edw. Scott, Register of E. TN
April 1, 1812 then received the state tax on this grant.   C M
Tax 164   Mattw. Rhea, C.S.C
(Regst): April 17, 1812

(Page)
(197)

STATE OF TENNESSEE	:	
WILLIE BLOUNT, GOV	:	LAND GRANT
TO	:	NO. 2016
JACOB STURM	:	

Date: Oct. 8, 1808
Consideration: An entry made in the office of the surveyor of the 6th
District of No. 600, founded on a warrant of No. 542, issued by the
Commissioner of 6th District of TN to Benjamin Key for 300 acres of land
dated Oct. 8, 1808. Entry dated Jan 7, 1811, 115 acres of which sd
warrant is vested in Jacob Sturm the enterer by assignment. There is
granted by TN to Jacob Sturm and his heirs a tract of land.
Land granted: A tract of land containing 29 acres in Washington District
on the north side of Holston River joining Nicholas Rogers' corner.
Surveyed Jan. 14, 1811
Granted by Gov. Willie Blount, R. Houston, Sec.
Edw Scott, Register of E. TN
Jacob Sturm is entitled to the within described tract of land. Registered
in my office Oct. 3, 1811
        Edw. Scott, Register
April 1, 1812, then received the state tax on this grant
5 cents 8 mills   Mattw. Rhea, C.S.C
Regst: April 17, 1812

----

(197)

JACOB MILLER of	:	
Washington Co, VA	:	
TO	:	DEED OF WARRANTY
HENRY KINGARY	:	

Date: Nov. 16, 1811
Consideration: $2000.00
Amt of land: 117* acres
Location: Sullivan Co, TN
Description: A tract of land on the waters of Steel Creek containing 107*,
exclusive of seven acres out of the within mentioned courses which Jacob
Miller had before the sealing and delivery of these presents sold to
Michael Hickman on which Hickman now lives, along Peter Hickman's line
to a marked white oak

Acknowledged: By Jacob Miller, Sullivan Co, TN, Nov, 1811
Test: Mattw. Rhea, C.S.C
Regst: (No date given)

(*Note: both amounts given)

(Page)
(199)
STATE OF TENNESSEE :
WILLIE BLOUNT, GOV. :   LAND GRANT
        TO   :   NO. 2019
JOHN MOTTAR   :

Date: Oct. 3, 1811
Consideration: An entry made in the office of the surveyor of the 6th
District of No. 455, founded on a certificate of No. 155 issued by the
Commissioner of E. TN to Samuel and Joseph McCorkle for 70 acres of
land dated Sept. 28, 1809, entry dated June 12, 1810, 15 acres of which
certificate is vested in John Mottern the Enterer by assignment. There is
granted by state of Tn unto John Mottern and his heirs a tract of land
containing 15 acres in the Washington District on the waters of Indian
Creek; beginning with Joshua Edward's line; surveyed Jan. 22, 1811
Granted by Willie Blount, Gov, R. Houston, Sec.
John Mottern is entitled to the within described tract of land. Rec'd in
my office Oct. 5, 1811.
                        E.W. Scott, Register of E. TN
April 1, 1812, then received the state tax on this grant
3 cts   Mattw. Rhea, C.S.C.
(Regst): April 5, 1812

----

(200)
STATE OF TENNESSEE :
WILLIE BLOUNT, GOV. :   LAND GRANT
        TO   :   NO. 1912
ISAAC BROWNLOW   :

Date: April 12, 1811
Consideration: An entry made in the office of the surveyor of the 6th
District of No. 204, dated Dec. 27, 1808, issued by Archibald Roane to
John Smith for 200 acres of land, dated April 7, 1808, by Smith to Samuel
Y. Balch to Isaac Brownlow, the enterer
Land granted: There is granted by the state of Tn a tract of land
containing 25 acres in the Washington District; beginning at Matthias
Little's corner thence crossing Indian Creek. Surveyed June 9, 1809.
Granted by Willie Blount, Gov, R. Houston, Sec.
The within named Isaac Brownlow hath title to the within named trats of
land. I do certify that this grant is recorded in my office, April 12, 1811.
                        E.W. Scott, Register of Land Office E. TN
Received March 27, 1812, Sullivan Co, TN.
5 cents tax d   Mattw. Rhea, C.S.C.
(Regst): April 27, 1812

----

(201)
STATE OF TENNESSEE :
WILLIE BLOUNT, GOV. :   LAND GRANT
        TO   :   NO. 2013
ABRAHAM LOONEY   :

Date: Oct. 3, 1811
Consideration: An entry made in the office of the surveyor of the 6th District No. 204, dated Dec. 27, 1808, issued by Archibald Roane to John Smith for 200 acres of land dated April 7, 1808, and assigned by Smith to Samuel Y. Balch and sd Balch to Isaac Brownlow, the enterer
Land granted: Granted by the state of TN to Abraham Looney and his heirs a tract of land containing 27 acres in the Washington District; beginning on a former survey of Looney
Granted by Willie Blount, Gov, R. Houston, Sec.
Abraham Looney is entitled to the within described tract of land. Recorded in my office Oct. 3, 1811
                 E.W. Scott, Register of E. TN
April 1, 1812, received state tax on this grant.
Test: Mattw. Rhea, C.S.C.
(Regst): April 27, 1812

(Page)
(202)

COMMONWEALTH OF VIRGINIA	:	
WM A. CABELL, GOV.	:	LAND GRANT
TO	:	NO. 21257
JOHN THOMPSON	:	

Date: April 10, 1808
Consideration: By virtue of a treasury warrant No. 21257
Amt of land: 200 acres by survey
Location: Washington Co
Description: By virtue of the above mentioned land ofice treasury warrant No. 21257, issued Dec. 12, 1783, there is granted by the Commonwealth to John Thompson a tract of land containing 200 acres dated May 12, 1803, on both sides of the Furnace Road
Wm A. Cabell, Gov.
John Thompson hath title to the within   Wm Pride Re Lott
April 1, 1812, then received the state tax on the grant
40 cents   Mattw. Rhea, C.S.C
(Regst): April 27, 1812

----

(202)

JAMES T. GAINES	:	
TO	:	DEED OF WARRANTY
JOSEPH EVERETT	:	

Date: Jan. 2, 1809
Consideration: $225.00
Amt of land: 75 acres
Location: Sullivan Co, TN
Description: a tract of land on the north side of Reedy Creek; beginning at a corner to David Ross' line, being part of a tract granted to Edmund Pendleton
Wit: John Pryors, Stephen Hicks, Robert Christian
Acknowledged: By T. Gaines, Sullivan Co, TN, Feb, 1812
Test: Mattw. Rhea, C.S.C
Regst: April 28, 1812

```
SARAH SHIPLEY & GEORGE ELMORE    :
          TO                     :         DEED OF WARRANTY
ELI SHIPLEY & BENJAMIN SHIPLEY   :
```

Date: March 19, 1808
Consideration: $200.00
Amt of land: 100 acres
Location: Sullivan Co, TN
Description: All that tract of land on the north side of the Holston River; containing 100 acres; being part of a tract of land granted by patent from the state of NC to Valentine Pope containing 300 acres dated Feb. 13, 1791, as will appear reference being thereunto
Wit: John A. Rogers, Jese Mills
Proven: By John A. Rogers, Hawkins Co, TN, Feb, 1812
Test: Richard Mitchell, Clk
Regst: April 28, 1812

----

(205)

```
WILLIAM HUGHES       :
      TO             :         DEED OF WARRANTY
SAMUEL MOORE         :
```

Date: Oct. 24, 1811
Consideration: $1200.00
Amt of land: 240 acres
Location: Sullivan Co, TN
Description: A tract of land containing 240 acres on both sides of Reedy Creek, joining Moore's meadow being part of a tract of land known by the name of Pendleton and Taylor's grant
Wit: Andrew Gains, Jacob Booher, Willie Cruts
(Regst): (No date given)

----

(206)

```
JAMES ANGELA         :
      TO             :         DEED OF WARRANTY
JOHN PUNCH           :
```

Date: Oct. 26, 1811
Consideration: $200.00
Amt of land: 2 acres
Location: Blountville, Sullivan Co, TN
Description: One lot of land on the side of the bridge and north side of the main street in Blountville being the lot next west from where George Punch now lives containing 1/2 acre which was conveyed to sd Angela by John Tipton by indenture bearing date Nov. 9, 1810. One other lot containing 12 acre adj. before mentioned lot on the west side thereof which was conveyed to Zachias Jones by Angela by indenture dated Nov. 9, 1810. One other lot containing 1 acre on the south side of the main street fronting the aforesaid two lots being the one known as Bonham's lot which was conveyed to Angela by John Tipton by indenture bearing date Nov. 9, 1810.
Wit: James H. Banneth*, Joseph W. Brownlow
Proven: By Joseph W. Brownlow, James H. Ganneth*, Sullivan Co, TN, Nov, 1811

Test: Mattw. Rhea, C.S.C.
Regst: April 28, 1812

(*Note: Name spelled both ways)

(Page)
(207)   STATE OF NORTH CAROLINA :
         SAMUEL ASHE, GOV.   :   LAND GRANT
                  TO   :   NO. 770
         JOHN HAWKINS   :

         Date: Nov. 17, 1797
         Consideration: 50 shillings for every 100 acres of land
         Amt of land: 5 acres
         Location: Sullivan Co, TN
         Description: A tract of land containing 5 acres in Sullivan Co, entered
         June 2, 1781, as the plot hereunto annexed doth appear
         Granted by Sam Ahse, Gov, by Commd. J. Glasgow, Sec.
         By virtue of a warrant to me directed No. 618, I have surveyed 5 acres
         of land for John Hawkins in Sullivan Co and territory south of Ohio
         (Meets and bounds)   Surveyed: Feb. 9, 1796
         Nicholas Hawkins)   By: John Anderson, C.S.
         Wm. Lynch   ) C C. STOKELEY DAVIDSON, E. D.
         State of TN, Sullivan Co, I do certify that I have received one cent tax
         on this deed, April 28, 1812.
                                        Mattw. Rhea, C.S.C.

(208)   JOHN TIPTON   :
                  TO   :   DEED OF WARRANTY
         JAMES ANGELA   :

         Date: Nov. 9, 1810
         Consideration: $40.00
         Amt of land: 1/2 acre
         Location: Sullivan Co, West end of the town of Blountville
         Description: A lot of ground at the west end of Blountville on the north
         side of the main road and divided from the lot now occupies by John
         Punch by an alley
         Wit: Elisha James, Thomas Johnson
         Acknowledged: By John Tipton, Sullivan Co, TN
         Test: Mattw. Rhea, C.S.C, by Robt Rhea, D.C.
         Regst: May 7, ?

----

(209)   STATE OF TENNESSEE   :
         WILLIE BLOUNT, GOV.   :   LAND GRANT
                  TO   :   NO. 672
         HARMON LATTURE   :

         Date: Sept. 8, 1808
         Consideration: An entry made in the office of the surveyor of the 6th
         District of No. 13 (or 134, difficult to read) dated Sept. 9, 1808, founded
         on a warrant of Nov. 1716 issued from Carter's office to Evan Shelby for
         400 acres dated Sept. 25, 1797, and adjudged valid on May 22, 1807, by
         the board of Commissioners for E. TN and assigned by Isaac Shelby,

Executor of Evan Shelby, dec'd, to Henry Harkleroad and by sd Harkleroad to George Emmert and by Emmert to Herman Latture. The entries for which this is a part. There is granted by the state of TN to Harmon Latture and his heirs a tract of land containing 50 acres
Description: A tract of land containing 50 acres in Washington District joining Joseph Bealor's corner, also joining Jacob Hasohs(sic) line, also Hugh Cummings' line, surveyed on March 1, 1809.
Seal affixed at Knoxville, Sept. 26, 1809
By the Gov. Willie Blount, R. Houston, Sec.
The within named Harmon Latture hath title to the within named tract of land. Recorded in my office. Certified Sept. 26, 1809.

E.W. Scott, Register Land Office E. TN
April 1, 1812, then rec'd state tax for this grant.
Test: Mattw. Rhea, C.S.C.
(Regst): May 9, 1812

(Page)
(210)

STATE OF TENNESSEE   :
WILLIE BLOUNT, GOV.   :   LAND GRANT
          TO   :   NO. 1851
LAURENCE SNAPP   :

Date: Sept. 30, 1809
Consideration: An entry made in the surveyor's office of the 6th District No. 347, Sept. 30, 1809, founded on a certificate of No. 62, issued by Archibald Roane to Jacob Casner for 20 acres dated Oct. 30, 1808, and assigned by Casner to John A. McKinney and by McKinney to David Yearsley and by Yearsley to Laurence Snapp, Jr, the enterer. There is granted by state of TN to Snapp, Jr, and his heirs a tract of land
Description: A tract of land containing 13 acres in the Washington District on the south side of Holston River; beginning at a post on the bank of the river, joining a former survey of sd Snapp's line; also joining John Moseley's line, also joining Slaughter's line, and along the river to the beginning. Surveyed Sept. 20, 1809. Seal of State of TN to be affixed at Knoxville, Dec. 30, 1810.
By the Gov. Willie Blount, R. Houston, Sec.
The within named Laurence Snapp hath title to the within described tract of land. I do certify that the grant is registered in my office. Given under my hand Dec. 13, 1810.

E.W. Scott, Register of Land for E. TN
April 1, 1812, then rec'd the state tax on this grant

Mattw. Rhea, C.S.C.
(Regst): May 11, 1812

----

(211)   STATE OF TENNESSEE   :
           WILLIE BLOUNT, GOV.   :   LAND GRANT
                     TO   :   NO. 2014
           SARAH BERRY   :

Date: Oct. 3, 1811
Consideration: An entry made in the office of the surveyor of the 6th District of No. 551, founded on a warrant of No. 542, issued by the Commissioner of E.TN to Benjamin Key for 300 acres of land dated Oct. 8, 1808. Entry dated Nov. 5, 1810, 10 acres of which warrant is vested in

Sarah Berry, the enterer, by assignment. There is granted by the state of
TN to Sarah Berry and her heirs a tract of land
Description: A tract of land containing 10 acres in the Washington District;
beginning with George Brown's line, and on an old corner of William
Worsham's then a direct line to the beginning. Great seal to be affixed at
Knoxville, Oct. 3, 1811
By the Gov. Willie Blount, R. Houston, Sec.
Sarah Berry is entitled to the within described tract of land. Recorded in
my office Oct. 3, 1811.

        E.W. Scott, Register of E. TN
April 1, 1812, rec'd state tax on this grant
Fee: 2 cts

        Mattw. Rhea, C.S.C.
(Regst): May 12, 1812

(Page)
 (212) MICHAEL OWEN   :
       TO   : QUIT CLAIM DEED
    DAVID OWEN   :

Date: April 3, 1812
Consideration: A valuable consideration
Amt of land: 155 acres
Location: Sullivan Co, TN
Description: A tract of land beginning at a red oak on the top of a hill
to a stake between the dwelling house and kitchen then (description
continued)*
Wit: John Anderson Rutledge
Acknowledged: In open court
Test: Mattw. Rhea, C.S.C.
Regst: June 2, 1812

(*Note: This is the end of this deed on the WPA copy)

    DAVID OWEN   :
       TO   : QUIT CLAIM DEED
    MICHAEL OWEN   :

Date: April 3, 1812
Consideration: A valuable consideration
Amt of land: 101 acres. Also mentioned as 151 acres and 20 acres
Location: Sullivan Co, TN
Description: A tract of land containing 101 acres; one of sd tracts joining
Andrew Crocket's line, also Robert Rutledge's containing 151 ares. The
other survey beginning at Abraham McClellands and joins Robert Rutledge's
line containing 20 acres
Wit: John Anderson, Robert Rutledge
Proven: By John Anderson, Robert Rutledge, Sullivan Co, May, 1812
Test: Mattw. Rhea, C.S.C
Regst: (No date given)

     ----

 (213) JACOB BOY   :
       TO   : DEED OF WARRANTY
    ADAM BOY   :
        82

Date: May 18, 1812
Consideration: In consideration of the natural love and affection which hath
and beareth unto Adam Boy, his son, also for the better maintenance and
preferment of the sd Adam Boy.
Amt of land: 83 acres
Location: Sullivan Co, TN
Description: A tract of land containing 83 acres; beginning on John Vance's
corner on the north bank of Holston River and with Vance's line to the
beginning
Wit: John Anderson
Acknowledged: By Jacob Boy, Sullivan Co, TN, May, 1812
Test: Mattw. Rhea, C.S.C.
Regst: June 10, 1812

(Page)
(214)

JOHN TIPTON   :
        TO   :   DEED OF WARRANTY
NICHOLAS RUSSELL   :

Date: Feb. 10, 1812
Consideration: For a valuable consideration
Amt of land: 1 acre
Location: Town of Blountville
Description: A lot containing 1 acre in the town of Blountville, No. 7;
beginning at a stake on the south side of Back Street and joining John
Rhea's lot
Acknowledged: John Tipton, Sullivan Co, TN, Feb. 1812
Regst: June 12, 1812

STATE OF NORTH CAROLINA :
ALEXANDER MARTIN, GOV. :   LAND GRANT
        TO   :   NO. 289
JOHN SNODGRASS   :

Date: Nov. 10, 1784
Consideration: 50 shillings for every 100 acres of land
Amt of land: 174 acres
Location: Sullivan Co, TN (formerly North Carolina)
Description: A tract of land containing 174 acres; beginning on William
Roger's line and joining Timothy Acuff's land, also joining John Adam's line
and Thomas Looney's corner
Granted by his Excellencys Comd. W. Williams, D. Sec.
Surveyed: a tract of land for John Snodgrass in Sullivan Co, NC; beginning
at a forked chestnut thence on Wm Rodger's line to a hickory Timothy
Acuff's corner and joining John Adams' line, also joining John Looney's
line, containing 174 acres.
Surveyed: Feb. 8, 1782   David Shelby, C.S.
(Regst): June 5, 181

----

(217)   JANE MOSS   :
              TO   :   DEED OF WARRANTY
          ROBERT COWAN   :

Date: Sept. 1, 1816(sic)
Consideration: $800.00 current money of TN
Amt of land: 80 acres
Location: Sullivan Co, TN
Description: A tract of land containing 80 acres on a branch of Beaver Creek, joining David Stuts line
Wit: Abraham McClellan, Mart Harkleroad
Proven: By Abraham McClellan, Martin Harkleroad, Sullivan Co, TN, May, 1812
Test: Mattw. Rhea, C.S.C.
Regst: June 15, 1812

(Page)
(218)   JOHN TIPTON   :
              TO   :   DEED OF WARRANTY
       JOHN RUSSELL   :

Date: Feb. 21, 1812
Consideration: $50.00
Amt of land: 1/2 acre
Location: Blountville, Sullivan Co, TN
Description: A lot of land, No. 7, in Blountville, containing 1/2 an acre at the west end of town; beginning at a stake joining the lot where the Acadmeu(sic) stands on the south side of the street
Wit: John Anderson, Robt. Blackmore
Acknowledged: By John Tipton, Sullivan Co, TN, May, 1812
Test: Mattw. Rhea, C.S.C
Regst: June 16, 1812

----

(219)   DAVID OWEN   :
              TO   :   DEED OF WARRANTY
       ROBERT RUTLEDGE   :

Date: April 3, 1812
Consideration: A valuable consideration
Amt of land: 155 acres
Location: Sullivan Co, TN
Description: A tract of land on White Top Creek, joining Andrew Crockett's line and the land of Conrad Sharretz to a stake between the dwelling house and kitchen thence on or near Abraham McClellan's line to the beginning
Wit: John Anderson, Michael Owens
Proven: By John Anderson, Michael Owen, Sullivan Co, TN, May, 1812
Test: Mattw. Rhea, C.S.C
Regst: June 16, 1812

----

(220)   GATEWOOD BLEVINS   :
              TO   :   DEED OF WARRANTY
       JOHN BLEVINS   :
       WM BLEVINS' HEIRS   :

Date: Jan. 2, 1812
Consideration: $50.00

84

Amt of land: Not stated
Location: Sullivan Co, TN
Description: - Parties hereto- Gatewood Blevins descendant from and heir of William Blevins commonly called Colonel Tate of Sullivan Co, and John Blevins, son of Wm Blevins, dec'd. All my individual share in and of the land belonging to the estate now in the possession of Ann Blevins, widow of William Blevins.
Wit: Caleb Morrell, Nathan Morrell, Jesse Morrell
Proven: By Caleb Morrell, Nathan Morrell, Sullivan Co, Tn, May, 1812
Test: Mattw. Rhea, C.S.C.
Regst: June 16, 1812

(Page)
(221)

JANE MOSS	:	
TO	:	DEED OF WARRANTY
ROBERT COWAN	:	

Date: Sept. 1, 1811
Consideration: $800.00
Amt of land: 96 acres
Location: Sullivan Co, TN
Description: A tract of land beginning on David Steel's line being a part of the tract of land where David Steel now lives
Wit: Martin Harkleroad, Abraham McClellan
Proven: By Martin Harkleroad, Abraham McClellan, Sullivan Co, TN, May, 1812
Test: Mattw. Rhea, C.S.C.
Regst: June 16, 1812

----

(222)

JOHN LYONS	:	
TO	:	DEED OF WARRANTY
MATTIE KING	:	

Date: March 30, 1807
Consideration: $240.00
Amt of land: 100 acres
Location: Sullivan Co, TN
Description: A tract of land on the south side of Holston River; beginning at John Bailey's corner then on Moses Cavet's line, then on Mack Osborne's line, then to Oakson Hofman's line
Wit: Jno Waller, Joseph Coin
Proven: By John Waller and Joseph Coin, Sullivan Co, TN, May, 1812
Test: Mattw. Rhea, C.S.C
Regst: June 18, 1812

HENRY SHARRITZ	:	
TO	:	DEED OF ANNUITY
CONRAD SHARITZ	:	

Date: Aug. 18, 1810
Consideration: $1400.00
Amt of land: 90 acres
Location: Sullivan Co, TN

Description: The annuity consists of a tract of land and the following products: an annuity of 15 bushels of wheat, 15 bushels of rye, 26 bushels of corn, 75 waight(sic) of pork, 75 waight of beef, $7.50 in specie, 7 bushels of potatoes, 7 bushels of turnups, 1 ton of good well cured hay, 13 waight of well hackled flax, 15 of toe, the house and all the old land incl. the old orchard, garden, potatoe patches, where I now live, also pasture for two cows, and one horse coling(sic) and haling(sic) firewood during my life and after my death the sd Henry Sharritz shall pay $5.00 yearly for five years to my wife, Anna Sharritz, in part of $100.00 in full of his dowery and is also to pay $200 ₤ VA currency to my 2 daughters 3 yrs after my deses(sic) Mary and Susanna, their heirs and assigns, 1/3 to be paid in spesy(sic) and the other to be paid in trade at cash price, to be received, taken and had and to be issuing out of all that massuage of a tract of land where Henry Sharritz now lives. Land on Sinking Creek on Yateses line. Sd land is to become the property of Conrad Sharrits Sr. and his assigns during the natural life of him the sd Conrad Sharrits. Sd annuity to be paid at or upon the first day of Dec, 1811, yearly by equal portions. And if it shall happen the sd anuity of the above mentioned wheat, rye, corn, oats, beef, pork, flax, toe, potatoes, turnops, hay, wood, and all the money and whiskey as above mentioned or any part thereof be behind or unpaid in part or in all by the space of 21 days next of the sd day or times, or terms of payment thereof at any time thereof it may be lawful for the sd Conrad Sharrats Sr. and his assigns to enter and distrain and impound to take, hold and keep until the sd annuity and the arrears if any thereof until all costs and charges have been paid. Henry Sharrets, his heirs, etc. shall well and truly pay to Conrad Sharrets, Sr, the sd annuity or yearly rent charge.
Wit: Henry Harkleroad, George Burkhart, Mart Harkleroad
Acknowledged: By Henry Sharets, Sullivan Co, TN, Aug, 1810
Test: Mattw. Rhea, C.S.C.
Regst: June 26, 1812

(Page)
(225)   CONRAD SHARETS, JR. :
                        TO   :   DEED OF ANNUITY
               CONRAD SHARETS, SR. :

Date: Aug. 18, 1810
Consideration: $2,970.00
Amt of land: 3,311 acres
Location: Sullivan Co, TN
Annuity: One annuity of 20 bushels of wheat, 20 bushels of rye, 40 bushels of corn, 40 cushels of oats, 100 weight of pork, 100 wt of beef, 15 wt of all hackled flax, 20 wt of tow, 10 bushels of turnups, 15 bushels of potatoes, 2 tons of good cured hay, $10.00 in cash, 30 gal of good whiskey, sufficient quantity of firewood all to be delivered at my house yearly and every year during my natural life and after my deses(sic) the sd Conrad Sharets, Jr. is to pay to my 2 oldest or their heirs 200 ???, that is to Elizabeth 100 and Catherine 100 1/3 of ech(sic) to be paid in specy(sic) and the balance in trade at cash price and is also to pay $10.00 in specy(sic) for 5 yrs after my deses to my wife, Ana Sharets, in part of 100 in full of his dowery all the above to be taken received yearly out of all that massuage of land where Conrad Sharets, Jr. now lives containing 3,311 acres; beginning at a hickory in the big road on John Peter's line, also joining John Sharets' line and Jacob Bealor's line, and George Bealor's

84

line. Sd property to remain the property of sd Conrad Sharrets, Jr. as long as sd annuity is paid during the lifetime of Conrad Sharrets, Sr. The annuity is to be paid yearly first payment to begin and be made on or before the first day of Dec. in the year 1811, and if it shall happen that the annuity be unpaid in part or in all by the space of 21 days next either of the sd days or times of payment thereof whereupon the same should or ought to be paid as aforesaid that then and so often and at any time thereafter it shall and may be lawful to and for the Conrad Sharets, Sr. and his assigns into and for the above mentioned messuage to enter and impound and the same impound to take, hold and keep the same impound until the sd annuity together with costs and charges shall be paid. Said land to stand for this annuity

Wit: Henry Harkleroad, George Burkhart, Martin Harkleroad
Acknowledged: By Conrad Sharets, Jr, Sullivan Co, TN, Aug, 1811
Test: Mattw. Rhea, C.S.C
Regst: June 27, 1812

(Page)

WILLIAM SKILLERN of :
Washington Co, VA   :
      TO   :   DEED OF WARRANTY
JOHN KENTON   :

Date: Feb. 24, 1812
Consideration: $100.00
Amt of land: 100 acres
Location: Sullivan Co, VA(sic)
Description: a tract of land on the waters of Reedy Creek being part of a tract of 560 acres granted to William Skillern by patent dated Feb. 28, 1800, from the Commonwealth of VA.
Wit: Jacob Wyzer, David Shaver, Lewis Peavler, William Messcan(sci)
Proven: By David Shaver, Lewis Peavler, Sullivan Co, TN, May, 1812
Test: Mattw. Rhea, C.S.C
Regst: July 5, 1812

----

(228) THOMAS ROCKHOLD   :
          TO   :   DEED OF WARRANTY
     SAMUEL PARMER   :

Date: Oct. 11, 1806
Consideration: $464.50
Amt of land: 108 acres
Location: Sullivan Co, TN
Description: A part of a tract of land being part of a tract of land where James Hawk(?) formerly lived on the north side of Holston River; beginning on Robert Cowan's line, also joining James King's ore bank
Wit: Hen Harkleroad, Albert Cowan, Geo Miller
Acknowledged: By Thomas Rockhold, Sullivan Co, TN, Feb, 1807
Test: Mattw. Rhea, C.S.C.
Regst: July 27, 1812

----

(229) JOHN SHARRETS   :
          TO   :   DEED OF ANNUITY
   CONRAD SHARRETS, SR :

Date: Aug. 18, 1810
Consideration: $2025.00
Amt of land: 225 acres
Location: Sullivan Co, TN
Annuity: One annuity of 15 bushels wheat, 15 bushels rye, 26 bushels corn, 26 bushels oats, 75 wt pork, 75 wt beef, 13 wt flax, 15 toe, 1 ton of good well cured hay, $7.50 in spacy(sic), 7 and 2 bus. potatoes, 10 bushels turnips, 10 gal whiskey, cutting and hauling sufitions(sic) quantity of firewood all to be delivered yearly and every year at my dwelling house as long and until my natural and after my deces the sd John Sharrets is to pay 200 Ł VA currency to 2 of my daughters, Margaretta and Bargary, their heirs or assigns each of them 100 1/3 to be paid in cash and the other part to be paid in trade at cash price is also to pay $5.00 for 5 yrs to my wife Anna Sharrets in part of $1..0.. in full of his dowery to be received taken had and issuing out of all that massuage or tract of land whereon the sd John Sharret now lives.
Description: Beginning on Thomas Shelby's corner, and on a line of Conrad Sharret, Jr, and on Noah Bealor's line, and on Martin Bealor's line containing 225 acres be the same more or less.
Terms: Sd annuity to be paid and payable at or upon the first day of Dec, 1811, yearly by equal and even portions and if it should happen that the sd annuity or any part thereof be behind or unpaid in part or in all be the space of either the sd days or times of payment thereof whereupon the same should or ought to be paid then it may be lawful to and for the sd Conrad Sharret, Sr, or his heirs to enter the sd premises and take hold and keep and impound the same to be held until annuity be paid, together with any costs or charges concerning the same shall be fully paid and satisfied. Messuage of land to be charged and chargeable with the annuity hereby granted.
Wit: Hen Harkleroad, Geo Burkhart, Martin Harkleroad
Acknowledged: By John Sharrets, Sullivan Co, TN, Aug, 1810
Test: Mattw. Rhea, C.S.C
Regst: July 27, 1812

(Page)
(232)

PHILLIP FOUST   :
      TO   :   DEED OF WARRANTY
BENJAMIN & AMOS WILSON :

Date: Nov. 16, 1807
Consideration: A valuable consideration
Amt of land: 120 acres
Location: Sullivan Co, TN
Description: a tract of land on the north fork of Reedy Creek; beginning on Jacob Hareses line and joining William Godard's corner and along Jacob Droke's line and on John Carathers' corner
Wit: Abner Hughes, John Anderson
Proven: Exhibited in open court the within deed of conveyance from Phillip Foust to Benjamin Wilson and Amos Wilson for 120 acres provey by Abner Hughes and John Anderson, Sullivan Co, TN, Nov, 1807
Test: Mattw. Rhea, C.S.C.
Regst: (No date given)

88

(233)   JAMES LAUGHLIN, SR. of Washington Co, VA   :
            TO   :   DEED OF WARRANTY
    JOHN CARSON of Washington Co, VA   :

Date: Feb. 14, 1807
Consideration: $350.00
Amt of land: 62 acres, 150 poles
Location: Sullivan Co, TN
Description: A tract of land beginning at a hickory on the bank of the
Holston River
Wit: Wm Owen, John Laughlin
Proven: By John Laughlin, William Owen, Sullivan Co, TN, Nov, 1811
Test: Mattw. Rhea, C.S.C
Regst: (No date given)

----

(234)   NICHOLAS HOUSER of Hawkins Co   :
            TO   :   DEED OF WARRANTY
    JONAS KEEN   :

Date: Oct. 15, 1802
Consideration: 200 ₤ lawful money of TN
Amt of land: By estimation, 300 acres
Location: Sullivan Co, TN
Description: All and every part of a tract of land on the waters of
Kendrick Creek on Houser's spring branch; on a conditional line between
Jonas Keen and John Waren and on James **
(**Note: The WPA copy did not have the complete deed)

----

(235)   PETER RADER   :
            TO   :   DEED OF WARRANTY
    RICHARD GAMMON   :

Date: Aug. 19, 1812
Consideration: A valuable consideration
Amt of land: 137 acres
Location: Sullivan Co, TN
Description: A tract of land beginning on John Hamilton's line and joining
Stephen Hicks' corner
Wit: John Anderson
Acknowledged: By Peter Rader, Sullivan Co, TN, Aug, 1812
Test: Mattw. Rhea, C.S.C.
Regst: Aug. 25, 1812

----

(236)   WILLIAM PRESLEY*   :
            TO   :   DEED OF TRUST
    GEORGE BURKHART & :
    WILLIAM WILLOUGHBY :

Date: aug. 17, 1812
Consideration: $100.00 debt to be paid Dec. 1, 1814, and $100.00 more to
be paid Dec. 1, 1815, and $1.00 in hand paid

Amt of land: A tract of land on both sides of Reedy Creek, joining
George Sower's line
Terms of trust: The sd trustee is hereby empowered at any time after
Dec. 1, 1815, to proceed to advertise and sell sd land at public vendue to
the highest bidder for case first giving notice by advertising at the
courthouse as Blountville and two other places; out of the money from sale
first to discharge the costs of sale then to discharge debt, the residue if
any shall return to William Priestly* for his use. If Priesly* will pay to
Jacob Booher the sum of $100.00 by Dec. 1, 1814, and $100.00 due by
Dec. 1, 1815, with proper costs then this deed is void, otherwise it
remains in full force
Acknowledged: By William Priestly*, Sullivan Co, TN, Aug, 1812
Test: Mattw. Rhea, C.S.C.
Regst: Aug. 28, 1812

(*Note: Name spelled three ways)

(Page)
   (237)**   WM PRIESTLY, Late, of :
               Washington Co, VA   :

(**Note: The above was written between two deeds; No other info given)

               LUDWICK RHINEHART   :
                     TO   :   DEED OF WARRANTY
               JOHN KING   :

               Date: Aug. 17, 1812
               Consideration: $167.65
               Amt of land: 50 acres
               Location: Sullivan Co, TN
               Description: A tract of land adj. a tract conveyed by John Sharp to John
               King; beginning at a forked white oak the beginning corner of a tract
               granted to Ludwick Rhinehart to John Gamble's line near the bank of
               Watauga River, and on John King's line
               Acknowledged: By Ludwick Rhinehart, Sullivan Co, TN, Aug, 1812
               Test: Mattw. Rhea, C.S.C.
               Regst: Aug. 28, 1812

----

   (239)   LEONARD YEAST   :
                     TO   :   DEED OF WARRANTY
               PETER CATRON   :

               Date: Nov. 17, 1811
               Consideration: A valuable consideration
               Amt of land: 254 acres
               Location: Sullvan Co, TN
               Description: A tract of land on the waters of Reedy Creek joining
               formerly James Haggard's line thence along John Catron's line
               Wit: John Catron, Valentine Catron
               Proven: By John Catron and Valentine Catron, Sullivan Co, TN, Aug, 1812
               Test: Mattw. Rhea, C.S.C.
               Regst: Aug. 29, 1812

```
MATTHEW RHEA          :
        TO            :     DEED OF WARRANTY
JAMES HAWLEY          :
```

Date: June 13, 1812
Consideration: $313.66
Amt of land: Not stated
Location: Sullivan Co, TN
Description: A tract of land purchased by Rhea from William Erwin to Wm by the last will and testament of David Erwin on the waters of Fall Creek, where the heirs of Erwin, dec'd, now lives
Wit: Ephraim Lewis, John Derting
Proven: By Ephraim Lewis and John Derting, Sullivan Co, TN, Aug, 1812
Test: Mattw. Rhea, C.S.C.
Regst: Aug. 31, 1812

```
IRESON LONGACRE       :
        TO            :     DEED OF WARRANTY
JOHN SHARP            :
```

Date: Aug. 14, 1812
Consideration: $366
Amt of land: 500 acres
Location: Sullivan Co, TN
Description: A parcel of land on the north side of Holston River; being part of a tract granted to Elizabeth Young in trust for the orphans of James Young, the larger tract containing 500 acres beginning at a creek on John Sharp's line and joining Robert Cowan's line to William Dulaney's corner; one undivided part of which supposed to be 168 1/2 acres was sold at public sale by Francis A Gaines, Sheriff of Sullivan Co, as the property of James Young on Aug. 14, 1801, at which time Ireson Longacre became purchaser by Sheriff's Deed dated Aug. 19, 1801, and Longacre doth sell over the above mentioned 168 1/2 acres to John Sharp
Acknowledged: By Ireson Longacre, Sullivan Co, TN, Aug, 1812
Test: Mattw. Rhea, C.S.C.
Regst: Aug. 31, 1812

----

(243)

```
CHARLES JONES         :
        TO            :     DEED OF WARRANTY
JONAS KEEN            :
```

Date: Aug. 29, 1805
Consideration: $133. 1/3
Amt of land: 40 acres
Location: Sullivan Co, TN
Description: A tract of land containing 40 acres on the waters of Kendrick's Creek; beginning at Jentry's old beginning corner
Wit: Elijah Matheny, John Jones
Acknowledged: By Charles Jones, Sullivan Co, TN, Aug, 1812
Test: Mattw. Rhea, C.S.C.
Regst: Aug. 13, 1812

SAMUEL GAMBLE   :
    TO   :   ARTICLES OF AGREEMENT
JOHN KING   :

Date: May 25, 1800
Consideration: $300.00
Amt of land: 17 3/4 acres
Agreement: Samuel Gamble is bound to John King for $300.00. The
condition of obligation is if Gamble shall permit King to hold his right in
fee simple to a tract of land on the north side of Watauga nearly a mile
from its junction and Holston containing by estimation 17 3/4 acres
conveyed to King by Anthony Sharp of KY; being part of land where
Gamble now lives; so that King be not injured respecting land and premises
by Gamble then the obligation be void, otherwise to remain in force.
Wit: James Gregg, Nathaniel Hale
Test: Mattw. Rhea, C.S.C
Regst: Aug. 31, 1812

----

(245)   JOHN STEWART   :
    TO   :   DEED OF WARRANTY
JONATHAN BRADLEY   :

Date: Nov. 28, 1810
Consideration: 190 ₺ VA currency
Amt of land: 35 acres and 30 poles
Location: Sullivan Co, TN
Description: A tract of land joining John King, Robert Alison and Florence
Hodge, the same being part of a tract where Robert Alison now lives on
the bank of Watauga River
Wit: Francis Hodge, William Engle
Proven: By Francis Hodge and Wm Engle, Sullivan Co, TN, Aug, 1812
Test: Mattw. Rhea, C.S.C.
Regst: Aug. 31, 1812

WALTER KING   :
    TO   :   DEED OF WARRANTY
ROBERT TRIBBETT   :

Date: April 3, 1812
Consideration: $150.00
Amt of land: 100 acres
Location: Sullivan Co, TN
Description: A tract of land on the south side of Holston River near
Robert Easley's and Aaron Bacon's lines
Proven: By Jonas Dean, Richard Basket, Sullivan Co, TN, Aug, 1819
Test: Mattw. Rhea, C.S.C.
Regst: (No date given)

----

(247)   DAVID MACHAN   :
    TO   :   DEED OF WARRANTY
JACOB STOFFEL   :

Date: Aug. 24, 1811
Consideration: A valuable consideration
Amt of land: 146 acres
Location: Sullivan Co, TN
Description: A tract on the waters of Steel Creek
Wit: John Anderson, Michael Hickman, Jacob Booher
Proven: By Michael Hickman, Jacob Booher, Sullivan Co, TN, Nov, 1811
Test: Mattw. Rhea, C.S.C.
Regst: Oct. 14, 1812

(Page)
(248)

MARTIN ROLLER   :
     TO   :   DEED OF WARRANTY
HENRY LOTS   :

Date: Dec. 8, 1804
Consideration: $100.00
Amt of land: 32 acres
Location: Sullivan Co, TN
Description: A tract of land joining Benjamin Shipley's corner
Wit: Henry Miller, John Jennings
Acknowledged: By Martin Roller, Sullivan Co, TN, Feb, 1805
Test: Mattw. Rhea, C.S.C.
Regst: Nov. 10, 1812

----

(249)

MARTIN ROLLER   :
     TO   :   DEED OF WARRANTY
HENRY LOTS   :

Date: Dec. 8, 1804
Consideration: $600.00
Amt of land: 104 acres
Location: Sullivan Co, TN
Description: A tract beginning at a white oak corner of Martin Roller's; a
dividing line between Roller and John Queenor's
Wit: Henry Miller, John Jennings
Acknowledged: By Martin Roller, Sullivan Co, Feb, 1806
Test: Mattw. Rhea, C.S.C.
Regst: Nov. 10, 1812

----

(251)

JAMES CLARK, SR, of Washington Co, TN :
     TO   :   DEED OF WARRANTY
WILLIAM MORTON   :

Date: Oct. 10, 1811
Consideration: $500.00
Amt of land: 195 acres
Location: Sullivan Co, TN
Description: A tract of land on the waters of Horse Creek incl. plantation
where John Clark now lives at the branch which is a dividing line between
this tract and George Vincent now being John Vincent's
Wit: Geo. Vincent, Jas Smith, Santhwill* Vincent
Proven: By Geo Vincent, Southerwell* Vincent, Sullivan Co, TN, Nov, 1811

Test: Mattw. Rhea, C.S.C.
Regst: Nov. 18, 1812

(*Note: Name spelled both ways)

(Page)

(252)   JOHN OLAR   :
                TO   :   DEED OF WARRANTY
         THOMAS HOPKINS   :

         Date: Sept 10, 1812
         Consideration: $2,000.00 current money of TN
         Amt of land: 300 acres
         Location: Sullivan Co, TN
         Description: All that tract of land on the north side of Holston River on
         the island flats incl. where he now resides, joining Thomas Titsworth's and
         James Duneral's corners
         Wit: John Pryor, Elisha Harbor, John Lynn, James Gaines
         Proven: By Elisha Harbor, Sullivan Co, TN, Nov, 1812
         Test: Mattw. Rhea, C.S.C.
         Regst: Nov. 18, 1812

                        ----

(254)   JONATHAN WEBB   :
                TO   :   DEED OF WARRANTY
         DAVID WEBB   :

         Date: Sept 25, 1810
         Consideration: A valuable consideration
         Amt of land: 90 acres
         Location: Sullivan Co, TN
         Description: A tract of land on the south side of Holston River, joining
         John Webb's old survey
         Wit: John Anderson, John Key, John Jennings
         Proven: By John Anderson, John Jennings, Sullivan Co, TN, Nov, 1812
         Test: Mattw. Rhea, C.S.C.
         Regst: Nov. 18, 1812

                        ----

(255)   WILLIAM PALLET   :
                TO   :   DEED OF WARRANTY
         THOMAS HOPKINS   :

         Date: Oct. 24, 1812
         Consideration: $1400.00 good and lawful money
         Amt of land: 207 acres
         Location: Sullivan Co, TN
         Description: All that tract on both sides of the road leading from Yancey's
         old place to Blountville, incl. the houses and other improvements in the
         occupation of William Pallet and where he now resides
         Wit: John Vaughan, John Lynn, Martin Roller, Robert Pallet
         Proven: By Robert Pallet, John Vaughan, Sullivan Co, TN, Nov, 1812
         Test: Mattw. Rhea, C.S.C
         Regst: March 1, 1813

                        ----

(257) JOHN TIPTON   :
            TO   :   DEED OF WARRANTY
       LAURENCE SNAPP   :

       Date: May 27, 1812
       Consideration: A valuable consideration
       Amt of land: 151 acres
       Location: 151 acres(sic)
       Description: A tract of land crossing Sinking Creek, a corner of George
       Rutledge's and near the wagon road
       Wit: John Anderson, Laurence Snapp
       Proven: By John Anderson, Laurence Snapp, Sullivan Co, TN, Nov, 1812
       Test: Mattw. Rhea, C.S.C.
       Regst: Nov. 25, 1812

                        ----

(258) CHARLES ALLIN   :
            TO   :   DEED OF WARRANTY
       WILLIAM ALLIN   :

       Date: Nov. 7, 1812
       Consideration: Natural love and affection
       Amt of land: 48 acres
       Location: Sullivan Co, TN
       Description: A tract of land on the south side of Holston River; part of a
       tract originally granted Henry Gauchee from the state of NC
       Wit: Nivean Biggs, Calvin Smith, Ily Runnels
       Proven: By Calvin Smith, Ily Runnels, Sullivan Co, TN, Nov, 1812
       Test: Mattw. Rhea, C.S.C.
       Regst: Nov. 28, 1812

                        ----

(259) JAMES HUGHES   :
            TO   :   DEED OF WARRANTY
       MARIAN BONHAM   :

       Date: Nov. 18, 1812
       Consideration: This indenture authorized by the last will and testament of
       David Hughes, dec'd
       Amt of land: 50 acres
       Location: Sullivan Co, TN
       Description: A tract of land containing 50 acres as directed by the above
       last will and testament
       Acknowledged: By James Hughes, Sullivan Co, TN, Nov, 1812
       Test: Mattw. Rhea, C.S.C.
       Regst: Nov. 30, 1812

                        ----

(260) THOMAS JACKSON   :
            TO   :   DEED OF WARRANTY
       JACOB & WILLIAM PENCE   :

       Date: Aug. 4, 1812
       Consideration: $500.00
       Amt of land: By estimation 110 acres

Location: Sullivan Co, TN
Description: All that tract joining the lands of George Roller, Jenkins
Murphy, formerly the widow Bailey's and Eatons Ridge
Wit: John Anderson, Jenkins Murphy, Thomas Titsworth
Proven: By John Anderson, Thomas Titsworth, Sullivan Co, TN, Aug, 1812
Test: Mattw. Rhea, C.S.C.
Regst: Dec. 1, 1812

(Page)
(261)

JONATHAN WEBB   :
        TO   :   DEED OF WARRANTY
DAVID WEBB   :

Date: Sept 25, 1810
Consideration: A valuable consideration
Amt of land: 91 acres
Location: Sullivan Co, TN
Description: A tract of land on the south side of Holston River along
Zachariah Cross and John Webb's lines
Wit: John Anderson, Elk. Key, John Jennings
Proven: By John Anderson, John Jennings, Sullivan Co, TN, Nov, 1812
Test: Mattw. Rhea, C.S.C.
Regst: Dec. 27, 1810

----

(262)

JOHN STEERS   :
        TO   :   DEED OF WARRANTY
JAMES BRIGHT   :

Date: Nov. 16, 1812
Consideration: A valuable consideration
Amt of land: 31 acres
Location: Sullivan Co, TN
Description: a tract of land on both sides of Horse Creek; beginning on
Stephen Easley's old patent and Elijah Bulter's(sic) lines
Wit: James Phagan
Acknowledged: By John Steers, Sullivan Co, TN, Nov, 1812
Test: Mattw. Rhea, C.S.C.
Regst: Dec. 27, 1812

----

(263)

CALEB SMITH   :
        TO   :   DEED OF WARRANTY
WILLIAM PIERCE   :

Date: Nov. 13, 1812
Consideration: $300.00
Amt of land: 1/2 of 220 acres being 110 acres
Location: Sullivan Co, TN
Description: One half of a tract of land containing 220 acres on both sides
of Horse Creek, beginning at Stephen Easley's old patent line and joining
Elisha Butler's old patent line, being part of two tracts of land granted by
NC to Stephen Easley containing 500 acres No. 41, dated Oct. 23,
1882(sic), the other part for 320 acres No. 199 dated Oct. 10, 1783

96

Wit: James Phagan
Acknowledged: By Caleb Smith, Sullivan Co, TN, Nov.
Regst: Dec. 28, 1812

(Page)
(265)

```
STATE OF TENNESSEE    :
WILLIE BLOUNT, GOV.   :     (LAND GRANT)
        TO            :     NO. 2632
JAMES KERR            :
```

Date: March 12, 1811
Consideration: By virtue of an entry made in the surveyor's office for the
6th District on March 12, 1811, No. 177, in part of a certificate No. 183,
issued by the register of the land office for E. TN on Jan. 8, 1811, in
favor of James Tathem, there is grated(sic) by the state of TN unto James
Kerr
Description: A tract of land containing 10 acres on the waters of Reedy
Creek; beginning at 3 Linn trees on Pendleton's old patent line running
along Peter Droke's line
Granted by: Willie Blount, Gov, W.G. Blount, Sec.
James Kerr is entitled to the within tract of land
Recorded in my office Oct. 9, 1812
                            Edw. Scott, Register of E. TN
Sullivan Co, TN, Nov, 1812
Test: Mattw. Rhea, C.S.C.
(Regst): Jan. 29, 1813

----

(266)

```
PETER CATRON          :
        TO            :     DEED OF WARRANTY
DAVID SHAVER          :
```

Date: Aug. 17, 1812
Consideration: A valuable consideration
Amt of land: 160 acres
Location: Sullivan Co, TN
Description: A tract of land on the waters of Reedy Creek along John
Ritchie's line and a corner of John Pitcher's and adj. Valentine Catron and
John Britton
Wit: John Anderson, Zach Weeks, Peter Catron
Proven: By John Anderson, Zach Weeks, Sullivan Co, TN, Nov, 1812
Test: Mattw. Rhea, C.S.C.
Regst: Feb. 1, 1813
State of TN, Sullivan Co, Register's office Feb. 1, 1815, this deed
registered in Book H, page ?

----

(267)

```
JOHN OLAR             :
        TO            :     DEED OF WARRANTY
THOMAS HOPKINS        :
```

Date: Sept. 10, 1812
Consideration: $2000.00 current money of TN
Amt of land: 300 acres
Location: Sullivan Co, TN

Description: all that tract of land on the north side of Holston River in the island flats where he now resides joining Thomas Titsworth and James Dunral and Christian
Wit: John Poyer, Elisha Harbour, John Lynn, Jas. Gaines
Proven: By Elisha Harbour, Sullivan Co, TN, Nov, 1812
Test: Mattw. Rhea, C.S.C.
Regst: Feb. 8, 1812

(Page)
(269)

```
HENRY RICHARDS      :
       TO           :    DEED OF WARRANTY
JAMES KERR          :
```

Date: Oct. 3, 1812
Consideration: $200.00
Amt of land: 202 acres
Location: Sullivan Co, TN
Description: A tract of land granted by NC to John Steel and by John Steel to Gilbert Kerr, dec'd, which tract contained 350 acres which bounded as aforesaid; Henry Richards reserves in consequences of a deed of gift made by Gilbert Kerr, dec'd, to Roady Welch who is now his present wife which sd land lies on the wagon road and on the east bank of Back Creek which sd last mentioned 155 acres sd Richards reserves to himself as being gift as aforesaid the residue being 202 acres which Henry Richards defends to James Kerr
Acknowledged: By E.E. Phipps, John Punch, Sullivan Co, TN, Nov, 1812
Test: Mattw. Rhea, C.S.C.
Regst: Feb. 10, 1813

```
STATE OF TENNESSEE   :
WILLIE BLOUNT, GOV.  :    LAND GRANT
       TO            :    NO. 2064
DAVID SHAVER         :
```

Date: Oct. 29, 1811
Consideration: An entry made in the office of the surveyor of the 6th District of No. 549, founded on a warrant of No. 2315, issued by Landon Carter to John Gest for 150 acres dated Sept. 19, 1781, entry dated Nov. 2, 1810, which warrant is assigned by Gist to John Thompson and by him to David Shaver, the bearer
Description: A tract of land containing 120 acres in Washington District on Young's run a branch of Reedy Creek joining Shaver's former survey.
Surveyed Nov. 10, 1810, seal affixed at Knoxville, Oct. 29, 1811
Granted by the Gov, R. Houston, Sec.
David Shaver is entitled to the within tract of land
Recorded in my office, Oct. 29, 1811
                    Edw. Scott, Register of E. TN
April 1, 1811, received the stae tax on this grant - 14 cents
Test: Mattw. Rhea, C.S.C.
(Regst): Feb. 11, 1813

```
ABRAHAM LOONEY, Executor of    :
David Looney, Dec'd.           :
        TO                     :      DEED OF WARRANTY
JOHN HAMILTON, Representative of :
John Spurgin, Dec'd.           :
```

Date: Nov. 17, 1812
Consideration: $860.00
Amt of land: By estimation, 210 acres
Location: Sullivan Co, TN
Description: a tract of land on the waters of Muddy Creek on a line formerly James Burgham's
Acknowledged: By Abraham Looney, Nov, 1812
Test: Mattw. Rhea, C.S.C.
Regst: Feb. 12, 1813

```
(273)   JOSEPH ELDER           :
            TO                 :      DEED OF WARRANTY
        WILLIAM THOMPSON       :
```

Date: Nov. 10, 1812
Consideration: A valuable consideration
Amt of land: Not stated
Location: Sullivan Co, TN
Description: A tract of land on the waters of Reedy Creek along a line formerly John Thompson's and Pendleton's old patent line
Wit: John Sinclair, Amos Sinclair
Proven: By John Sinclair, Amos Sinclair, Sullivan Co, TN, Feb, 1813
Test: Mattw. Rhea, C.S.C.
Regst: Feb. 15, 1813

```
(274)   JAMES HALL             :
            TO                 :      BILL OF SALE
        PETER EARLY            :
```

Date: Jan. 4, 1813
Consideration: $600.00
Sale: James Hall delivers to Early one healthy negro woman named Charlot 19 yrs old, and child named Ned abt 2 yrs old
Wit: Richard Hammer, Nathaniel Hall
Acknowledged: By James Hall, Sullivan Co, TN, Feb, 1813
Test: Mattw. Rhea, C.S.C.
Regst: Feb. 15, 1813

```
        JOHN TIPTON, JR.       :
            TO                 :      DEED OF WARRANTY
        PHILIP SNAPP           :
```

Date: Feb. 18, 1808
Consideration: $150.00
Amt of land: 1/4 acre
Location: Town of Blountville, Sullivan Co, TN

Description: One lot, No. 13, containing 1/4 acre
Acknowledged: By John Tipton, Sullivan Co, TN, Feb, 1813
Test: Mattw. Rhea, C.S.C.
Regst: Feb. 23, 1813

(Page)
(275)   JAMES KAIN   :
            TO   :   DEED OF WARRANTY
        PATRICK WRIGHT   :

        Date: May 20, 1811
        Consideration: $40.00
        Amt of land: 1 1/2 acres and 10 1/2 poles
        Location: Sullivan Co, TN
        Description: A tract of land adj. the plantation where Wright now lives
        incl. the spring near the line; beginning at a corner of Wright's survey
        Wit: John Jennings, Alexander Gitgood, James Kain
        Acknowledged: By James Kain, Sullivan Co, TN, May, 1811
        Test: Mattw. Rhea, C.S.C.
        Regst: Feb. 23, 1813

----

(276)   ARCHABALD TAYLOR   :
            TO   :   DEED OF WARRANTY
        JACOB COOK   :

        Date: Nov. 19, 1812
        Consideration: A valuable consideration
        Amt of land: 130 acres
        Location: Sullivan Co, TN
        Description: A tract of land beginning at a hickory near Pendleton's patent
        line a corner of John Foust and George Pearce
        Wit: John Pryor, Elisha Harbour, Thos. Morrison
        Acknowledged: By John Pryor, Thos Morrison, Sullivan Co, TN, Feb, 1813
        Test: Mattw. Rhea, C.S.C.
        Regst: (No date given)

----

(277)   JACOB AKARD   :
            TO   :   BILL OF SALE
        WILLIAM WILSON   :

        Date: Feb. 16, 1813
        (Consideration): $400.00
        (Sale): Rec'd of William Wilson for $400.00 in full for a negro woman
        named Edna and her female child, Dellah, slaves for life
        Wit: John Punch
        Acknowledged: By Jacob Akard, Sullivan Co, TN, Feb, 1813
        Test: Mattw. Rhea, C.S.C.
        Regst: (No date given)

```
WILLIAM SCOTT          :
       TO              :     DEED OF WARRANTY
GEORGE MILHORN         :
```

Date: Dec. 29, 1812
Consideration: $35.00
Amt of land: 20 acres
Location: Sullivan Co, TN
Description: A tract of land on the waters of Watauga River; beginning on David Dyer's, the dec'd George Milhorn's, and William McKinley's lines and with the same to the beginning
Acknowledged: By William Scott, Sullivan Co, TN, Feb.
Test: Mattw. Rhea, C.S.C.
Regst: Feb. 26, 1813

```
(279)    JACOB EMERT            :
              TO               :     DEED OF WARRANTY
         JOHN SMITH CARPENTER   :
```

Date: Jan. 20, 1813
Consideration: $500.00
Amt of land: 278 acres
Location: Sullivan Co, TN
Description: A tract of land beginning on Samuel Smith's line then along George Emert's* and joining John Wert Miller's corner and on George Emert*, Sr's line and Frame's and Scott's corners
Wit: Benjamin Webb, George Wolford
Acknowledged: By Jacob Emmert*, Sullivan Co, TN, Aug, 1812
Test: Mattw. Rhea, C.S.C.
Regst: Feb. 27, 1813

(*Note: Name spelled both ways)

```
(280)    JOHN GARLAND & JAMES HURLEY  :
              TO                       :     DEED OF WARRANTY
         JAMES JORDAN GEORGE           :
```

Date: Sept. 15, 1812
Consideration: $200.00
Amt of land: 34 acres
Location: Sullivan Co, TN
Description: A tract of land where Hurley now lives on the south bank of Holston River
Wit: Thomas Majors, William Blevins, William R. Cowan
Proven: By Thomas Majors, William R. Cowan, Sullivan Co, TN, Feb, 1813
Test: Mattw. Rhea, C.S.C.
Regst: March 1, 1813

```
(281)    MOSES HUMPHREYS &     :
         JOHN McCALL*          :     BILL OF SALE &
              TO               :     DEED OF TRUST
         STEPHEN HICKS         :
```

Date: Nov. 3, 1810
Consideration: $105.00
Description: (Bill of Sale) Moses Humphreys and John McFall* both sold one negro woman, Hannah, to Stephen Hicks for $105.00, in hand paid
Witness our hands and seals Nov. 3, 1810
Condition: If Moses Humphreys shall on March 1, ensuing the date hereof deliver unto Stephen Hicks ont(sic) likely negro boy between the age of 12 and 15 yrs, then the above obligation to be void; Stephen shall pay Moses Humphreys in 9 months from March 1, next, $223.39 for negro is Hicks should like sd boy after having 3 months service of boy; sd boy is to be an American and at the expiration of 3 months service is Stephen should not like boy then Moses is to receive sd negro again and pay to Stephen $120.00
Wit: James Phagan
Proven: By James Phagan, Sullivan Co, TN, Feb, 1813
Test: Mattw. Rhea, C.S.C.
Regst: March 1, 1813

(*Note: Name spelled both ways)

(Page)

JOHN GARLAND   :
       TO   :   DEED OF WARRANTY
GEORGE BROOKS   :

Date: April 4, 1812
Consideration: $800.00
Amt of land: 140 acres
Location: Sullivan Co, TN
Description: A tract of land where Garland now lives on south bank of Holston River joining William Dulaney's line
Wit: Benjamin Pemberton, Thos. Pemberton, Lett Stafford
Proven: By Benjamin & Thos Pemberton, Sullivan Co, Tn, Feb, 1813
Test: Mattw. Rhea, C.S.C.
Regst: March 1, 1813

----

(282)   GASPER MIERS   :
           TO   :   DEED OF WARRANTY
        PHILLIP KITE   :

Date: Sept 25, 1812
Consideration: $800.00
Amt of land: 120 acres
Location: Sullivan Co, TN
Description: A tract of land on the north bank of the Holston River and joining John Olar's and Philip Rite's lands
Wit: Jenkins Murphy, George Roller
Proven: By Jenkins Murphy, George Roller, Sullivan Co, TN, Feb. 1813
Regst: March 1, 1813

----

(283)   This deed typed on Page 255, Page 85 of notes.

WILLIAM BLEVINS, JR.   :
JAMES BLEVINS   :
       TO   :   BILL OF SALE
WILLIAM WILSON   :

Date: Sept 7, 1811
Consideration: 400 -
Sale: William Blevins, Jr. and James Blevins have sold to William Wilson one negro boy named David aged 14 yrs for the sum of 400 - to me in hand paid, the receipt is acknowledged
Wit: John Phagan, Job Key, James Phagan
Proven: By James Phagan, Job Key, Sullivan Co, Aug, 1812
Test: Mattw. Rhea, C.S.C.
Regst: (No date given)

JACOB MILLER   :
       TO   :   DEED OF WARRANTY
GEORGE BURKHART   :

Date: Dec. 5, 1812
Consideration: $100.00
Amt of land: 40 poles
Location: Sullivan Co, TN
Description: A lot of land laid off by Wallace Willoughby and numbered 5th on the west bank of Sinking Creek
(Wit): W.W. Willoughby, Isaac Stoffel, Jacob Booher
Proven: By Wallace Willoughby, Jacob Booher, Sullivan Co, TN, Feb, 1813
Test: Mattw. Rhea, C.S.C.
Regst: March 1, 1813

JAMES KING   :
       TO   :   DEED OF WARRANTY
SAMUEL HAMPTON   :

Date: Jan. 18, 1813
Consideration: $1000.00
Amt of land: 250 acres
Location: Sullivan Co, TN
Description: a tract of land on Beaver Creek which was granted by the state of NC to Thomas Wallace by patent No. 358, dated Nov. 10, 1804, running with John Malone south and Joseph Collins' and John Rhea's lines
Wit: Washington Lewis, James Ware, James King, Jr.
Proven: By James King, Jr, James Ware, Sullivan Co, TN, Feb, 1813
Test: Mattw. Rhea, C.S.C.
Regst: March 1, 1813

----

(287)   JOHN GARLAND & JAMES HURLEY :
            TO   :   DEED OF WARRANTY
JAMES JORDAN GEORGE   :

Date: Sept. 15, 1812
Consideration: $124.00

Amt of land: 30 acres
Location: Sullivan Co, TN
Description: A tract of land where Hurley now lives on the south bank of
the Holston River
Wit: Thomas Majors, William Blevins, William R. Cowan
Proven: By Thomas Majors, William R. Cowan, Sullivan Co, TN, Feb, 1813
(Regst): (No date given)

(Page)
(288)   JOHN KINGSTON   :
              TO   :   DEED OF WARRANTY
         JOHN BURCH   :

Date: Nov. 23, 1812
Consideration: $400.00
Amt of land: 100 acres
Location: Sullivan Co, TN
Description: A tract of land containing by estimation 100 acres
Wit: Stephen Hicks, David Shaver, Jacob Wyzer
Proven: By David Shaver and Jacob Wyzer, Sullivan Co, TN, Feb, 1813
Test: Mattw. Rhea, C.S.C.
Regst: March 2, 1813

----

(289)   PETER EARLY   :
              TO   :   DEED OF WARRANTY
         JAMES HALL   :

Date: Jan. 4, 1813
Consideration: $1200.00
Amt of land: 300 acres
Location: Sullivan Co, TN
Description: a tract of land on both sides of Horse Creek beginning at
Michael Light's corner white oak on Stephen Easley's old patent line; being
part of 2 tracts of land granted by NC to Stephen Early, one containing
500 acres No. 41 dated Oct. 23, 1782, the other for 330 acres No. 199
dated Oct. 10, 1783
Wit: Rich'd Hammer, George Marden, Nathaniel Hall
Acknowledged: By Peter Early, Sullivan Co, TN, Feb, 1813
Test: Mattw. Rhea, C.S.C.
Regst: March 2, 1813

----

(290)   HENRY BORDEN of Shenandoah Co, VA   :
              TO   :   DEED OF WARRANTY
         JOHN TIPTON   :

Date: Oct. 18, 1803
Consideration: $150.00
Amt of land: 1/4 acre
Location: Town of Blountville, Sullivan Co, TN
Description: One lot, No. 13, in the town of Blountville
Wit: Laurence Snapp

Proven: By Laurence Snapp, Sullivan Co, Tn, Feb, 1813
Test: Mattw. Rhea, C.S.C.
Regst: March 2, 1813

(Page)
(291)

SETH PORTERFIELD   :
        TO   :   DEED OF WARRANTY
SAMUEL PROTERFIELD   :

Date: Dec. 6, 1812
Consideration: $100.00
Amt of land: Supposed to contain 45 acres
Location: Sullivan Co, TN
Description: A tract of land where Seth no lives joining Lowry's corner
Wit: James Kerr, Patrick Niel
Proven: By James Kerr, Patrick Niel, Sullivan Co, TN, Feb, 1813
Test: Mattw. Rhea, C.S.C.
Regst: March 2, 1813

----

(292)   COMMONWEALTH OF VIRGINIA   :
         JAMES MONROE, GOV.   :   LAND GRANT
                 TO   :   (NO. Not given)
         SAMUEL BYSHEARS

Date: Oct. 22, 1800
Consideration: By virtue of 2 land office warrant to wit 50 acres by
Treasury Warrant No. 20702, issued Nov. 11, 1788, and 50 acres by
preemption warrant No. 2390, issued March 17, 1783
Amt of land: 100 acres
Location: Washington Co, VA
Description: A tract of land containing 100 acres by survey dated May 4,
1796, in Washington Co on the waters of Reedy Creek, a soth branch of
Holston River; beginning on a line of James Igou's land
                          Jas. Monroe
Samuel Byshears hath title to the within
                          Wm Price, Re. L. Off.
Regst: March 3, 1813

----

(293)   COMMONWEALTH OF VIRGINIA   :
         JAMES MONROE, GOV.   :   LAND GRANT
                 TO   :   (NO. Not Given)
         WALLACE WILLOUGHBY   :

Date: Oct. 22, 1800
Consideration: By virtue of a land office Treasury Warrant No. 10261,
issued Dec. 22, 1781
Amt of land: 134 acres
Location: Washington Co, VA
Description: A tract of land containing 134 acres by survey, dated April
18, 1798, in Washington Co, on the waters of Sinking Creek, a north
branch of Holston River and on a survey made in the name of Andrew
Willoughby

                          Jas. Monroe

Wallace Willoughby hath title to the within
(Regst): (No date given)

JOHN WEAVER   :
     TO   :   DEED OF WARRANTY
FRANCES HAWLEY   :

Date: Sept 30, 1800
Consideration: $100.00
Amt of land: 15 acres
Location: Sullivan Co, TN
Description: A tract of land containing 15 acres beginning on Samuel
Moore's south line near the big road then along a conditional line on the
top of Eatons Ridge, same being part of a tract of land Moore purchased
of Isaac Agee
Wit: John Jennings, George Waver, W.B. Childress
Proven: By John Jennings, George Weaver, Sullivan co, TN, Nov, 1811
Test: Mattw. Rhea, C.S.C.
Regt: March 3, 1813

----

(295)   STATE OF TENNESSEE   :
           WILLIE BLOUNT, GOV. :   LAND GRANT
                TO   :   NO. 2311
           NICHOLAS MOTTON   :

Date: June 7, 1812
Consideration: An entry made in the office of the survey of the 6th
District of No. 312, dated Sept. 4, 1819, founded on a warrant of No.
1808, issued by Archabald Roane to John Smith for 200 acres dated April
11, 1808, 60 acres of which is entered in Nicholas Matton, the entry is
granted by the state of TN to Nicholas Motton
Description: A tract of land containing 60 acres in the Washington District
on the south side of the Holston joining Benjamin Webb's and Greenway's
lines
Survey: March 3, 1810
Great seal of state affixed at Knoxville, June 15, 1812
                    Willie Blount, Gov, W.G. Bount, Sec.
Nicholas Motton is entitled to the within described tract of land, Recorded
in my office June 15, 1812
                    Edw. Scott, Register of E. TN
Rec'd March, 1813, the tax on this grant - 12 cents
Test: Mattw. Rhea, C.S.C.
(Regst): March 3, 1813

----

(296)   STATE OF TENNESSEE   :
           WILLIE BLOUNT, GOV. :   LAND GRANT
                TO   :   NO. 2070
           JOSHUA MILLER   :

Date: July 14, 1809

Consideration: An entry made in the office of the Surveyor of the 6th
District, No. 228, founded ona warrant of No. 1808, issued to John Smith
for 200 acres of land dated July 14, 1809, which warrant is issued by
John Smith to Samuel Y. Balch and by Balch to isaac Brownlow, 11 acres
of which are assigned to Isaac Brownlow by Joshua Miller, the enterer
Description: There is granted by the state of TN to Joshua Miller hiers a
tract of land containing 8 acres in the Washington District in an island of
Holston River, surveyed Aug. 17, 1809

                          Willie Blount, Gov, R. Houston, Sec
Joshua Miller is entitled to the within described tract of land, Recorded in
my office Oct. 29, 1811

                          Edw. Scott, Register of E. TN
Rec'd tax on this grantd
Test: Mattw. Rhea, C.S.C.
(Regst): March 3, 1813

(Page)
   (297)   STATE OF TENNESSEE   :
                WILLIE BLOUNT, GOV.   :   LAND GRANT
                     TO   :   NO. 2069
                GEORGE WEBB   :

Date: Oct. 29, 1811
Consideration: An entry made in the office of the surveyor of the 6th
District of No. 462, founded on a warrant of No. 149, issued to John Nard
for 200 acres dated July 6, 1808. Entry dated March 3, 1810, issued by
Jacob Knave, Representative of John Knave to Samuel J. Balch and by him
to Isaac and William Brownlow and by them to John McCorkle and 27
acres assigned by Samuel McCorkle to George Wevv, the enterer.
Description: There is granted by the state of TN to George Webb and his
heirs a tract of land containing **
(**Note: WPA copy of deed not completed)

   (298)   STATE OF TENNESSEE   :
                WILLIE BLOUNT, GOV.   :   LAND GRANT
                     TO   :   NO. 2063
                DAVID SHAVER   :

Date: Oct. 29, 1811
Consideration: An entry made in office of Surveyor of the 6th District of
No. 550, founded on a warrant of No. 2315, issued by Landon Carter to
John Gist for 150 acres dated Sept. 19, 1781, entry dated Nov. 2, 1810,
and assigned to Gist by John Thompson and by him to David Shaver the
enterer
Description: There is granted by TN to David Shaver and his heirs a tract
of land containing 36 acres in Washington District on the waters of Reedy
Creek incl. the poplar flats surveyed Nov. 7, 1810

                          Willie Blount, Gov, R. Houston, Sec.
David Shaver is entitled to the within described tract of land. Recorded in
my office Oct. 29, 1811

                          Edw. Scott, Register of E. TN
April 1, 1812, rec'd state tax on this grant - 6 cents
Test: Mattw. Rhea, C.S.C.
Regst: March 10, 1813

STATE OF NORTH CAROLINA :
RICHARD (DOBBS) SPAIGHT, GOV. : LAND GRANT
       TO : NO. 644
RICHARD LAIN :

Date: Dec. 5, 1794
Consideration: 50 shillings for every 100 acres
Amt of land: 66 acres
Location: Sullivan Co, NC
Description: A tract of land containing 66 acres; beginning at alexander
Cavett's corner on the south side of Holston River
Richard Dobbs Spaight, By his Excellys Comd. J. Glasgow, Sec.
Rec'd Feb. 27, 1813 tax on this grant - 13 cents 2 mills
                    Mattw. Rhea, C.S.C.
SURVEY NO. 541
By virtue of a warrant to me directed containing 66 acres entered April
29, 1780, No. 541. I have surveyed for Richard Lane April 17, 1794, 66
acres south the River Ohio; beginning at Alexander Cavett's corner
shugar(sic) tree on the south side of Holston River then up Holston River
to the various courses as it meanders to a corner gum tree to a straight
line to the beginning.
Platted by a scale of 100 equal parts to the inch.
              S. George Vincent, C.S.
(Wit): Wm Parker, Henry Bond, C. Bears
(Regst): March 11, 1813

WILLIAM COPASS :
       TO : DEED OF WARRANTY
JOHN COPASS :

Date: March 26, 1811
Consideration: $300.00
Amt of land: 95 acres
Location: Sullivan Co, TN
Description: All that tract of land on the waters of Kendrick Creek
beginning at William Copass' corner
Wit: Thomas Copass, William Copass
Regst: March 12, 1813

STATE OF TENNESSEE :
WILLIE BLOUNT, GOV. : LAND GRANT
       TO : NO. 2318
LEONARD HART :

Date: June 17, 1812
Consideration: An entry made in the office of the Surveyor of the 6th
District, Nov. ?, 18??, founded on a warrant of No. 224, issued by William
Snodgrass to Leonard Hart for 239 acres, dated Feb. 1, 1796.
Description: There is granted by state of TN to Leonard Hart a tract of
land containing 130 acres in the Washington District on the south side of
Holston River; beginning at a corner to Hart's former survey then to
Webb's corner to a stake on Cunningham's line

Surveyed: Nov. 15, 1808, by Gov. Willie Blount, W.G. Blount, Sec.
Leonard Hart is entitled to the within tract of land. Recorded in my
office June 17, 1812

        Edw. Scott, Register of E. TN

(?Note: No specific date given)

(Page)
(302) STATE OF TENNESSEE :
    WILLIE BLOUNT, GOV. : LAND GRANT
      TO   : NO. 2322
    LUDWICK RHINEHART :

Date: June 18, 1812
Consideration: A special entry made in Carter's office of No. 2587, July 5,
1780, of a warrant of the same number and date issued by John Carter to
David Dyro for 200 acres of land and assigned by Dyer to Ludwick
Rhinehart, there is granted to Rhinehart and his heirs
Description: A tract containing 200 acres in the Washington District in the
fork of Watauga and Holston Rivers; beginning near William Hodge's line
formerly Gideon Rucker's, to a stake on Samuel Gamble's line on the ridge
road (adj) John Sharp's line
Surveyed Sept. 9, 1808

      Willie Blount, Gov, W.G. Blount, Sec.

      ----

(304) DAVID MACHON :
      TO   : DEED OF WARRANTY
    PETER BURKHART :

Date: Aug. 24, 1811
Consideration: A valuable consideration
Amt of land: 208 acres
Location: Sullivan Co, TN
Description: A tract of land containing 208 acres on the waters of Steel's
Creek joining David Steel's land at the Blountsville wagon road
Wit: John Anderson, Michael Hickman, Jacob Booher
Proven: By Michael Hickman, Jacob Booher, Sullivan Co, TN, Nov, 1811
Test: Mattw. Rhea, C.S.C.
Regst: March 15, 1813

      ----

(305) JOHN TIPTON :
      TO   : BILL OF SALE WITH SECURITY
    SAMUEL CARITHERS* :

Date: March 6, 1811
Consideration: $130.00
Sale: A negro boy named Jim to Samuel Carithers*
Terms: If John Tipton shall pay to Samuel Carrithers* the sum of $130.00
before May 24, next, with interest then the above obligation be void,
otherwise to remain in full force
Wit: James Rhea, Phillip Snapp

Proven: By James Rhea, Phillip Snapp
Test: Mattw. Rhea, C.S.C.
Regst: (No date given)

(*Note: Name spelled both ways)

(Page)
(306) JOHN ANDERSON, E.R. DULANEY,   :
       GEORGE RUTLEDGE, Commissioners   :
                   TO   :   COMMISSIONER'S DEED
       JOHN RHEA   :

Date: Nov. 19, 1812
Consideration: A valuable consideration
Amt of land: 2 acres
Location: Blountville, Sullivan Co, TN
Description: Certain lots, Nos. 5 & 6, of land containing 2 acres on the south side of sd town
Signed & delivered in our presence; John Anderson, E.R. Dulaney, George Rutledge
Acknowledged: By (sd Commissioners), Sullivan Co, TN, Nov, 1812
Test: Mattw. Rhea, C.S.C.
Regst: (No date given)

----

(307) JOHN ANDERSON, E.R. DULANEY,   :
       GEORGE RUTLEDGE, Commissioners   :
                   TO   :   DEED OF WARRANTS
       JOHN RHEA   :

Date: Aug. 23, 1812
Consideration: A valuable consideration
Amt of land: Lot No. 25
Location: Town of Blountville
Description: A lot, No. 25, in sd town
April 22, 1813 - John Anderson, E.R. Dulaney, George Rutledge
Acknowledged: By (sd Commissioners), Sullivan Co, TN, Nov, 1812
Test: Mattw. Rhea, C.S.C.
(Regst): (No date given)

       BENJAMIN & WILLIAM DOWNS :
                   TO   :   DEED OF WARRANTY
       PHILLIP SNAPP   :

Date: Nov. 9, 1799
Consideration: $1535.00
Amt of land: 347 acres
Location: Sullivan Co, TN
Description: A tract of land containing 347 acres beginning at 3 white oaks, a corner at Stephen Hicks' land, then across Muddy Creek, a corner of John Tipton's land
Wit: John Tipton, John Williams
Proven: By John Williams, Sullivan Co, TN, Nov, 1799
(Regst): April 22, 1813

110

STATE OF NORTH CAROLINA :
SAM ASHE, GOV.   :   LAND GRANT
       TO   :   NO. (Unable to read)
BENJAMIN DOWNS   :

Date: Nov. 17, 1797
Consideration: 50 shillings for every 100 acres
Amt of land: 26 acres
Location: Sullivan Co, TN
Description: See survey, entered April 29, 1781
Survey: By virtue of a warrant of No. 538, I have surveyed 25 acres for
Benjamin Downs, to corner of James Brigham's then adj. Mc Hampton's land
then straight to the beginning
Surveyed: March 17, 1796, and plated by a scale of 100 poles to an inch
                    by John Anderson, D.S.
Mich'l Hampton and William Downs, C.C., Stockley Donelson, S.E.D.
Granted: By command of Sam Ashe, Gov., J. Glasgow, Sec.
April 28, 1813, rec'd the tax on this deed
Test: Mattw. Rhea, C.S.C.
(Regst): (No date given)

----

(310)   WILLIAM ARMSTRONG of Hawkins Co   :
             TO   :   DEED OF WARRANTY
        JOHN TIPTON   :

Date: Oct. 9, 1811
Consideration: $1330.00
Amt of land: 200 acres
Location: Sullivan Co, TN
Description: William Hawkins(sic) of Hawkins Co to John Tipton; a tract of
land beginning at what was formerly James Brigham's and joining what was
formerly Joseph Kincaid's now George Rutledge's line,
Wit: D. Yearsley, S. Powel
Proven: By D. Yearsley, Samuel Powel, Sullivan Co, TN, Feb, 1812
Test: Mattw. Rhea, C.S.C
Regst: April 28, 1813

----

(311)   JOHN TIPTON   :
             TO   :   DEED OF WARRANTY
        GEORGE WHITE   :

Date: Feb. 22, 1809
Consideration: $85.00
Amt of land: 1 acre
Location: Sullivan Co, TN
Description: A piece of land near the town of Blountville; beginning at a
stake joining Jacob Sturm
Acknowledged: By John Tipton, Sullivan Co, TN
Test: Mattw. Rhea, C.S.C, by Robt. Rhea, D.C.
Regst: (No date given)

```
BENJAMIN WILSON, AMOS WILSON,   :
& ANN WILSON                     :
        TO                       :        DEED OF WARRANTY
JACOB DROKE                      :
```

Date: Aug. 10, 1812
Consideration: For a valuable consideration
Location: Sullivan Co, TN
Description: a tract of land on the north fork of Reedy Creek; adj. Jacob Harris and William Goddard
Wit: James Spencer, John Carithers, Solomon Crotsinger
Proven: By John Carrithers, David Crotsinger, Sullivan Co, TN, May, 1813
Test: Mattw. Rhea, C.S.C.
Regst: June 4, 1813

```
(313)    JOHN TIPTON              :
            TO                    :        DEED OF WARRANTY
         JAMES RHEA               :
```

Date: Sept. 1, 1809
Consideration: $100.00
Location: Sullivan Co, TN
Description: Two lots, Nos. 56 and 57, in the town of Blountville containing 1 acre on the northside of Main Stree
Wit: James H. Barnett, John Rader
Acknowledged: By John Tipton, Sullivan Co, TN, May, 1813
Test: Mattw. Rhea, C.S.C.
Regst: June 6, 1813

```
(314)    JOHN TIPTON              :
            TO                    :        BILL OF SALE
         STEPHEN HICKS            :
```

Date: April 14, 1813
Sale: Rec'd Blountville April 14, 1813, of Stephen Hicks $300 in full for a yellow boy named Jim
Wit: D. Yearsley, J. Punch
Acknowledged: By John Tipton, Sullivan Co, TN, May, 1813
Regst: June 5, 1813

```
HENRY SELLS              :
    TO                   :        DEED OF WARRANTY
MARTIN BOOHER            :
```

Date: April 5, 1813
Consideration: A valuable consideration
Amt of land: 24 acres
Location: Sullivan Co, TN
Description: A tract of land on the waters of Beaver Creek adj. George Brown, James King, and John Sells

Wit: John Anderson, George Brown, Samuel Sells
Acknowledged: By Henry Sells, Sullivan Co, Tn, May, 1813
Test: Mattw. Rhea, C.S.C.
Regst: June 12, 1813

(Page)
(315)   JOHN ACUFF   :
            TO   :   DEED OF WARRANTY
         ELISHA JAMES   :

         Date: April 23, 1813
         Consideration: A valuable consideration
         Location: Sullivan Co, TN
         Description: A tract of land containing 35 acres adj. Thomas Craft
         Wit: John Anderson, William Anderson
         Acknowledged: By John Acuff, Sullivan Co, TN, May, 1813
         Test: Mattw. Rhea, C.S.C.
         Regst: June 12, 1813

----

(316)   JOHN CAWOOD   :
            TO   :   BILL OF SALE
         JACOB STURM   :

         Date: March 16, 1813
         Consideration: $300.00
         Location: Sullivan Co, TN
         Sale: John Cawood sold to Jacob Sturm one negro woman named Ruth for
         $300.00
         Wit: James Phagan, Alexander S. Gunnings
         Acknowledged: By John Cawood, Sullivan Co, TN, May, 1813
         Test: Mattw. Rhea, C.S.C.
         Regst: June 21, 1813

----

(317)   JAMES KAINE   :
            TO   :   DEED OF WARRANTY
         ROBERT EARLY   :

         Date: May 21, 1813
         Consideration: $650.00
         Amt of land: 142 1/2 acres
         Location: Sullivan Co, TN
         Description: A tract of land on both sides of Fall Creek
         Acknowledged: By James Kaine, Sullivan Co, TN, May, 1813
         Test: Mattw. Rhea, C.S.C.
         Regst: July 9, 1813

----

(318)   THOMAS CAPPS, SR.   :
            TO   :   DEED OF WARRANTY
         THOMAS CAPPS, JR.   :

         Date: May 22, 1805
         Consideration: $300.00

113

Location: Sullivan Co, TN
Description: A tract containing 268 acres adj. Key and Wicke
Wit: John Anderson, William Connole
Acknowledged: By Thomas Capps, Sr, Sullivan Co, TN, May, 1805
Test: Mattw. Rhea, C.S.C.
Regst: July 21, 1813

(Page)
(319)

STATE OF NORTH CAROLINA :
ALEXANDER MARTIN, GOV.   :   LAND GRANT
            TO   :   NO. 337
JOHN DEVER   :

Date: Nov. 10, 1784
Consideration: 50 shillings for every 100 acres
Location: Sullivan Co, NC
Description: A tract of land containing 537 acres on the north side of
Holston River on the waters of Fall Creek
Aug. 5, 1813, Rec'd state tax - $1.00
Test: Mattw. Rhea, C.S.C.
Regst: Aug. 6, 1813
SURVEY: March 10, 1782, Sullivan Co, NC. In pursuance of a warrant, No.
781 dated April 22, 1782, I have surveyed for John Dever 537 acres on
the north side of Holston River on the waters of Fall Creek, adj. Edward
David, Rowland, Thomas Ramsey, James Blithe
                              Stokley Davidson
Plated by the scale of 100 poles an inch
Aug. 5, 1813, Rec'd state tax on grant - $1.70
                              Mattw. Rhea, C.S.C.
Regst: Aug. 6, 1813

----

(321)

WILLIAM, JONATHAN, NATHAN, CALEB,   :
& MARTHA MORRELL, JOHN BLEVINS, &   :
SAMUEL MILLARD, Heirs of John Blevins,   :   DEED OF WARRANTY
Son of William Blevins   :
            TO   :
WILLIAM ODELL   :

Date: May 7, 1813
Consideration: $11.00 each in hand paid
Location: Sullivan Co, TN
Description: A tract containing 59 acres conveyed to Jonahtan Morrell,
dec'd, by John Shelby incl. where William Odell now lives on the south
side of Holston River adj. Stephen Wallin on the river bank and Thomas
Morrell's corner
Wit: Stephen Walling, Nicholas Deloch, Edmond Morrell
Proven: By Stephen Walling, Michael Deloach, Sullivan Co, TN, May, 1813
Test: Mattw. Rhea, C.S.C.
Regst: Aug. 11, 1813

----

(322)

JOHN BASKETT   :
            TO   :   DEED OF WARRANTY
RICHARD BASKETT   :

114

Date: Nov. 25, 1812
Consideration: $300.00
Location: Sullivan Co, TN
Description: A tract of land containing 100 acres on the south side of
Holston River adj. Henry Hughes, Isaac Agee, William Fitzgerald, John
Bickley, and Joseph Clark
Wit: Joseph Clark, Thomas Clark, Charles Baskett
Proven: By Joseph Clark, Thomas Clark, Sullivan Co, TN, May 1813
Test: Mattw. Rhea, C.S.C.
Regst: Aug. 17, 1813

(Page)
(324)   RICHARD & JOHN BASKETT* :
         TO   :   DEED OF WARRANTY
    JOSEPH CLARK   :

Date: Nov. 24, 1812
Consideration: $300.00
Location: Sullivan Co, TN
Description: A tract of land containing 100 acres on the south side of
Holston River on Kendrick's Creek; being part of the land Basket
purchased from Walter James, adj. Isaac Agee
Wit: Charles Basket*, Thomas Clark
Regst: Aug. 18, 1813

(*Note: Name spelled both ways)

(325)   STATE OF TENNESSEE   :
         WILLIE BLOUNT, GOV. :   LAND GRANT
              TO   :   NO. 713
         JAMES OFFIELD   :

Date: Sept. 8, 1808
Consideration: An entry made in the office of the Surveyor of the 6th
District of No. 121 dated Sept. 8, 1808, founded on a warrant, No. 1404,
issued by John Carter to James Offield for 400 acres dated Sept. 12, 1779
Location: Sullivan Co, District of Washington
Description: A tract of land containing 30 acres on the south bank of
Holston River corner to a former survey of Offield
Granted by Willie Blount, Gov, R. Houston, Sec.
Offield hath title to the within named tract of land. Recorded in my
office Feb. 3, 1810
                        E.W. Scott, Register of Land for E. TN
Aug. 18, 1813 rec'd tax on this grant
                        Mattw. Rhea, C.S.C.
Regst: Aug. 8, 1913(sic)

----

(326)   STATE OF TENNESSEE   :
         WILLIE BLOUNT, GOV. :   LAND GRANT
              TO   :   NO. 712
         JAMES OFFIELD   :

Date: Feb. 3, 1810
Consideration: An entry made in the office of the 6th District of No. 125,

dated Sept. 8, 1808, founded on a warrant of No. 1604, issued by John Carter to James Offield.
Location: Sullivan Co, District of Washington
Description: A tract of land containing 270 acres on the north side of Holston River, surveyed Dec. 7, 1808
Granted by Willie Blount, Gov, R. Houston, Sec.
James Offield hath title to the within described tract. Recorded in my office Feb. 3, 1810

E.W. Scott, Register of Land E. TN
Aug. 18, 1813, rec'd tax on this grant

Mattw. Rhea, C.S.C.
Regst: Aug. 19, 1813

(Page)
(327)

JOHN TIPTON	:	
TO	:	BILL OF SALE
NICHOLAS FAIN	:	

Date: April 15, 1813
Sale: Rec'd of Nicholas Fain, $400.00 the full amt, for a negro man named Joshua abt 28 yrs old
Attest: Henry Earnest, Rich'd. Gammon
Acknowledged: By John Tipton, Sullivan Co, TN, Aug, 1813
Test: Mattw. Rhea, C.S.C.
Regst: Aug. 19, 1813

JONATHAN LEWIS & NANCY,	:	
His wife, of Franklin Co, Ind. Terr	:	
TO	:	POWER OF ATTORNEY
DAVID & GEORGE LEWIS of	:	
Franklin Co, Ind. Terr	:	

Date: July 13, 1813
Parties: Jonathan Lewis and Nancy, my wife, of the Luisiana(sic) Territory, and Franklin Co. to David and George Lewis of same
Power of Attorney: The sd parties of the first do appoint their brothers, parties of the second part, out lawful attorney for us; to ask and receive any money due us and to sell all our rights and titles of certain tracts of land, sd land left to us by our father, Nathaniel Lewis, and to made good title for the same as if we were personally present
Test: Charles Waldridge
Indiana* Territory, Franklin Co: Be it remembered that on July 30, 1813, Saml Rockefeller, one of the justices of the peace in sd county aforesaid Jonathan Lewis and Nancy, his wife, the within grantor and acknowledged the within power of attorney to be their voluntary act for the purposes therein contained; Nancy apart from her husband, relinquished her right of dowery in the within named premises   Saml. Rockefeller
Indiana* Territory, Franklin Co: I, Enoch McCarty, Clerk of the court of Common Pleas for the county aforesaid do certify that Saml Rockefeller was acknowledged to which certificate he affixed his name as an acting justice of the peace   Enoch McCarty, Clk, July 30, 1813
Sullivan Co, TN, Aug, 1813, the within power of attorney was subscribed in court
Test: Mattw. Rhea, C.S.C.
Regst: Aug. 21, 1813

(*Note: Unsure if it should be Indian or Indiana Territory)

JOHN SCOTT & JOSEPH SCOTT, ADM.   :
        TO   :
WILLIAM HALL of Greene Co.   :

Date: Aug. 20, 1813
Consideration: A valuable consideration
Location: Sullivan Co, TN
Description: A tract of land containing 140 acres on the south side of
Holston River adj. Nancy Shete and Milhorn
Wit: John Anderson
Acknowledged: By John & Joseph Scott, Sullivan Co, TN, Aug, 1813
Test: Mattw. Rhea, C.S.C.
Regst: Sept. 10, 1813

----

(329)   JOHN TIPTON   :
            TO   :   DEED OF WARRANTY
         GEORGE GROSS   :

Date: Jan. 4, 1811
Consideration: $500.00
Location: Blountville, Sullivan Co, TN
Description: A lot, No. 42, in town of Blountville, containing 1/2 acre at
the east end of town
Wit: Jacob Jett, James Anglea
Acknowledged: By John Tipton, Sullivan Co, TN, Aug, 1813
Test: Mattw. Rhea, C.S.C.
Regst: Sept. 10, 1813

----

(330)   JACOB WADDLE   :
            TO   :   DEED OF WARRANTY
         HARMAN LATTURE   :

Date: June 29, 1813
Consideration: A valuable consideration
Location: Sullivan Co, TN
Description: a tract of land containing 51 acres on the waters of Reedy
Creek adj. David Shaver and a former survey of Waddle
Wit: John Tipton, Walter Jones, John Anderson
Acknowledged: By Jacob Waddle, Sullivan Co, TN, Aug, 1813
Test: Mattw. Rhea, C.S.C.
Regst: Sept. 10, ????

(?Note: Year not given - Probably 1813)

(331)   JOSEPH SMITH   :
            TO   :   DEED OF WARRANTY
         JOHN CHESTER   :

Date: Jan. 15, 1813
Consideration: $200.00
Location: Sullivan Co, TN

Description: A tract of land containing 50 acres on the clear fork of
Horse Creek; beginning at a hickory tree on John Crawford's line.
Wit: Jacob Molock, Samuel Smith, John Chester
Acknowledged: By Joseph Smith, Sullivan Co, Aug, 1813
Test: Mattw. Rhea, C.S.C.
Regst: Sept. 11, 1813

(Page)
(332)   JENKINS MURPHY   :
                TO   :   DEED OF WARRANTY
           WILLIAM DICKSON   :

           Date: Aug. 10, 1813
           Consideration: $325.00
           Location: Sullivan Co, TN
           Description: A tract of land containing 75 acres
           Wit: Thomas Titsworth, Philip Kite
           Proven: By Titsworth and Kite, Sullivan Co, TN, Aug, 1813
           Test: Mattw. Rhea, C.S.C.
           Regst: Sept. 13, 1813

----

(333)   RICHARD MURRELL, SR.   :
                TO   :   DEED OF WARRANTY
           RICHARD MURRELL, JR.   :

           Date: Aug. 16, 1813
           Consideration: $400.00 current money of sd state
           Location: Sullivan Co, TN
           Description: A tract of land containing 100 acres on the waters of Horse
           Creek; begin part of the tract of land Murrell, Sr. now lives on
           Wit: Nathan Peoples, John Peoples, Frederick Titsworth
           Proven: By John Peoples, Frederick Titsworth, Sullivan Co, TN, Aug, 1813
           Test: Mattw. Rhea, C.S.C.
           Regst: Sept. 13, 1813

----

(334)   JAMES PHAGAN, Sheriff :
                TO   :   SHERIFF'S DEED OF WARRANTY
           JOHN SCOTT   :

           Date: Aug. 21, 1813
           Consideration: $154.30
           Location: Sullivan Co, Tn
           Purpose: William N. Gale in the court of Pleas and Qtr Session recovered
           a judgment against Jacob Emmert and John Scott, Jr. for the sum of
           sum of $134.35, with costs and afterwards a writ of execution issued on
           judgement to writ which came to hands of James Phagan, Sheriff, request-
           ing him that of the goods and lands of Jacob and John to make the
           aforesaid sum and which writ the High Sheriff returned to sd court with
           his return thereon that he had lived on the tract of land where Jacob
           Emmert, Jr, and a writ requiring Sheriff to expose land to public sale to
           satisfy debt of Wm N. Gale to John Scott

Description: A tract of land containing 100 acres granted to Jacob Emmert
Acknowledgement: By James Phagan, Sullivan Co, TN, Aug, 1813
Test: Mattw. Rhea, C.S.C.
Regst: Sept. 14, 1813

(Page)
(336)
```
JOHN PITCHER                      :
        TO                        :       DEED OF TRUST
SAM'L MOORE, MICHAEL DECKERT      :
and AMBROSE GAINES                :
```

Date: Jan. 25, 1813
Consideration: $273.74
Location: Sullivan Co, TN
Description: John Pitcher, in order to secure payment of above sum to
Moore, Deckert and Gaines, which they signed bonds for viz: 3 bonds to
David Shaver for $101.03 and 1 bond to Matthias Cleark and Mary Clerk
for $85.00 and $1.00 in hand paid to him by Moore, Deckert and Gains;
Pitcher hath sold to Moore, Deckert and Gaines, 2 tracts of land and one
of 109 acres on both sides of the great road adj. the land of David
Shaver and Sally Kilshaw and incl. where Pitcher now lives, also an entry
of 60 acres adj. Pitcher
Terms: Moore, Deckert and Gaines shall within 12 months sell the aforesaid
tract of land after advertising to highest bidder and proceeds to first pay
all charges attending sale and then the debts mentioned.
Wit: Samuel Edgeman, James Edgeman, Susannah Edgeman
Test: Mattw. Rhea, C.S.C.
Regst: Sept. 15, 1813

---

(338)
```
THOMAS MILLER          :
        TO             :       DEED OF WARRANTY
JOSHUA MILLER          :
```

Date: Nov. 2, 1812
Consideration: A valuable consideration
Location: Sullivan Co, TN
Description: A tract of land containing 291 acres beginning at John Miller
and adj. Edward Cox, George Melone, Widow Hawkins
Wit: Edward Cox, Thos Hamilton
Proven: By Edward Cox, John Hamilton, Sullivan Co, TN, Aug, 1813
Test: Mattw. Rhea, C.S.C.
Regst: Sept. 20, 1813

---

(339)
```
JAMES BRIGHT          :
        TO            :       QUIT CLAIM DEED
PHILIP FOUST          :
```

Date: Oct. 19, 1801
Consideration: A valuable consideration
Amt of land: 250 acres
Location: Sullivan Co, TN
Description: Land on the waters of Reedy Creek where Foust now lives
Wit: Isaac Jone, John Anderson

Proven: By Isaac Jone, John Anderson, Sullivan Co, TN, Nov, 1807
Test: Mattw. Rhea, C.S.C.
Regst: Oct. 1, 1813

```
STATE OF TENNESSEE    :
WILLIE BOUNT, GOV.    :    LAND GRANT
         TO           :    NO. 2104
JOHN WADDLOW          :
```

Date: Nov. 4, 1811
Consideration: An entry made in Adair's office of No. 219 dated March 9,
1780, founded on a warrant issued by James Gaines of dated Sept. 26,
1783, which warrant issued to John Anderson and assigned to John Waddlow
Amt of land: 100 acres
Location: Sullivan Co, District of Washington
Description: A tract of land in Washington District on a branch called
Young's Run on the Virginia line, surveyed June 22, 1809
Granted: By Gov. Willie Blount, R. Houston, Sec.
John Waddlow is entitled to within tract of land, Recorded in my office
Nov. 4, 1811
                    Edw. Scott, Register of E. TN
Oct. 30, 1811, rec'd tax on within grant
Test: Mattw. Rhea, C.S.C.
Regst: Oct. 30, 1813

```
(340)    SALLY KELSHAW & JOHN BRITTEN* :
             TO                   :    DEED OF WARRANTY
         JOHN PITCHER             :
```

Date: May 13, 1809
Consideration: 109 ₺
Amt of land: 100 acres
Location: Sullivan Co, TN
Description: A tract of land on both sides of the great road adj. Jacob
Yeast and John Kelshaw, dec'd, and incl. where John Pitcher now lives
Wit: Ambrose Gaines, William Wallace, Thos, McCauley
Acknowledged: By Sally Kelshaw, John Brotten*, Sullivan Co, TN, May, 1809
Test: Mattw. Rhea, C.S.C.
Regst: Nov. 5, 1813

```
(341)    CHARLES ALLEN       :
             TO               :    DEED OF WARRANTY
         WILLIE ALLEN         :
```

Date: Nov. 7, 1812
Consideration: Natural love and affection which I have and bear to my son
Amt of land: 25 acres
Location: Sullivan Co, TN
Description: A tract of land on the south side of Holston River joining
Charles Allen's line

Wit: Vivian Riggs, Calvin Smith, Hy M. Runnels
Proven: By Calvin Smith, Hy Runnels, Sullivan Co, TN, Nov, 1812
Test: Mattw. Rhea, C.S.C.
Regst: Nov. 15, 1813

(Page)

(342)

GABRIEL GOAD   :
         TO   :   DEED OF WARRANTY
WILLIAM GOAD   :

Date: Jan. 25, 1800
Consideration: 26 £ current money
Amt of land: 79 acres
Location: Sullivan Co, TN
Description: A tract of land on the Horse Creek adj. Patten Goad, up the creek to the school house hollow
Wit: Jonathan Bachman, Patrick Smiley
Proven: By Patrick Smiley, Sullivan Co, Tn, Feb, 1802
Test: Mattw. Rhea, C.S.C.
Regst: Nov. 15, 1813

----

(343)

ROBERT CHRISTIAN   :
         TO   :   DEED OF WARRANTY
WILLIAM TRIGG, CHARLES S. :
CARSON & JOHN LYNN   :

Date: May 15, 1813
Consideration: $50.00
Amt of land: 150 sq poles
Location: Sullivan Co, TN
Description: A lot of ground in Christiansville Boatyard joining Robert Christian and a line 16 ft wide is to be left between fences
Wit: Joseph Everitt, David Geyer
Proven: By Joseph Everitt, David Geyer, Sullivan Co, TN, May, 1813
Test: Mattw. Rhea, C.S.C.
Regst: Nov. 18, 1813

----

(344)

WALLACE WILLOUGHBY :   SURVEY

Date: Nov. 5, 1813
Survey: This plat represents 10 acres I have surveyed for Wallace Willoughby assignee of William Rockhold assignee of Alfred M. Carter for himself and Elizabeth Carter, heirs of John Carter, dec'd. This survey made by virtue of an entry made in the surveyor's office of the 6th District on July 13, 1812, No. 1370, by warrant issued by Archibald Roane, Commissioner of E. Tn, Nov. 20, 1810, No. 2855.
Description: Situated on both sides of Sinking Creek
Chain Carriers: Jacob Booher, Andrew Brown
I assign all my right and title of the with return of survey unto George Burkhart and Jacob Booher for value rec'd as witness my hand and seal, Nov. 5, 1813
(Regst): (No date given)

HENRY SHARRETTS*   :   SURVEY

Date: Nov. 5, 1813
Survey: I have surveyed 20 acres, by a scale of 50 poles to the inch, for Henry Sharretts assignee of William Willoughby assignee of William Rockhold assignee of Alfred M. Carter for himself and Elizabeth Carter heirs of John Carter, dec'd. This survey made by virtue of an entry made in the surveyor's office of the 6th District Feb. 26, 1813, No. 1620, made by a warrant issued by Archibald Roane, Commissioner for E. Tn, Nov, 20, 1810, No. 2855.
Description: On the waters of Sinking Creek adj. Wallace Willoughby, Conrad Sharret
Chain Carriers: Jacob Booher, Andrew Brown
                                John Anderson, D.S.
I assign over all my right and title of the within to George Burkhart and Jacob Booher for value rec'd of them, Nov. 5, 1813
                                Henry Sharrett*
Wit: John Anderson and Nathan Willett
Proven: By John Anderson, Nathan Willett, Sullivan Co, TN, Nov, 1813
Test: Mattw. Rhea, C.S.C.
Regst: Nov. 19, 1813

(*Note: Name spelled both ways)

JOHN PITCHER   :   SURVEY

Date: Nov. 1, 1813
Survey: I have surveyed 60 acres for John Pitcher assignee of Joseph Everett. This survey made by virtue of an entry made in the surveyor's office of the 6th District on Oct. 8, 1812, No. 1484. Certificate issued by Edw. Scott, reg. of land office for E. TN, No. 39, Jan. 22, 1810.
Description: On the waters of Reedy Creek adj. John Lynn
Chain Carriers: Carter Waddle, John Waddlow
                                John Anderson, D.S.
I assign over all my right and title of the within survey to John Lynn for value rec'd, Nov. 17, 1813
                                John Pitcher
Wit: John Anderson
Acknowledged: Sullivan Co, TN, Nov, 1813
Test: Mattw. Rhea, D.C.
Regst: Nov. 19, 1813

----

(346)   DAVID & GEORGE LEWIS,   :
         JONATHAN LEWIS   :
                 TO   :   DEED OF WARRANTY
         JAMES RHEA   :

Date: Aug. 20, 1813
Consideration: $50.00
Amt of land: 72 acres
Location: Sullivan Co, TN
Parties: David and George Lewis as well for themselves as attorneys for Jonathan Lewis all of the Indiana Territory and Washington Lews of Maddison Co and Mississippi Terroroty. Heirs of Nathan Lewis, dec'd, of the

one part and John Rhea of the other part
Description: Four undivided shares of a parcel of land containing 72 acres
adj. a corner formerly Job Keyes and John Tipton
Wit: John Tipton, D.C. Yearsley, John Rhea
Acknowledged: By David & George Lewis for themselves and as Attorneys
for Jonathan Lewis, Sullivan Co, TN, Aug, 1813
Test: Mattw. Rhea, C.S.C.
Regst: Nov. 30, 1813

(Page)
(347)　　　PETER HUFLUCK* & DAVID HARRY :
　　　　　　　　TO　　　　　　　　　　　　:　　　POWER OF ATTORNEY
　　　　HENRY PORTSMAN*　　　　　　　:

Date: Oct. 25, 1813
Consideration: Divers good cause
Power of Attorney: Whereas John Portsman, dec'd, did by his last will and
testament appoint Peter Hufluck David Harry, Thomas C. Brent and Michael
McKennan, all of Washington Co, MD, his Executors; and Thomas C. Brent
and Michael McKennan would not act but relinquished their right agreeable
to the laws of this state and Hufluck and Harry having taken upon
themselves the duties of Executors agreeable to sd will. Now, Hufluck and
Harry appoint Henry Protzman*, one of the heirs of John Protsman, at
present of the state of KY, our true and lawful attorney for the use and
benefit of the heirs of John Protsman, dec'd, to sue for and recover from
all persons whatsoever are indebted to estate all funds of money debts and
demand which are now due and owing and to have all lawful ways and
means in our name or otherwise for the recovery thereof and to agree for
other sufficient discharges for we in our names and in every effect as we
ourselves might
Wit: Jacob Schuebly, Adam Ott
Maryland, Washington Co, SS: Be it remembered that on Oct. 12, 1813,
Peter Huflick* and David Harry appeared before two Justices of the Peace
for the aforesaid county and acknowledged the foregoing power of attorney
to be their act and deed for the purpose and use therein mentioned
　　　　　　　　　　　　　　Jacob Schuebly
　　　　　　　　　　　　　　Adam Ott
Certified: Oct. 25, 1813, Washington Co, MD
　　　　　　　　　　　　　　O.H. Williams, Clk.
Washington Co, MD, SS: I, John Buchanan, Chief Judge of the 5th Judicial
District of MD, certify that this attestation by oath Holland Williams, Clk
of Washington Co Court is in due form. Oct. 5, 1813, Elizabeth town.
　　　　　　　　　　　　　　Jno. Buchanan
Bombon(sic) Co Clerk's office for Nov. 13, 1813; This letter of Attorney
from Peter Hufluck and David Harry to Henry Protzman was this day
produced to me and together with the certificate thereon was duly
recorded.
　　　　　　　　　　　　Att. Tho P. Smith, D.C.B.C.
(Regst): Dec. 2, 1813

(*Note: Names spelled both ways)

```
JOHN PROTZMAN                          :
      TO                               :
MARY, His wife, His four Children;     :
JOHN, MARY & KITTY PROTZMAN            :          WILL
and POLLY McKURNAN. DAVID HARRY,       :
PETER HEFFLEY, THOMAS C BRENT and      :
Son-in-Law Michael McKurnan, Executors :
```

Date: June 29, 1804

Will: In the name of God, Amen. John Protzman of Washington Co, MD, being very weak of body, but of perfect and sound and sidposing mind, memory and underatanding, I do make and order this my last will and testament. It is my will and I do order all my debts and funeral charges be fully paid and satisfied. ITEM: I do will and bequeath to my beloved wife, Mary, during her life provided whe remain single and unmarried all that house and lot of gound situated in Elizabeth Town between the house of Mr. Douglass and Mr. Capp, likewise the meadow ground in Roburs addition to Elizabeth Town with three feather beds of her choice and 1/3 part of the residue of my household furniture. It is also my will and desire that as soon as so much of my debts and the money rising from the sale of my property can be collected that my Executors pay unto my beloved wife the sum of 300 ₤ and should she marry, it is my desire that my executors require immediate security of her for the payment of sd sum of 300 ₤ to my children at her decease. ITEM: I give to my beloved wife, Mary, during her life, a mulatto girl named Nancy with her off spring and at the death of my wife, it is my wish that the mulatto girl Nancy be free and discharged from servitude, her issue to be at the disposal of my wife. ITEM: I give to my daughter, Kitty, two cows of her choice and a side saddle to be paid for by my executors out of my estate. It is my wish that my two sons, John and Henry, be sent to a good English School for the terms of 18 months. Their expences, boarding, clothing and schooling be paid out of my estate by my executors, and lastly I will and order that the residue of my estate both real and personal shall be disposed of by my executors at public sale and the money arising be equally divided among my four children, John Protzman, Henry Protzman, Kitty Protzman, and Polly McKernan, share and share alike and finally, I do hereby appoint my friends David Harry and Peter Feffley(sic), Thomas C. Brent, and my son-in-law Michael McKernan, executors to my last will and testament.

                    June, 23, 1804   John Protzman
Wit: Leonard Shaffer, Nicholas Parrott, David Stephens
Proven: By Parrott and Stephens, Aug. 11, 1804,
                              Certified: Thomas Bilo, Reg.
Proven: By Peter Heffley and David Harry, Oct. 31, 1804
                              Certified: Thomas Bilo, Reg
Test: George C. Smoot, Reg. Washington Co, MD
(Regst): Dec. 2, 1813

```
DAVID LEWIS & GEORGE LEWIS,     :
JONATHAN & NANCY LEWIS          :
       TO                       :          DEED OF WARRANTY
JAMES RHEA                       
```

Date: Aug. 20, 1813

Consideration: $500.00
Location: Sullivan Co, TN
Parties: David Lewis and George Lewis for themselves and as attorneys in fact for Jonathan and Nancy Lewis, all of the Indiana Territory and heirs of Nathan Lewis, dec'd.
Description: Three undivided shares of a tract of land on both sides of Beaver Creek containing 300 acres being part of a grant of land of 400 acres. From the state of NC to Nathan Lewis in his lifetime 100 acres of which we bequeathed to David Lewis by Nathan Lewis, which tract of land of 400 acres as aforesaid is bounded as follows: beginning at a white oad on George Hemses corner to bank of Beaver Creek and adj. Webb
Signed: David Lewis, George Lewis, Jonathan Lewis, Nancy Lewis, his wife, by their attorneys David and George Lewis
Acknowledged: By Jonathan and Nancy Lewis, Sullivan Co, TN, Aug, 1813
Test: Mattw. Rhea, C.S.C.
Regst: Dec. 6, (No year given)

(Page)
(353)

SAMUEL MOORE   :
        TO   :   DEED OF WARRANTY
ALVIN SOPER   :

Date: Oct. 14, 1813
Consideration: $1000.00
Amt of land: 200 acres
Location: Sullivan Co, TN
Description: A tract of land adj. John Mackey and north corner to George Rutledge
Wit: David Yearsley, Matthew Rhea, Jr.
Proven: By Yearsley and Rhea, Sullivan Co, TN, Nov, 1813
Test: Mattw. Rhea, C.S.C.
Regst: Dec. 7, 1813

MOSES, ELLENOR, JOHN &   :
MARY BARBER   :
        TO   :   DEED OF WARRANTY
JAMES RHEA   :

Date: Feb. 16, 1813
Consideration: $400.00
Location: Sullivan Co, TN
Description: All their claim to two undivided shares of a tract of land on both sides of Beaver Creek and containing 300 acres being part of a grant of land from the state of NC to Nathan Lewis in his lifetime of 400 acres, 100 acres of which grant off the east end was bequeathed by Nathan Lewis to David Lewis which tract of 400 acres is bounded as follows: Beginning at George Himes' corner, then south bank of Beaver Creek then south to Webb's corner
Wit: Matthew Rhea, Jr, Joseph McLin, Cyrus Humphries, Mattw. Rhea
Proven: Joseph McLin, Cyrus Humphreys, Sullivan Co, TN, Aug, 1813
Test: Mattw. Rhea, C.S.C.
Regst: Dec. 7, (1813)

125

ELIZABETH LEWIS, Widow of William :
Lewis, Dec'd, and JOBES MILLER :
     TO   :   DEED OF WARRANTY
WILLIAM DURY :

Date: Aug. 25, 1813
Consideration: $25.00 for the performance of which we bind ourselves our heirs
Location: Sullivan Co, near town of Blountville
Description: William Lewis, dec'd husband of Elizabeth Lewis, was entitled to 1/7 part of 72 acres as one of the heirs of Nathan Lewis, dec'd, his father; being part of a tract of 200 acres granted to Nathan Lewis, dec'd, in his lifetime by NC by a grant dated Feb. 27, 1796. And whereas the sd William, dec'd, has left 6 children who are infants named Matilda, Elizabeth, Cansberry, Nathan, Edna & William Lewis, his lawful heirs who are entitled to the 1/7 part of sd premises. If Elizabeth and John or either of them shall make a good title in the fee simple to William Dury and heirs to the before mentioned 1/7 part of the 72 acres. As the heirs of Wm Lewis, dec'd, shall arrive at full age or as soon as the youngest child of Lewis shall arrive at full age then this obligation to be void otherwise to remain in full force
Wit: David Yearsley, Joseph Cook
Proven: By Yearsley, Cook, Sullivan Co, TN, Nov, 1813
Test: Mattw. Rhea, C.S.C.
Regst: Dec. 8, 1813

----

(356)

MARY LEWIS, Widow of David Lewis, :
WILLIAM, GEORGE, JONATHAN & :
WASHINGTON LEWIS, MOSES BARBER :   DEED OF CONVEYANCE
& WIFE, ELLENOR BARBER, JOHN :
BARBER & Wife, MARY, & :
WILLIAM DURY :

Date: Feb. 27, 1813
Consideration: $100.00
Location: Sullivan Co
Description: A tract of land being part of a tract of 200 acres granted to Nathan Lewis, now dec'd, in his lifetime. Grant dated Feb. 27, 1796, containing 72 acres
Wit: Joseph Brownlow, Joseph Cook, Julius Ford
Proven: By Joseph Cook, Julius Ford, Sullivan Co, TN, Nov, 1813
Test: Mattw. Rhea, C.S.C.
Regst: Dec. 10, 1813

----

(358)

JOHN & ELIZABETH BRITTON,CATHARINE :
SMITH, Daughters of John Kelshaw, dec'd. :
     TO   :   DEED OF WARRANTY
JOHN LYNN, Acting partner of Lynn & :
Trigg and Carson

Date: Nov. 19, 1813
Consideration: $1.00 was respectively paid
Location: (Blank)

Description: Have sold unto John Lynn all of our two undivided (blank line). Shares of the land possessed by John Kilshaw, which was conveyed by Sally Kilshaw and John Britton to John Pitcher by indenture dated May 13, 1809. By these presents forever relinquish and quit claim to our sd undivided moities as aforesaid unto John Lynn
Wit: J. Punch, Jr Punch
Acknowledged: By John Birtton, Elizabeth Britton, Catharine Smith
Test: Mattw. Rhea, C.S.C.
Regst: Dec. 11, 1813

(Page)
(359)   JOHN PITCHER   :
             TO   :   DEED OF WARRANTY
      JOHN LYNN, Acting partner :
      Lynn, Trigg, & Carson   :

Date: Nov. 19, 1813
Consideration: A valuable consideration
Location: Sullivan Co, TN
Description: A tract of land containind 109 acres
Wit: J. Punch, John Anderson
Acknowledged: By John Pitcher, Sullivan Co, TN, Nov, 1813
Test: Mattw. Rhea, C.S.C.
Regst: Dec. 11, 1813

----

(360)   JACOB AKARD   :
            TO   :   BILL OF SALE
      ADAM AKARD   :

Date: Nov. 13, 1813
Consideration: $163.00
Description: I, Jacob Akard, do sell unto Adam Akard allmy household furniture and plantation utensils, one mare and cow, two yrs old heiffer, three yearling calves and one young calf, two head of sheep, twelve head hogs
Wit: George Burkhart, Nathan Willett
Proven: By George Burkhart and Nathan Willet
Test: Mattw. Rhea, C.S.C.
Regst: Dec. 13, 1813

----

(361)   JACOB AKARD, SR.   :
            TO   :   DEED OF WARRANTY
      ADAM AKARD   :

Date: Nov. 5, 1813
Consideration: 200 lbs. lawful money
Location: Sullivan Co
Description: 190 acres on the waters of Beaver Creek, where J Akard lives
Wit: George Burkhart, Nathan Willett
Proven: By George Burkhart, Nathan Willett, Sullivan Co, TN, Nov, 1813
Test: Mattw. Rhea, C.S.C.
Regst: Dec. 14, 1813

----

(362)   JOB KEY & JACHIES* JONES :
              TO   :   DEED OF WARRANTY
          JOHN JACKSON   :

          Date: Nov. 17, 1813
          Consideration: A valuable consideration
          Location: Sullivan Co
          Description: Land where Martha Key, widow, now lives, on which is to be
          equal share with a brother and three sisters. Who do by these presents
          grant unto John Jackson all right Job Key and Zachies* Jones have
          Wit: (No names given)
          Acknowledged: By Job Key, Zachies Jones, Sullivan Co, TN, Nov, 1813
          Test: Mattw. Rhea, C.S.C.
          Regst: Dec. 14, 1813

(*Note: Name spelled both ways)

(362)   JOHN SPURGIN   :
              TO   :   BILL OF SALE
          JAMES PHAGAN   :

          Date: Sept. 27, 1813
          Consideration: $500.00
          (Description): I, John Spurgin, have sold unto James Phagan one negro man
          named Solomon aged 23 yrs for the sum of $500.00
          Wit: George Burkhart, James Kerr
          Acknowledged: By John Spurgin
          Test: Mattw. Rhea, C.S.C.
          Regst: Dec. 14, 1813
                              ----

(363)   JAMES ENGLISH   :
              TO   :   DEED OF WARRANTY
          JOSEPH EVERETT   :

          Date: May 17, 1813
          Consideration: $1200.00
          Location: Christiansville* Boatyard
          Description: One acre in Christianville* Boatyard
          Wit: David George, John Simpson
          Proven: By David George, John Smpson, sullivan Co, TN, May, 1813
          Test: Mattw. Rhea, C.S.C.
          Regst: (No date given)
                              ----

(364)   THOMAS CAPPS   :
              TO   :   DEED OF LAND
          WALTER GAINS

          Date: Aug. 31, 1813
          Consideration: A valuable consideration
          Location: Sullivan Co
          Description: 170 acres on the waters of Week
          Wit: John Anderson, Zach Wicks, Samuel Bouder
          Proven: By John Anderson, Zachariah Wicks, Sullivan Co, TN, Nov, 1813

Test: Mattw. Rhea, C.S.C.
Regst: Jan. 1, 1814

(Page)
(365)   JACOB GITT   :
              TO   :   DEED OF WARRANTY
         ANDREW CROCKETT   :

         Date: Oct. 2, 1813
         Consideration: $150.00 current money of Virginia
         Location: Middle Town, Sullivan Co
         Description: One house and lot, No. 28, in Middle town, 1/4 acre being
         part of land formerly owned by Samuel McCorkle
         Wit: John Miller, Benjamin Slickler
         Acknowledged: By Jacob Gitt
         Test: Mattw. Rhea, C.S.C.
         Regst: (No date given)

----

(366)   HENRY MAUK   :
              TO   :   DEED OF WARRANTY
         JOSEPH CLARK   :

         Date: July 10, 1813
         Consideration: $80.00
         Location: Sullivan Co
         Description: 47 acres of water and land below Funks Ferry incl. outer side
         of river, all the fish, dams, and traps
         Wit: Eli Shipley, Harman C. Vie(sic), John Childress
         Proven: By Eli Shipley, John Childress, Sullivan Co, Tn, Nov, 1813
         Test: Mattw. Rhea, C.S.C.
         Regst: July 6, 1814

----

(367)   JAMES HAGGARD   :
              TO   :   DEED OF WARRANTY
         HENRY MAUK   :

         Date: May 15, 1813
         Consideration: $500.00
         Location: Sullivan Co
         Description: A tract of land on the south side of Holston River behind
         part of Alexander Calvett(sic) old tract
         Wit: Alexander Gitgood, James Wright, George Willard
         Proven: Sullivan Co, TN, May, 1813
         Test: Mattw. Rhea, C.S.C.
         Regst: Jan. 14, 1814

----

(368)   THOMAS WHITE   :
              TO   :   DEED OF WARRANTY
         JOHN THOMAS   :

         Date: Oct. 16, 1813
         Consideration: $310.00

Location: 108 acres where Thomas White now lives
Wit: Frederick Weaver, Thomas Mayors
Proven: Thomas Mayors, Frederick Weaver, Sullivan Co, TN, Nov, 1813
Test: Mattw. Rhea, C.S.C.
Regst: Jan. 18, 1813

(Page)
369)   HENRY SHARRATTS   :
                TO   :   DEED OF WARRANTY
        JACOB BOOKER(sic)   :

Date: Nov. 16, 1813
Consideration: A valuable consideration
Location: Sullivan Co, TN
Description: 51 acres on Sinking Creek
Wit: John Anderson, Nathan Willett
Acknowledged: By Henry Sharratts, Sullivan Co, TN, Nov, 1813
Test: Mattw. Rhea, C.S.C.
Regst: Jan. 18, 1813

----

(370)   EDWARD GOSUCH   :
                TO   :   DEED OF WARRANTY
        JESSE COX   :

Date: Feb. 20, 1806
Consideration: $40.00
Location: Sullivan Co
Description: 25 1/2 acres in county aforesaid
Wit: (No names given)
Acknowledged: By Edward Gosuch, Sullivan Co, Feb, 1806
Test: Mattw. Rhea, C.S.C.
Regst: Jan. 18, 1814

----

(370)   GEORGE BURKHART   :
                TO   :   DEED OF CONVEYANCE
        NATHAN WILLETT   :

Date: Nov. 17, 1813
Consideration: A valuable consideration
Location: Sullivan Co, TN
Description: 3 acres and 3 qrtrs in state and county aforesaid
Wit: (No names given)
Acknowledged: By George Burkhart
Test: Mattw. Rhea, C.S.C
Regst: Jan. 18, 1814

----

(371)   JACOB GITT   :
                TO   :   DEED OF WARRANTY
        ANDREW CROCKITE   :

Date: Oct. 2, 1813
Consideration: $150.00 current money of VA

130

Location: Middle Town, Sullivan Co
Description: One lot, No. 28, in Middletown, 1/4 acre, land Samuel
McCorkle formerly owned
Wit: John Miller, Benjamin Strickler
Acknowledged: By Jacob Gitt
(Regst): (No date given)

(Page)
(372)   ABRAHAM FRIEND and Wife, ELIZABETH :
            TO   :   DEED OF WARRANTY
    GEORGE HOUSER   :

Date: March 14, 1807
Consideration: A valuable consideration
Location: Sullivan Co
Description: 157 acres to wit: 108 acres in Washington Co and 49 acres in
Sullivan Co and on the head waters of Back Creek
Wit: John Anderson, Jacob Bark*
(Proven): By John Anderson, Jacob Back*, Sullivan Co, TN, May, 1807
Test: Mattw. Rhea, C.S.C.
Regst: Feb. 14, 1814

(*Note: Name spelled both ways)

(373)   STATE OF TENNESSEE :
    ARCHIBALD ROANE   :   LAND GRANT
          TO   :   NO. 2325
    JOHN NAVE   :

Date: May 20, 1809
Consideration: Entry made in office of Surveyor of 6th District, No. 267,
dated May 20, 1807. Founded on a warrant No. 149, issued by Archibald
Roane to John Nave for 200 acres; assigned by Jacob Knane(sic)
Representation of John Nave to Samuel Y. Balch and by him to Isaac and
William Brownlow and by him to John McCorkle. 50 acres is assigned by
McCorkle to John Allison the enterer. There is granted by TN to John
Allison and his heirs
Description: 32 1/2 (acres) in Washington District
Surveyed: Dec. 7, 1809
To be affixed at Knoxville, June 18, 1812, By Gov. Willie Blount, W.
Blount, Sec.
                            Edw Scott, Reg. of E. Tn
Feb. 18, 1814, tax paid - 06 & 4 mills
Test: Mattw. Rhea, C.S.C.
Regst: Feb. 21, 1814

----

(374)   STATE OF TENNESSEE :
    JOHN CARTER   :   LAND GRANT
          TO   :   NO. 3076
    JAMES HENRY   :

Date: Feb. 24, 1810
Consideration: An entry made in office of surveyor of 6th District, No.
417, on a warrant No. 2662, issued by John Carter to James Henry for

100 acres dated Nov. 12, 1780; 40 acres of which is vested in William
Feam*, the enterer
Description: Granted by state of TN to William Fram* and his heirs 40
acres in Washington District and the wters of Watauga River
Affixed at Knoxville, Oct. 30, 1811. by Gov. Willie Blount

                         Edw. Scott, Reg. of E. TN

Test: Mattw. Rhea, C.S.C.
Regst: Sept. 22, 1814

(*Note: Name spelled both ways)

(Page)
(375)   SARAH NEWTON   :
            TO   :   DEED OF WARRANTY
     JOHN HOUSLEY   :

Date: Feb. 19, 1814
Consideration: $152.08
Location: Sullivan Co
Description: All my undivided right of dower to 300 acres where Cate
Hashband, Charles Newton, dec'd, resided at the time of his death, to have
my undivided right in the tract of land to John Housley
Wit: J. Brownlow, W. Keyes
Proven: By J. Brownlow, Washington Keyes, Sullivan Co, TN, Feb, 1814
Test: Mattw. Rhea, C.S.C.
Regst: Feb. 22, 1814

----

(377)   ZACKARIAH WELKS*   :
            TO   :   DEED OF WARRANTY
     GEORGE WOLFORD   :

Date: Feb. 22, 1814
Consideration: A valuable consideraton
Location: Sullivan Co
Description: 14 acres on the waters of Reedy Creek
Wit: John Anderson
Acknowledged: By Zackariah Weeks*, Sullivan Co, TN, Feb, 1814
Regst: Feb. 23, 1814

(*Note: Name spelled both ways)

(378)   WALTER JAMES   :
            TO   :   DEED OF WARRANTY
     GEORGE WOLFORD   :

Date: Feb. 22, 1814
Consideration: A valuable consideration
Location: Sullivan Co, TN
Description: 20 acres on the waters of Reedy Creek
Wit: John Anderson
Acknowledged: By Walter James, Sullivan Co, TN, Feb, 1814
Test: Mattw. Rhea, C.S.C.
Regst: Feb. 23, 1814

NICHOLAS RUSSELL   :
          TO   :   DEED OF CONVEYANCE
WILLIAM DURY   :

Date: Jan. 27, 1814
Consideration: A valuable consideration
Location: Town of Blountville, Sullivan Co
Description: A lot, No. 7, containing 1 acre
Wit: Mattw. Rhea, Jr, Benjamin Strickler
Acknowledged: By Nicholas Russell, Sullivan Co, TN, Feb, 1814
Test: Mattw. Rhea, C.S.C.
Regst: Feb. 28, 1814

----

(380)   WM SCOTT   :
          TO   :   DEED OF WARRANTY
HARMAN ARANTS   :

Date: May 18, 1813
Consideration: $44.86
Location: Sullivan Co
Description: 14 acres in Sullivan Co
Wit: (No names given)
Acknowledged: By Wm Scott
Test: Mattw. Rhea, C.S.C.
Regst: April 13, 1814

----

(381)   STATE OF TENNESSEE   :
COMMISSIONERS OF E. TN   :   LAND GRANT
          TO   :   NO. 2021
ISAAC PULLARD   :

Date: Oct. 27, 1810
Consideration: Of entry made in the office of the Surveyor of the 6th
District, No. 546, founded on a warrant, No. 1532, issued by the
Commissioners of E. TN to Isaac Pullard for 100 acres, 14 acres of which
is vested in John Early, the enterer by assignment then is granted by TN
to John Early. Sd 14 acres in Washington District on the waters of Horse
Creek
To be affixed at Knoxville, Oct. 3, 1811 by Gov. Willie Blount, R.
Houston, Sec.   Edw. Scott, Reg. of E. TN
March 29, 1814, tax on within grant
Test: Mattw. Rhea, C.S.C.
Regst: April 18, 1814

----

(382)   JOHN TIPTON   :
          TO   :   DEED OF WARRANTY
JOHN GIFFORD   :
Date: July 15, 1812
Consideration: $100.00
Amt of land: 1/2 acre
Location: Town of Blountville, Sullivan Co
Description: 1/2 acre lot, No. 44, in the plot of sd town

133

Wit: Robert Blackmore, Wm Dulaney
Acknowledged: By John Tipton, Sullivan Co, Tn, Nov, 1812
Regst: April 18, 1814

(Page)
(382)

JOHN ALLISON   :
      TO   :   DEED OF WARRANTY
FINLEY ALLISON   :

Date: Feb. 21, 1814
Consideration: $76.67
Amt of land: By estimation, 23 acres
Location: Sullivan Co
Description: A parcel of land in sullivan Co, aforesaid John Allison and Finley Allison, also the land of Robert Allison
Wit: Jas. L. Taylor, E.R. Dulaney
Proven: By Ja. L. Taylor, E.R. Dulaney, Sullivan Co, TN, Feb, 1814
Test: Mattw. Rhea, C.S.C.
Regst: April 29, 1814

----

(383)

DAVID PERRY, SR.   :
      TO   :   DEED OF CONVEYANCE
DAVID PERRY, JR.   :

Date: June 7, 1813
Consideration: $500.00
Amt of land: 189 acres
Location: Sullivan Co
Description: All that tract of land in county aforesaid (Except as have after Excepted) (And Bounded)
Wit: Nathan Shipley, Enoch Shipley
Acknowledged: By David Perry, Sr, Sullivan Co, TN, Feb, 1814
Test: Mattw. Rhea, C.S.C.
Regt: April 29, 1814

----

(385)

BENJAMIN BIRDWELL :
      TO   :   DEED OF CONVEYANCE
DAVID SAXTON   :

Date: Aug. 4, 1810
Consideration: $100.00
Amt of land: 97 acres
Location: Sullivan Co, TN
Description: 97 acres on the south side of Holston River
Wit: Walter King, Jacob Farry
Proven: Benjamin Birdwell, David Saxton, Sullivan Co, Tn, Feb, 1814
Test: Mattw. Rhea, C.S.C.
Regst: May 12, 1814

----

(386)

MOSES LOONEY   :
      TO   :   DEED OF WARRANTY
ELIJAH CROSS   :

Date: Feb. 17, 1812
Consideration: A valuable consideration
Amt of land: 100 acres
Location: Sullivan Co
Description: 100 acres on the north side of Holston River
Wit: Zackariah Cross, Jese Cross
Proven: By Zackariah Cross, Jese Cross, Sullivan Co, TN, May, 1814
Test: Mattw. Rhea, C.S.C.
Regst: May 10, 1814

(Page)
(388)

```
STATE OF TENNESSEE        :
ARCHIBALD ROANE           :       LAND GRANT
        TO                :       NO. 2946
ANDREW GREER, Heirs of    :
```

Date: July 24, 1812
Consideration: An entry made in the surveyor's office of the 6th District,
No. 1378, founded on a certificate of No. 30, issued by Archibald Roane
to the heirs of Andrew Greer for 2480 acres, dated July 19, 1808, 20
acres of which are assigned to John Kennedy, the enterer
Description: There is granted by the state of TN to John Kennedy and his
heirs, a tract of land containing 30 acres in Sullivan Co,
To be affixed at Knoxville, Oct. 4, 1813 by Gov. Willie Blount, W.G.
Blount, Sec.

                        Edw. Scott, Reg. of E. TN
May 17, 1814, rec'd tax on this grant
Test: Mattw. Rhea, C.S.C.
Regst: Oct. 4, 1813

----

(389)
```
BENJAMIN WEBB             :
        TO                :       DEED OF GIFT
JACOB & BENJAMIN WEBB,    :
Grandsons                 :
```

Date: March 25, 1814
Consideration: Natural love and affection and also for diver other good
causes
Amt of land: 240 acres
Location: Sullivan Co
Description: Benjmain Webb hath given unto Jacob and Benjamin Webb all
claim to 240 acres and land I now live on. Sd land to be equally divided
between Jacob and Benjamin and not to have possession until after my
decease
Wit: Samuel McCorkle, Nicholas Motton, Andrew Crockett
Test: Mattw. Rhea, C.S.C.
Regt: (No date given)

----

(390)
```
STATE OF TENNESSEE   :
REGISTER OF E. TN     :       LAND GRANT
        TO            :       NO. 2947
ADAM HUNTSMAN         :
```

Date: June 1, 1812
Consideration: An entry made in the surveyor's office of the 6th District No. 1311, founded on a certificate of No. 234, issued by the register of E. TN to Adam Huntsman for 10 acres, April 6, 1814; 5 acres of which are assigned to Tedance Lane, the enterer.
Description: Granted by state of TN to Tedance Lane 5 acres on the north side of Holston River
To be affixed at Nashville, Oct. 4, 1813, by Gov. Willie Blount, W.G. Blount, Sec.
March 17, 1814, rec'd tax on this grant
Test: Mattw. Rhea, C.S.C.
Regst: May 18, 1814

(Page)
(391)

JOHN JONES   :
        TO   :   DEED OF WARRANTY
WILLIAM JONES   :

Date: Nov. 16, 1804
Consideration: $333.00
Amt of land: 97 acres
Location: Sullivan Co, TN
Description: A parcel of land to incl the double springs and Capt Clark's muster(sic) ground
Wit: Jonas Keen, Matthew Keen
Acknowledged: By John Jones, Sullivan Co, TN, Feb, 1814
(Regst): (No date given)

----

(392)

JONATHAN WEBB   :
        TO   :   DEED OF CONVEYANCE
ZACKARIAH CROSS &   :
ELIJAH CROSS, JR.   :

Date: Sept. 25, 1810
Consideration: A valuable consideration
Amt of land: 90 acres
Location: Sullivan Co
Description: 90 acres on the south side of Holston River
Wit: John Anderson, Elk. Key, John Jennings
Proven: By Ezekiel Key, John Jennings, Elijah Cross, Sullivan Co, May,1814
Test: Mattw. Rhea, C.S.C
Regst: (No date given)

----

(393)

RICHARD GAMMON   :
        TO   :   DEED OF WARRANTY
PETER RADER   :

Date: May 19, 1814
Consideration: A valuable consideration
Amt of land: 130 acres
Location: Sullivan Co
Description: 130 acres in Sullivan Co

Wit: Nicholas Fain
Acknowledged: By Richard Gammon, Sullivan Co, TN, May, 1814
Test: Mattw. Rhea, C.S.C.
Regst: May 19, 1814

(Page)
(394)   HENRY SEGLER, JR.   :
                TO   :   DEED OF CONVEYANCE
           GEORGE WALLARD   :

Date: June 12, 1812
Consideration: $500.00
Amt of land: 150 acres
Location: Sullivan Co, TN
Description: On south side of Holston River
Wit: Andrew Shell, Michael Queen, Samuel Jones
Proven: By Andrew Shell, Samuel Jones, Sullivan Co, TN, May, 1814
Test: Mattw. Rhea, C.S.C.
Regst: May 31, 1814

----

(395)   WASHINGTON LEWIS   :
                TO   :   DEED OF CONVEYANCE
           JAMES RHEA   :

Date: April 26, 1814
Consideration: $12.50
Amt of land: 72 acres
Location: Sullivan Co, TN
Description: Washington Lewis does sell to James Rhea all his claim, as
heir of Nathan Lewis, dec'd, to one undivided seventh share of a piece of
land near town of Blountville containing 72 acres
Wit: Wm King, Thomas Mayor, Hacker Cross, Joshua Johnson
Proven: Bu Thomas Mayor, Hackanah Cross, Sullivan Co, TN, May, 1814
Test: Mattw. Rhea, C.S.C.
Regst: June 2, 1914

----

(396)   WASHINGTON LEWIS   :
                TO   :   DEED OF CONVEYANCE
           JAMES RHEA   :

Date: April 26, 1814
Consideration: $200.00
Amt of land: 300 acres
Location: Sullivan Co, TN
Description: Washington Lewis hath sold to James Rhea all claim to one
undivided piece of land on both sides of Beaver Creek; being part of a
grant of land of 400 acres from NC to Nathan Lewis; 100 acres which was
bequeathed by him to David Lewis
Wit: Wm King, Thomas Mayors, Joshua Johnson, Zackariah Cross
Proven: By Thomas Mayors, Zackariah Cross, Sullivan Co, Tn, May, 1814
Test: Mattw. Rhea, C.S.C.
Regst: June 3, 1814

(Page)
(398)

DAVID AND GEORGE LEWIS :
        TO   :   DEED OF CONVEYANCE
JAMES RHEA   :

Date: Aug. 20, 1813
Consideration: $179.70
Amt of land: 400 acres
Location: Sullivan Co, TN
Description: As to my farm made to deeds of conveyance to James Rhea
of Sullivan Co for my two undivided shares of two tracts of land, a tract
of 72 acres near the town of Blountville; the other is part of a grant for
400 acres from the state of NC to Nathan Lewis, dec'd, 100 acres of
which was bequeathed by Nathan Lewis to David Lewis and to hims said of
my share of the undivided to wit 300 acres was by the sd David and
George on the day and year aforesaid conveyed to james Rhea .
Wit: Benjamin Smith, John Cox
Proven: Sullivan Co, TN, May, 1814
Test: Mattw. Rhea, C.S.C.
Regst: June 4, 1814

----

(400)

HIGGINS COPPINGER   :
        TO   :   DEED OF CONVEYANCE
JAMES BOYD   :

Date: Feb. 29, 1814
Consideration: $100.00
Amt of land: 20 acres
Location: Sullivan Co, TN
Description: 20 acres on the south side of Holston River
Wit: John Anders(sic), William Boyd
Acknowledged: By Higgins Coppinger, Sullivan Co, TN, Feb, 1814
Test: Mattw. Rhea, C.S.C
Regst: June 28, 1814

----

(402)

COMMISSIONERS OF EAST TN :
        TO   :   LAND GRANT
MOSES ROBERTSON   :

Date: March 9, 1808
Consideration: An entry made in the office of the Surveyor of the 6th
District of No. 38, founded on a certificate of No. 7, issued by the
Commissioners of E. Tn to Moses Robertson for 148 acres dated Aug. 15,
1897, 18 acres which is vested in John Willingford, the enterer
Description: Granted by the state of TN to John Willingford and his heirs
18 acres in Washington District on the south side of Holston River
To be affixed at Knoxville, Oct. 27, 1811, by Gov. Willie Blount, R.
Houston, Sec.
                        Edw. Scott, Reg. of E. TN
May 6, 1814, tax paid - 3 cents and 6 mills
Test: Mattw. Rhea, C.S.C.
Regst: June 16, 1814

EMBREW. ELISHU AND   :
ELIJAH EMBRU.   :
    TO   :   ARTICLE OF AGREEMENT
JOHN SPURGIN   :

Date: Feb. 22, 1811
Purpose of Agreement: To give to Embrew the right of digging, washing,
and taking away the oar(sic) from the oar bank lying within a few poles
of Spurgin's house. It being the bank which Walter King has generally got
oar(sic)f from, known by Spurgin bank. Embrew also to have privileges of
timber war said oar bank. Also to have a road said road to run by
Spurgin, born straight through his field wide enough for two wagons to
pass each other. Said road to lead through Spurgin's land toward the great
road that leads to Sanpp Ferry
Consideration: Sd Embrew to pay to Spurgin, 1/3 of a dollar per ton for
every ton of oar(sic) prepared for the furnace from this bank to be paid
as sd Spurgin may request at pactolos(sic) iron works. Except as much bar
iron as Spurgin may need for his own private use at the above rate this
contract to continue for 20 years from this date.
Wit: Miles Davis, jacob Slaughter, Martin Slaughter
Acknowledged: By John Spurgin, Elishue Embrew, Sullivan Co, TN, Nov,
1813
Test: Mattw. Rhea, C.S.C.
Regst: June 25, 1814

----

(404)   JOHN ACUFF   :
          TO   :   DEED OF CONVEYANCE
       JOHN ACUFF   :

Date: Oct. 28, 1813
Consideration: A valuable consideration
Amt of land: 24 1/2 acres
Location: Sullivan co, TN
Description: 24 1/2 acres in sd county and state
Wit: Timothy Hamilton, Elishu James, Thos. Jackson
Proven: By Elishu James, Thomas Jackson, Sullivan Co, TN, May, 1814
Test: Mattw. Rhea, C.S.C.
Regst: June 28, 1814

----

(405)   CHARLES JONES   :
          TO   :   DEED OF WARRANTY
       JOHN JONES   :

Date: March 7, 1813
Consideration: A valuable consideration
Amt of land: 83 acres
Location: Sullivan Co, TN
Description: 83 acres on the waters of Clear Creek
Wit: William Baskett, William Hulse
Acknowledged: By Charles Jones, Sullivan Co, TN, Feb. 1814
Test: Mattw. Rhea, C.S.C.
Regst: June 29, 1814

----

(406)   WALTER KING   :
               TO   :   DEED OF CONVEYANCE
          HIGGINS COPPINGER   :

          Date: AUG. 14, 1813
          Consideration: $500.00
          Amt of land: 300 acres
          Location: Sullivan Co, TN
          Description: Land containing 300 acres on the south side of Holston River
          Wit: James B. Boyd, William Boyd
          Proven: By James & William Boyd, Sullivan Co, TN, Feb, 1814
          Test: Mattw. Rhea, C.S.C.
          Regst: July 1, 1814

                              ----

(407)   JACOB LADY   :
               TO   :   DEED OF WARRANTY
          DAVID ROLLER   :

          Date: Feb. 24, 1814
          Consideration: A valuable consideration
          Amt of land: 82 acres
          Location: Sullivan Co, TN
          Description: Land containing 82 acres
          Wit: John Anderson, William Anderson
          Proven: By John & William Anderson, Sullivan Co, TN, May, 1814
          Test: Mattw. Rhea, C.S.C.
          Regst: July 1, 1814

                              ----

(407)   JACOB LADY   :
               TO   :   DEED OF WARRANTY
          DAVID ROLLER   :

          Date: Feb. 24, 1814
          Consideration: A valuable consideration
          Amt of land: 164 acres
          Location: Sullivan Co, TN
          Description: Land containing 164 acres more or less
          Wit: John Anderson, William Anderson
          Test: Mattw. Rhea, C.S.C.
          Regst: July 10, 1814

                              ----

(409)   STATE OF TENNESSEE :
          ARCHIBALD ROANE   :   LAND GRANT
               TO   :   NO. 2994
          THOMAS NICHOLS   :

          Date: Feb. 23, 1811
          Consideration: An entry made in the surveyor's office of the 6th District
          of No. 594, Feb. 23, 1811. Founded on a warrant of No. 594, issued to
          Archibald Roane to Thomas Nichols for 150 acres, oct. 24, 1809. 28 acres
          of which is assigned to William Lock the enterer.

Description: Land containing 28 acres in Sullivan Co.
To be affixed at Nashville, Oct. 9, 1813, by Gov. Willie Blount
Recorded: Feb. 4, 1814
June 8, 1814, rec'd tax on this grant   Scott, Reg. of E TN
Test: Mattw. Rhea, C.S.C.
Regst: July 2, 1814

(Page)
    (409)
```
STATE OF TENNESSEE    :
ARCHIBALD ROANE       :    LAND GRANT
        TO            :    NO. 2659
ISAAC HICKS, Dec'd    :
```

Date: May 25, 1809
Consideration: By virtue of a duplicate warrant, No. 1058, dated may 25, 1809, issued by Archibald Roane, Commissioner for E TN, to Isaac Hicks, dec'd, entered in the surveyor's office of the 6th District by No. 1112, March 9, 1812
Description: Land containing 136 acres, granted to Benjamin Webb assigned to Isaac Hicks' heirs
Affixed at Nashville, Oct. 9, 1812 Recorded Oct. 9, 1812, By Gov. Willie Blount, W.G. Blount, C.S.C.
                    by Edw. Scott, Reg. E TN
July 4, 1814, rec'd tax on within grant
Test: Mattw. Rhea, C.S.C.
Regst: July 4, 1814

----

(411)
```
JOHN HUGHES and Wife, SUFFEY HUGHES :
        TO                          :    DEED OF CONVEYANCE
JOHN DONALDSON                      :
```

Date: Nov. 18, 1811
Consideration: 100 lb. lawful money of VA
Amt of land: 200 acres
Location: Sullivan Co, TN
Description: Land containing 200 acres, by estimation, on the waters of Holston River and on both sides of Indian Creek
Wit: David Donaldson, john Swink, Matthias Swink
Acknowledged: Privately by Suffey   Chesley Kenney, C.C.
Relinquishment of Dower: Oct. 26, 1812, this deed of bargain and sold between John and Suffey Hughes to John Donaldson
Certified to Sullivan Co Court, Nov. 10, 1812
                    Erasmus Stribbing, Clk of Augusta Co Court
I, Alexander Robertson, presiding justice of the peace for Augusta Co Court certify that the foregoing certificate and attestations of Erasmus Stribbing, Clk of sd court is in due form, Nov. 15, 1812
                    Alex Robertson
Test: Mattw. Rhea, C.S.C.
Regst: July 1, 1814

----

(412)
```
ROBERT CHRISTIAN     :
        TO           :    DEED OF WARRANTY
JAMES ENGLISH        :
```

Date: May 17, 1813
Consideration: $25.00
Amt of land: 1/2 acre
Location: Sullivan Co, TN
Description: One lot containing 1/2 acre in Christiansville Boatyard
Wit: Joseph Everett, David Glyer
Proven: By Joseph Everett, David Glyer, Sullivan Co, TN, May, 1813
Test: Mattw. Rhea, C.S.C.
Regst: July 6, 1814

(Page)
(413)

JAMES ENGLISH	:	
TO	:	DEED OF WARRANTY
JOSEPH EVERETT	:	

Date: May 17, 1813
Consideration: $12.00
Amt of land: 1 acre
Location: Sullivan Co, TN
Description: One lot containing 1 acre in Christiansville Boatyard
Wit: David Glyer, John Simpson
Proven: By Glyer & Simpson, Sullivan Co, TN, May, 1813
Test: Mattw. Rhea, C.S.C.
Regst: July 7, 1814

----

(414)

ROBERT CHRISTIAN	:	
TO	:	DEED OF WARRANTY
BENJAMIN EVERETT, SR	:	

Date: May 15, 1813
Consideration: $25.00
Amt of land: 1/2 acre
Location: Sullivan Co, TN
Description: One lot containing 1/2 acre in Christiansville Boatyard
Wit: Joseph Everett, David Glyer
Proven: By Everett, Glyer, Sullivan Co, TN
Test: Mattw. Rhea, C.S.C.
Regst: July 7, 1814

----

(415)

STATE OF NORTH CAROLINA	:	
MOSES & SAMUEL LOONEY &	:	LAND GRANT
SAMUEL LOONEY(sic) and	:	NO. 483
SAMUEL JOHNSTON, GOV.	:	

Date: July 10, 1788
Consideration: 50 shillings for every hundred acres
Amt of land: 394 acres
Location: Sullivan Co
Description: Land containing 394 acres and improvement and island in holston on Holston River
By his Excellys Comd. J. Glasgow, Sam Johnston, Sec.
(Regst): (No date given)

GRANT SURVEY

A tract of land surveyed for Moses and Samuel Looney, Oct. 26, 1785. Enterer in Washington Co joining old Rentfrow incl. an improvement and island in Holston, enterer Oct. 6, 1779. Situate in NC, Sullivan Co on Holston River.

Chain Carrier: N.B. Elijah Cross, Wm Cross

George Vincent, D.S.

This certifies that I have amended and corrected the errors in this patent grant of No. 483, July 10, 1788, for 394 acres of land agreeable to an order issued from Sullivan Co court dated, July 18, 1809 and certified by Mattw. Rhea. Clerk and have stricken out the ward (Six) (East) (Twenty) and have inserted on line there of the word (Three) (West) and (Seventy) and recorded the same with the certificate of survey as corrected at full truth in my office, Oct. 10, 1809.

R. Houston, Sec.

Aug. 5, 1813, rec'd state tax on this grant - seventy nine cents.

GRANT: seventy nine cents

Test: Mattw. Rhea, C.S.C.

Regst: July 8, 1814

------------------d

(417)

STATE OF NORTH CAROLINA :
ALEXANDER MARTIN, GOV. : LAND GRANT
      TO : NO. 64
WILLIAM PEMBERTON :

Date: Oct. 23, 1788
Consideration: Fifty shillings for every hundred acres
Amt of land: 200 acres
Location: Sullivan Co
Description: Land containing 200 acres on both sides of Sinking Creek
By his Excellys Comd. J. Glasgow, Sec. Alex Martin

----

(417)

LAND SURVEY

May 15, 1781. Surveyed for William Pemberton
Land in Sullivan Co, NC, on both sides of Sinking Creek

Stockely Donaldson, D.S.
David Shelby, C.S.

Sec. Office, TN

This is to certify that I have amended and corrected the errors in this patent grant, No. 64, Oct. 23, 1783, for 200 acres. Agreeable to an order from Sullivan Co Court dated Sept. 18, 1809, and certified by their clerk by striking out the word (East) in the fourth time and inserting in line there of the word (West) and rec'd the same with the certificate of survey as corrected. At full rights in my office Oct. 10, 1809

R. Houston, Sec.

Regst: July 9, 1814

----

(418)

STATE OF TENNESSEE :
LANDON CARTER : LAND GRANT
      TO : NO. 2063
JOHN GEST :

Date: Nov. 2, 1810
Consideration: An entry made in the surveyor's office of the 6th District
of No. 550, founded on a warrant of No. 2315, issued by Landon Carter to
John Gest for 150 acres, Sept. 19, 1781. Entry dated Nov. 2, 1810, and
assigned by Gest to John Thompson and by him to David Shaver, the
enterer
Description: There is granted by state of TN to David Shaver and his
heirs, land containing 30 acres in Washington District, Sullivan Co, on the
waters of Reedy Creek.
To be affixed at Knoxville, Oct. 29, 1811, by Gov. Willie Blount, R.
Houston, Sec., Recorded Oct. 29, 1811
                              Edw. Scott, Reg. of E TN
April 1, 1812, rec'd state tax on this grant - 6 cents
Test: Mattw. Rhea, C.S.C.
Regst: July 11, 1814

----

(419)   THOMAS CARRIER   :
                 TO   :   DEED OF LAND
            NATHAN & CALEB MORRELL :

Date: aug. 17, 1813
Consideration: $300.00
Amt of land: 25 acres
Location: Sullivan Co
Description: Land containing 25 acres on the south side of Holston River
Wit: Thomas, Edmund, and Daniel Morrell
Proven: By Thomas & Edmund Morrell, Sullivan Co, TN, Feb, 1814
Test: Mattw. Rhea, C.S.C.
Regst: July 11, 1814

----

(420)   HARMAN LATTURE   :
                 TO   :   QUIT CLAIM DEED
            JONAS NICELY   :

Date: Feb. 20,1810
Consideration: A valuable consideration
Amt of land: 50 acres
Location: Sullivan Co
Description: Land containing 50 acres by virtue of a grant dated Sept. 26,
1809, No. 672
Wit: John Anderson
Acknowledged: By Harman Latture, Sullivan Co, Feb, 1810
Test: Mattw. Rhea, C.S.C, by Robt. Rhea, D.C.
Regst: July 11, 1814

----

(421)   RICHARD BASKETT   :
                 TO   :   DEED OF CONVEYANCE
            BENJAMIN BIRDWELL   :

Date: March 16, 1814
(Consideration): (None given)
Amt of land: 100 acres

Location: Sullivan Co, TN
Description: Land on the south side of Holston River on Kendricks Creek
incl. a grist mill and saw mill
Wit: Joseph Clark, David Paxton*, William Smith
Proven: By Joseph Clark, David Saxton*, Sullivan Co, TN, May, 1814
Test: Mattw. Rhea, C.S.C, by Robt Rhea, D.C.
Regst: (No date given)

(*Note: Both names given)

(Page)

(421)   STATE OF TENNESSEE   :
         WILLIAM SNODGRASS   :   LAND GRANT
                 TO   :   NO. 2318
         LEONARD HART   :

         Date: Feb. 1, 1796
         Consideration: An entry made in the surveyor's office of the 6th District,
         No. ?, founded on a warrant of No. 224, issued by William Snodgrass to
         Leonard Hart for 239 acres, Feb. 1, 1796
         Description: Land containing 130 acres in Washington District on the south
         side of Holston River
         To be affixed at Knoxville, June 17, 1812, by Gov. Willie Blount, W.G.
         Blount, Sec., Recorded June 17, 1812
                                        Edw. Scott, Reg. of E TN
         March 17, 1813, rec'd tax on this grant
         Test: Mattw. Rhea, C.S.C.
         Regst: July 14, 1814

         ----

(422)   JOHN PUNCH   :
                 TO   :   MORTGAGE
         ISAAC ROBBINS   :

         Date: Dec. 15, 1813
         Consideration: $729.15
         Amt of land: Not stated
         Location: Sullivan Co
         Description: Land on the north side of the main road in the new addition
         attached to the town of Blountville
         Condition as follows: Should john Punch discharge a certain hand or bill
         mingle dated Nov. 25, in the present year, for $729.15 to be done on or
         before March 1, next, in the event the obligation to be made null and
         void, as respects as force and virtue otherwise to be and remain in full
         force and effect for the said Isaac to have forever the lot of ground
         Wit: E.R. Dulaney, T.V. Rockhold
         Proven: By William Rockhold, Elkanah R. Dulaney, Sullivan Co, TN, Feb,
         1814
         Test: Mattw. Rhea, C.S.C, by Robt Rhea, D.C.
         Regst: July 14, 1814

         ----

(423)   JOHN PUNCH   :
                 TO   :   DEED OF CONVEYANCE
         LIBBURN HENDERSON, Heirs   :
         Heirs of Will King, Dec'd.   :

                              146

Date: April 11, 1814
Consideration: A valuable consideration
Amt of land: Not stated
Location: Sullivan Co
Description: Oct. 26, 1811, James Angel conveyed to John Punch two lots of ground which by reference to the Register's office of Sullivan Co, Book H, pgs 200 and 207. One moity was intended to secure to William Trigg the surveying executors of William King, dec'd. A sum of money due to the sd William in his lifetime for merchand. On bought and secured at the Blountville store of William, dec'd. The other moety for the use and benefit of John Punch to secure a certain sum of money then due to John from James Angel non(sic) therefore for the purpose of transfering to the legal heirs of William King, dec'd, (individual) in the aforesaid two lots of land

John Punch doth by these presents sell to Libburn L. Henderson, in trust or executore aforesaid, for the use of the heirs and to their only use intrust to L.L. Henderson. I, John Punch, do warrant and defend the one half of all the lots of ground that James Angel conveyed to me as aforesaid which does appear of record in the Register's office as aforesaid unto him the sd L.L. Henderson for the purpose aforesaid
Wit: T.W. Rockhold, Law'r. Snapp, Jr.
Proven: By William Rockhold, Lawrence Snapp, Jr, Sullivan Co, Tn, May, 1814
Test: Mattw. Rhea, C.S.C, by Robt. Rhea, D.C.
Regst: July 4, 1814

(Page)
(424)

JOHN PUNCH	:	
TO	:	DEED OF TRUST
PETER MAYO	:	

Date: Dec. 23, 1813
Purpose: John Punch is indebted to the concern of Smith, Trigg and Carson of the state of VA in the sum of 1451 2s- 10 1/2 D. VA currency for which he has executed his obligation or bill single dated Nov. 16, 1813. By which he binds himself in 90 days thereafter to pay the sd concern the sum of A 145-2c 10 1/2 D. And where as also Punch stands indebted to the firm of Henderson & Trigg of the county and state aforesaid by open accounty(sic) our rent commencing from the year 1810 to the present date which after deducting the credit thereon leaves a balance due the sd firm of 109.49 dollars
In order to secure payment of debts totaling 177 L, 19s, 10 1/2 D. With interest in consideration further sum of 1.00 to him the sd John Punch paid by sd Peter Mayo following land to be sold.
Amt of land: (A)- 120 acres (B)- 1 house & lot in Blountville (C)- all my right in and 2 other lots, buildings ther on containing 1/2 acre
Description: (A)- one tract of land in Sullivan Co, TN, within 3 miles of Blountville, containing 120 acres surveyed by John Anderson, April 23, 1813, (B)- One house and lot in the town of Blountville, being the same conveyed to me by John Phagan, 1813, (C)- All my right in and two other lots, buildings thereon which was purchased of James Angela by myself 1/2 for my own benefit. The other 1/2 for William King, dec'd, and conveyed to me by deed dated Oct. 26, 1811, containing 1/2 acre, which was conveyed to Punch by Angela

147

Condition: If Punch fails to pay sd Smith, Trigg and Carson, their heirs or assigns the above amt. with interest thereon acquiring in 12 months from this date and also to the sd Henderson & Trigg with interest the amt. of their sd account by Dec. 23, 1814. Then this obligation to be void otherwise the sd Mayo in trust aforesaid shall proceed by public sale to sell the land, houses and lots to make the sum of 177 L. - 17s 10-(sic) As aforesaid with the expense of drawing and making of this deed and 5 Commissioners for selling the same at some public place in Blountville. Should there be any surplus over the above amts, Punch is to receive the same

Wit: W. Rockhold, James H. Barnett
Proven: By William Rockhold, James Barnett, Sullivan Co, TN, May, 1814
Test: Mattw. Rhea, C.S.C, by Mattw.(sic) Rhea, D.C
Regst: July 15, 1814

(Page)
(426)

WILLIAM DELANEY	:	
TO	:	DEED OF GIFT
His Children- ELIZABETH, NANCY R,	:	
SARAH G, & JOHN R. DELANEY*	:	

Reason: On acct of one and infirmity known the certainty of death and the uncertainty of time thereof
Consideration: Love and affection for the sd children
No. of negroes - 25, with their increase
Amt of land: All that is my just right in Hawkins Co and all in Duck River, Ranare(sic) Co, 100 acres on Holston River. To my son, John Delaney- the tract of land I now live on and 3 negroes. To Elizabeth Delaney- the following negroes; Jordan, Mary, Grace, Harry, James, Joseph, Tom and Will with all their issue and increase. To Nancy R. Delaney- Ishmas, Jane Munday, Caya, Charles, Sirah, Fan, with all their issue and increase. To Sarah G. Dulaney*- Hanner, Pat Rody, Lear, Ned, Ben, Edy, with their issue and increase. To John R. Dulaney- Jacob, Suck and Stephen with their increase.
Description: The aforesaid land in Hawkins Co and Duck Renare(sic) Co and 100 acres of land adjoiner of land on south side of Holston River adj. John Carwood when the title to the 100 acres is adjusted my daughters to share sd land equally
To my son John- I give the sd tract I live on now and all the lands adjoining the same
The Reservation same shall be their property at my death. I do receive my living out of the above property
Wit: Samuel Hopkins, W. Rockhold
N.B. always during my daughters living single they are to have ther living out of my plantation
Wit: Samuel Hopkins, W. Rockhold
Acknowledged: By William Delaney, Sullivan Co, TN, Feb, 1814
Test: Mattw. Rhea, C.S.C, by Mattw.(sic) Rhea, D.C.
Regst: July 16, 1814

(*Note: Name spelled both ways)

(427)	MICHAEL CROWBARGER & ENE, His wife	:	
	TO	:	DEED OF WARRANTY
	THOMAS HOPKINS	:	

Date: May 10, 1813
Consideration: $300.00
Amt of land: 33 acres
Location: Sullivan Co
Description: Land containing 33 acres on the south side of Holston River
incl. the first bottom below the mouth of Horse Creek, and bounded by
Bay's Mounty
Wit: Joseph Everett, R. Netherland, David Glyer
Proven: By R. Netherland, Joseph Everett, Sullivan Co, TN, May, 1813
Test: Mattw. Rhea, C.S.C
Regst: July 18, 1814

(Page)
(428)   THOMAS HOPKINS   :
               TO   :   DEED OF WARRANTY
         MICHAEL CROWBARGER :

Date: May 10, 1813
Consideration: $500.00
Amt of land: 200 acres
Location: Sullivan Co, TN
Description: Land on the waters of Reedy Creek
Wit: Joseph Everett, R. Netherland, David Glyer
Proven: By Joseph Everett, R. Netherland, Sullivan Co, TN, May, 1813
Test: Mattw. Rhea, C.S.C
Regst: July 18, 1814

----

(429)   LARKIN CLEVELAND and FANNY, His wife :
               TO   :   DEED OF GIFT
         Our Daughter, LUCINDA LESTER, Wife of :
         German Lester   :

Consideration: Natural love and affection which we bear toward our
daughter, Lucinda Lester, wife of German Lester
Larkin Cleveland and Fanny, his wife, do grant unto German Lester and
his heirs forever all right which (they) have in and to the estate of David
Wright, dec'd, father of Fanny who formerly resided near the iron works
on the north fork of Holston River, E TN
Wit: Samuel Jones, Jas. Reed
Giles Court, TN, April, 1814
        The within Deed of Gift from Larkin and Fanny cleveland to German
Lester, was produced in open court at sd turn and proven to be the act
and deed of Larkin and Fanny Cleveland by the oaths of Samuel Jones and
James Reed. Examined in court privately from her husband, Fanny
Cleveland says she voluntarily executed sd deed.
                        Cert. by James Berry, Clk of Giles Circuit Court
                        April 16, 1814
Thomas Sturat, one of the judges of the Circuit Court of TN, now by law
presiding in the 5th Circuit, which incl. Giles Co, certify the above is in
due form and legal signed and sealed
                        Thomas Sturat
                        April 16, 1814
Regst: July 18, 1814

149

(430)   SAMUEL HAMPTON   :
              TO   :   DEED OF WARRANTY
      ELISHA COLE   :

Date: Feb. 16, 1813
Consideration: $100.00
Amt of land: Not stated
Location: Sullivan Co
Description: The tract of land sold by John Wallace to Job Key and by Key to James King and by King to Samuel Hampton which lies on the east side of Beaver Creek, adj. Elisha Cole present residence (of Wallace Grant) to the brink of the creek, with all right to land
Acknowledged: By Samuel Hampton, Sullivan Co, TN, Feb, 1813
Test: Mattw. Rhea, C.S.C.
Regst: July 20, 1814

----

(431)   STATE OF TENNESSEE   :
      (ARCHIBALD ROANE)   :   LAND GRANT
              TO   :   NO. 1576
      JOB KEY   :

Date: Oct. 15, 1808
Consideration: An entry made in the Surveyor's office of the 6th District of No. 164, dated Oct. 15, 1808, founded on a duplicate warrant of No. 495, issued by Archibald Roane to Job Key for 640 acres dated Feb. 9, 1808. 180 acres of which was assigned by job Key to Jonathan Webb, the enterer
Description: Land containing 180 acres in Washington Dictrict on the south side of Holston River being an occupant claim. Surveyed Aug. 25, 1808. To be affixed at Knoxville, July 2, 1810, by Gov. Willie Blount, R. Houston, Sec. Recorded July 2, 1810
                          Edw. Scott, Reg. of E TN
July 22, 1814, tax paid on within grant
Test: Mattw. Rhea, C.S.C.
Regst: July 22, 1814

----

(432)   SOLOMON SMITH   :
              TO   :   BILL OF SALE
      JOHN GIFFORD   :

Date: July 21, 1814
Consideration: $310.00
    Solomon Smith sold unto John Gifford one negro girl named Lucy aged 11 yrs for $310.00
Wit: James Phagan, Abraham Looney
Proven: By James Phagan, Abraham Looney, Sullivan Co, TN, May, 1814
Test: Mattw. Rhea, C.S.C, by Mattw.(sic) Rhea, D.C.
Regst: July 26, 1814

----

(432)   WILLIAM DULANEY   :
              TO   :   BILL OF SALE
      JOHN GIFFORD   :

Date: Sept. 30, 1813
Consideration: $450.00
    William Dulaney sold to John Gifford one negro fellow named Samuel
aged 28 yrs for $450.00
Wit: J. Gitt, Elk. R. Dulaney
Proven: By Elkanah Dulaney, Jacob Gitt, Sullivan Co, TN, May, 1814
Test: Mattw. Rhea, C.S.C, by Mattw.(sic) Rhea, D.C
Regst: July 26, 1814

(Page)
(432)   ROBERT BIRDWELL   :
              TO   :   BILL OF SALE
         JONATHAN BAUGHMAN   :

         Date: Dec. 31, 1811
         Consideration: $600.00
             Robert Birdwell hath bargained to Jonathan Baughman one negro boy
         named Abram
         Wit: Robert Allison, Wm Birdwell
         Proven: By Samuel Powell, Jugh(?) Martin, Sullivan Co, TN, Feb, 1811
         (1812?)
         Recorded: Vol. 5, pg 405
         Test: Mattw. Rhea, C.S.C, by Mattw(sic) Rhea, D.C.
         Regst: July 26, 1814

----

(433)   JOHN WEAVER   :
              TO   :   DEED OF CONVEYANCE
         THOMAS HOWLEY   :

         Date: Sept. 13, 1811
         Consideration: $500.00
         Amt of land: 83 acres
         Location: Sullivan Co, TN
         Description: Land containing 83 acres in Sullivan Co
         Wit: John Jennings, George Weaver, W.B. Childress
         Proven: By John Jennings, George Weaver, Sullivan Co, TN, Nov, 1811
         Test: Mattw. Rhea, C.S.C.
         Regst: July 27, 1814

----

(433)   GEORGE ROLLER   :
              TO   :   DEED OF WARRANTY
         HENRY MAGERT   :

         Date: Feb. 17, 1807
         Consideration: $150.00
         Amt of land: 140 acres
         Location: Sullivan Co
         Description: Land containing 140 acres more or less
         Wit: Robert Benhaw, Jr, John Jennings
         (Proven): By John Jennings, George Weaver, Sullivan Co, TN
         Test: Mattw. Rhea, C.S.C.
         Regst: July 27, 1814

151

(433)　　GEORGE ROLLER　　　　　　　:
　　　　　　　　TO　　　　　　　　　　　:　　　DEED OF WARRANTY
　　　　　　HENRY MAGERT　　　　　　:

Date: Feb. 17, 1807
Consideration: $150.00
Amt of land: 140 acres
Location: Sullivan Co
Description: Land containing 140 acres more or less
Wit: Robert Benhaw, Jr, John Jennings
Acknowledged: By George Roller in open court
Regst: July 29, 1814

----

(434)　　JOHN HART　　　　　　　　:
　　　　　　　　TO　　　　　　　　　　:　　　DEED OF WARRANTY
　　　　　　LEONARD HART　　　　　:

Date: Aug. 24, 1812
Consideration: $250.00
Amt of land: 531 acres
Location: Sullivan Co
Description: A tract of land in Sullivan Co, being part of two tracts of
land, one granted to John Pitner for 401 acres and the other granted to
Leonard Hart for 130 acres
Wit: James Gregg, John Smith
Proven: By James Gregg, John Smith, Sullivan Co, TN, May, 1813
Test: Mattw. Rhea, C.S.C.
Regst: July 29, 1814

----

(434)　　STATE OF TENNESSEE　　　　　　:
　　　　　　ARCHIBALD ROANE　　　　　　　:　　　LAND GRANT
　　　　　　　　TO　　　　　　　　　　　　:　　　NO. 2995
　　　　　　WM TYRELL & GEORGE GORDON　　:

Date: Feb. 4, 1812
Consideration: An entry made in the surveyor's office of the 6th District
of No. 991, dated Feb. 4, 1812, founded on a certificate of No. 93, issued
by Archibald Roane to Wm Tyrell and George Gordon for 381 acres, dated
Jan. 25, 1809, 40 acres which is assigned to John Blevins
Description: State of TN granted to John Blevins and is heirs a tract of
land containing 40 acres. Surveyed Feb. 28, 1812.
To be affixed at Nashville, Oct. 9, 1813, by Gov. Willie Blount, W.G.
Blount, Sec. Recorded Nov. 20, 1813
　　　　　　　　　　　　　　　Edw. Scott, Reg. of E TN
Test: Mattw. Rhea, C.S.C
Regst: Aug. 16, 1814

----

(435)　　JOHN BROWN　　　　　　　　　:
　　　　　　　　TO　　　　　　　　　　　:　　　DEED OF CONVEYANCE
　　　　　　PATRICK HENRY MADISON　　　:

Date: Oct. ?, 1813 (No day given)

Consideration: $10.00
Amt of land: 480 acres
Location: Sullivan Co, TN
Description: Land on the waters of Holton River containing, by survey, 480 acres
Franklin Circuit Court:
        At the courthouse in Frankfort, Oct. 18, 1813
The within deed of sale from John Brown to Patrick Henry Madison was acknowledged by John Brown to be his act and ordered to be certified.
        I, Francis O. Blair, Clerk do affix my private seal
Commonwealth of Kentucky:
        I, Henry Davidge(sic), one of the judges for sd commonwealth, certify that Francis P. Blair is the clerk of sd court and that the above attestation is in due form, Oct. 25, 1813
                                        Henry Davidge, C.J.C.
Within deed of conveyance is certificate of the clerk of Franklin Circuit Court as also the cert. of Henry Davidge, one of the Circuit Judges of the Commonwealth of KY, it is ordered by the court that it be admitted to Registrator.
Aug. 17, 1814, rec'd tax on within deed from Samuel May - 96 cents, also 75 cents
Test: Mattw. Rhea, C.S.C, by Mattw(sic) Rhea, D.C.
Regst: Aug. 17, 1814
Being part of a tract of land granted to John Buckanan for 1200 acres by patent dated May 20, 1750, and conveyed by William Preston, Executor of sd Buckanan, unto Evan Shelby and John Shelby by them conveyed to John Brown by deed dated Aug. 12, 1783

(Page)
(437)   THOMAS HOPKINS   :
                    TO   :   DEED OF CONVEYANCE
        JOSEPH POWEL, JR.   :

        Date: Aug. 17, 1814
        Consideration: $1,400.00 of lawful money
        Amt of land: 207 acres
        Location: Sullivan Co
        Description: Land on both sides of the road leading from Yancy aold place to Blountville incl. the houses and other improvements in the occupation of Thomas Hopkins
        Wit: (No names given)
        Acknowledged: By Thomas Hopkins, Sullivan Co, TN, Aug, 1814
        Test: Mattw. Rhea, C.S.C.
        Regst: Aug. 19, 1814
                        ----

(438)   JOHN TIPTON   :
                    TO   :   DEED OF CONVEYANCE
        JAMES RHEA   :

        Date: Aug. 16, 1814
        Consideration: $110.00
        Amt of land: 1 acre and 2 square poles
        Location: Sullivan Co, TN

Description: Land adj the land of James Rhea on the north side of the
main street of Blountville containing one acre and two square poles
Wit: John Jennings, William Anderson
Acknowledged: By John Tipton, Sullivan Co, TN, Aug, 1814
(Wit): (No names given)
(Regst): (No date given)

(Page)
(438)

JOHN TIPTON   :
    APPOINTED BY   :   POWER OF ATTORNEY
GEORGE & JOSEPH GREENWAY   :

Date: Sept. 9, 1810
Purpose: John Tipton of Blountville, Sullivan Co, TN, on Sept 9, 1810,
appointed by George and Joseph Greenway, attorney duly authorized to
dispose of, in their names, two entries of land made by John Webb, dec'd,
their father in law in his name in his lifetime in John Armstrong's office
of 2500 acres each one entry of No. 2545, the other of No. 2548, both
entries purporting to have been made May 25, 1784, likewise authorizing
one to draw warrants thereon or do whatsoever else I, John Tipton, might
think proper in disposing of sd warrants as reproven to sd power will fully
appear and whereas the sd John Tipton did afterwards make application to
the legislature of the state of TN, for an act to authorize the drawing sd
warrants and which was granted and the Commissioners authorized to issue
duplicated there for since which I sold to Thomas Hopkins of Sullivan Co,
TN
Description: 3,300 acres of good land warrants in consideration of which he
paid me $1,670.00. Being desirous of transfering and putting him in
possesion of the warrant and it being at this time inconvient to me to
attend in person at the Commissioner's office where the greater part of
the warrants and at this time, I do hereby constitute inpower and appoint
my friend, Thomas McCarry, of the town of Knoxville and Nathan Shipley
of Washington Co or either of them to make free use of my name in
transferring and subscribing my name as attorney in fact for George and
Joseph Greenway, in presence of their power in me virted to each and
every duplicate warrant in their name issued by the Commissioners of E
TN. Remaining in Commissioners' office at Knoxville from the before
recitted two warrants of 2500 acres each to the before mentioned Thomas
Hopkins then deliver the same to him for me and in my name the whole
amt which I advised is about 2753 acres containing in 27 warrants the
before named Thomas McCarry or Nathan Shipley as hereby refuse to and
fully authorized to transfer over to him this aforesaid Thomas McCarry of
Hopkins all the claim of them George and Joseph Greenway as before
mentioned to the same which shall be as good and valid to all interest
and purpose as if done in my own hand.
Wit: John Anderson, James P. Nulse
Test: Mattw. Rhea, C.S.C
Regst: Aug. 19, 1814

----

(439)   GEORGE & JOSEPH GREENWAY   :
                APPOINT   :   POWER OF ATTORNEY
    COL. JOHN TIPTON, Attorney   :

Date: Sept. 9, 1813

Purpose: George and Joseph Greenway, do appoint Colonel John Tipton our
Attorney and we do hereby authorized him in our names to dispose to such
persons as he may think proper our interest (in) two entries made by John
Webb, our father-in-law, dec'd, in his lifetime in Armstrong office of 2500
acres each one entry ofNo. 2545; and the other 2548 both entries made
May 25, 1784. No. 2548 John Webb 2500 in Green Co on the waters of
Mississippi River
Description: Entry claim or Survey No. 2547 thence running several courses
so as to incl the complement the other May 25, 1784, No. 2545, John
Webb. 2500 in Green Co on the east side of Mississippi River. John May
deem expediment to enable him affectually to dispose of sd entries or to
draw warrants thereon or to do whatever else with sd entries that John
may think proper and as may best suit him and to recover payment and to
give all such receipts in our name as may be deemed necessary and with
the sd Geo & Joseph Greenway and our heirs well at all times hereafter
ratify confirm and make good all and every such act as John shall and
may do in the presences.
Wit: (No names given)
Acknowledged: By Joseph Wallace, Chairman of Court of Pleas and Qrtr
Session
    I certify that Joseph Wallace was acting J.P. in Sullivan Co, Sept.
10, 1813
Test: Mattw. Rhea, C.S.C
Regst: Aug. 19, 1814

----

(440)

JOHN TIPTON	:	
TO	:	DEED OF CONVEYANCE
JOHN RHEA	:	

Date: Aug. 16, 1814
Consideration: $1,000.00
Amt of land: 69 acres
Location: Sullivan Co, TN
Description: Land adj. the town of Blountville containing 69 acres
Wit: John Jennings, William Anderson
Acknowledged: By John Tipton
Test: Mattw. Rhea, C.S.C
Regst: Aug. 20, 1814

----

(441)

AQUILLA CROSS	:	
TO	:	DEED OF CONVEYANCE
PHILLIP HOBBAUGH	:	

Date: Aug. 11, 1814
Consideration: $850.00
Amt of land: 118 acres
Location: Sullivan Co, TN
Description: Land containing 118 acres more or less
Wit: Thos Cawood, George R. Cowan
Acknowledged: By Aquilla Cross, Sullivan Co, TN, Aug, 1814
Test: Mattw. Rhea, C.S.C.
Regst: Aug. 20, 1814

----

(442)   JOSEPH CLARK   :
                   TO   :   DEED OF CONVEYANCE
        HENRY MAUK   :

Date: Aug. 15, 1814
Consideration: $100.00
Amt of land: 30 acres
Location: Sullivan Co
Description: Land containing 30 acres more or less
Wit: Thomas Morrison, William Hester
Proven: By Thomas Morrison, William Hester, Sullivan Co, TN, Aug, 1814
Test: Mattw. Rhea, C.S.C.
Regst: Aug. 20, 1814

----

(442)   JOHN STEADMAN   :
                   TO   :   DEED OF CONVEYANCE
        ROBERT TRIBET   :

Date: Aug. 2, 1814
Consideration: $350.00
Amt of land: 60 acres
Location: Sullivan Co, TN
Description: Land containing 60 acres on the waters of Horse Creek
Wit: William Basket, Lot O. Gott, Henry Hartman
Proven: By William Baskett, Henry Hartman, Sullivan Co, TN, Aug, 1814
Test: Mattw. Rhea, C.S.C.
Regst: Aug. 20, 1814

----

(443)   JOHN STEADMAN   :
                   TO   :   DEED OF CONVEYANCE
        HENRY HARTMAN   :

Date: Aug. 2, 1814
Consideration: $200.00
Amt of land: 60 acres
Location: Sullivan Co, TN
Description: Land containing 60 acres in aforesaid county and state
Wit: William Baskett, Lot O. Gott, Robert Trivett(sic)
Proven: By William Baskett, Robert Trivett, Sullivan Co, TN, Aug, 1814
Test: Mattw. Rhea, C.S.C, by his D.C.
Regst: Aug. 20, 1814

----

(444)   HENRY SHUMAKER   :
                   TO   :   DEED OF CONVEYANCE
        DANIEL SHUMAKER   :

Date: Aug. 15, 1814
Consideration: $150.00
Amt of land: 72 acres
Location: Sullivan Co

Description: One half of a tract containing 72 acres more or less, the whole tract being likely the property of John Shumaker*, dec'd, and one half heretofore conveyed by Judith Shoemaker* and Jeremiah Shoemaker* to the sd Daniel
Wit: (No names given)
Acknowledged: By Henry Shumaker, Sullivan Co, TN, Aug, 1814
Test: Mattw. Rhea, C.S.C, by his D.C.
Regst: Aug. 20, 1814

(*Note: Names spelled both ways)

(Page)
(445)
SAMUEL BAUGHMAN   :
      TO   :   DEED OF CONVEYANCE
His Sons- NATHAN &   :
JONATHAN BAUGHMAN   :

Date: Aug. 10, 1814
Consideration: $1400.00
Amt of land: Not stated
Location: Sullivan Co, TN
Description: Land except a meadow lying on Clear Creek which I hold during my and my wife's natural life then to be given up into the hand of my sons and heirs forever. The mills and all other improvement together with the balance of sd tract of land to be the present use of sd Jonathan and Nathan Baughman and heirs forever the land and premises
Wit: Jacob Molock, John Mays, Robert B. Wallace, John Chester
Proven: By Jacob Molock, John Mays, Sullivan Co, Tn, Aug, 1814
Test: Mattw. Rhea, C.S.C, by his D.C.
Regst: Aug. 20, 1814

----

(445)
GEORGE MOLOCK*   :
      TO   :   DEED OF CONVEYANCE
JONATHAN BAUGHMAN   :

Date: Nov. 8, 1813
Consideration: $600.00
Amt of land: 90 acres
Location: Sullivan Co
Description: Land containing 90 acres on Horse Creek incL all the lands and improvements where Thomas McLane now lives and joining and running by the lines that George Vincent surveyed for George Morelock* and part of a tract of land on sd creek granted to Vachel Dillingham by patent under the seal of the state of NC, together with the houses, buildings way, woods, water courses, mines, minerals, hereditaments and appurtenances ways appertaining there unto with all
ents issues and profits there of and all the estate property claim and demand whatsoever of him or by him the sd George Morelock
Wit: John Mays, Thomas Pierce, Jacob Morelock
Proven: By Jacob Morelock, John Mays, Sullivan Co, TN, Aug, 1814
Test: Mattw. Rhea, C.S.C, by his deputy
Regst: Aug. 20, 1814

(*Note: Name spelled both ways)

157

JOHN TIPTON   :
        TO   :   DEED OF CONVEYANCE
JOHN FELLYERS   :

Date: Aug. 15, 1814
Consideration: $150.00
Amt of land: (228 acres)
Location: Sullivan Co
Description: Land on the north side of Holston River incl. the plantation where the sd Stephen now lives being part of two tracts of land granted to John Chrisman, dec'd, containing 228 acres more or less
Wit: Joseph W. Looney, Frederick Hull
Proven: By Joseph W. Looney, Frederick Hull, Sullivan Co, TN, Aug, 1814
Test: Mattw. Rhea, C.S.C, by his deputy
Regst: Aug. 20, 1814

----

(448)   SAMUEL HAMPTON   :
        TO   :   DEED OF CONVEYANCE
BENJAMIN PHILLIPS   :

Date: Aug. 16, 1814
Consideration: A valuable consideration
Amt of land: 40 acres
Location: Sullivan Co, TN
Description: Land containing 40 acres in state and county aforesaid
Wit: John Anders(on)
Acknowledged: By Samuel Hampton, Sullivan Co, TN, Aug, 1814
Test: Mattw. Rhea, C.S.C, by his deputy
Regst: Aug. 20, 1814

----

(449)   SAMUEL JOBE, JOHN COX, WILLIAM JACKSON   :
GEORGE JACKSON, THOMAS BARRON,   :
LYDDA JAKE & DORCAS JOBE   :   QUIT-CLAIMED
        TO   :DEED OF CONVEYANCE
JACOB, ZACHARIAH, JAMES &   :
GEORGE JOBE   :

Date: May 13, 1808
Consideration: A valuable consideration
Amt of land: 230 acres
Location: Sullivan Co, TN
Purpose: To release and convey for ever quit claimed their shares of an undivided estate in fee simple to them belonging by descent.
Description: Land occupied by the aforesaid Jacob Jobe, dec'd, on a branch of Kinderick Creek, containing 230 acres
Wit: Charles Jones, James Boyd, Nathan Shipley
Proven: By Charles Jones, James Boyd, Sullivan Co, Tn, Aug, 1814
Test: Mattw. Rhea, C.S.C, by his deputy
Regst: Aug. 20, 1814

----

(450)

```
ISAREL W. BONHAM        :
        TO              :    DEED OF CONVEYANCE
JAMES HUGHES            :
```

Date: Oct. 10, 1813
Consideration: $200.00
Amt of land: 50 acres
Location: Sullivan Co, TN
Description: Land on the west end originally part of the plantation on
which the sd James Hughes now liveth with the appurtenances and all the
_____ title claim interest and demand of him the sd Isarel W. Bonham
either in law or equity to have and to hold the sd 50 acres of land with
the appurtenances unto him the sd James Hughes his heirs and assigns
forever
Wit: Timothy Millard, George Hughes
Proven: By Timothy Millare, George Hughes, Sullivan Co, TN, May, 1814
Test: Mattw. Rhea, C.S.C, by his deputy
Regst: Aug. 20, 1814

----

(451)

```
STATE OF TENNESSEE      :
COMMISSIONERS OF E TN   :    LAND GRANT
        TO              :    NO. 1586
JAMES OFFILL            :
```

Date: April 24, 1807
Consideration: An entry made in Carter's office of No. 648, dated Nov. 28,
1778, founded on a warrant of the same number and adjudged valued by
the commissioners of E TN, april 24, 1807, for 97 acres of land
Description: There is granted by the state of TN to James Offill the
enterer and his heirs, a certain tract containing 97 acres in the
Washington District on the south side of Holston River
To be affixed at Knoxville, June 8, 1810, by Gov. Willie Blount, R.
Houston, Sec, Recorded June 30, 1810
                        Edw. Scott, Reg of E TN
Aug. 18, 1814, rec'd tax on within grant - 19 cents and 4 mills
Test: Mattw. Rhea, C.S.C, by his deputy
Regst: Aug. 20, 1814

----

(452)

```
JOHN MAYOR             :
        TO             :    DEED OF CONVEYANCE
JACOB WORK             :
```

Date: Oct. 30, 1797
Consideration: $333 and 1/3 dollars
Amt of land: 300 acres
Location: Sullivan Co, TN
Description: Land which I claim as the legal heir of Jacob Mayor, dec'd,
on the north side of Holston River
Wit: Nathaniel Taylor, Jacob Fleenor
Proven: By Jacob Fleenor, Sullivan Co, Nov, 1797
Test: Mattw. Rhea, C.S.C.

Carter Co May, 1814:
        Proven by Nathaniel Taylor and admitted May 11, 1814
                            Geo Williams, C.C.C.
Sullivan Co, TN, Aug, 1814: The within Deed of Conveyance was proven in
open court by the oath of Jacob Fleener
Test: Mattw. Rhea, C.S.C, by his deputy
Regst: Aug. 20, 1814

(Page)
(453)   JOSEPH TORBET   :
                    TO   :   DEED OF CONVEYANCE
               JOHN KING & JOHN ALISON   :

Date: Oct. 15, 1810
Consideration: $90.00
Amt of land: 59 1/4 acres
Location: Sullivan Co
Description: Sell unto King and Alison in behalf of the heirs of Isaac King,
dec'd, all his undivided moity or half of a tract of land adj. John and
Robert Alison
Wit: James Gregg, Frances Hodge
Proven: By James Gregg, Frances Hodge, Sullivan Co, TN, Aug, 1814
Test: Mattw. Rhea, C.S.C, by his deputy
Regst: Aug. 20, 1814

----

(454)   LEONARD HART   :
                    TO   :   DEED OF WARRANTY
               JOHN SMITH   :

Date: aug. 24, 1812
Consideration: $200.00
Amt of land: 86 acres
Location: Sullivan Co
Description: Land adj. Smith and David Webb; being part of a tract of 130
acres granted to aforesaid Hart
Wit: James Gregg, John Hart
Proven: By James Gregg, John Hart, Sullivan Co,TN, May, 1813
Test: Mattw. Rhea, C.S.C.
Regst: Aug. 20, 1814

----

(454)   JACOB HARTMAN   :
                    TO   :   DEED OF WARRANTY
               ABRAHAM HEDRICK   :

Date: Nov. 21, 1814
Consideration: $40.00
Amt of land: Not stated
Location: Sullivan Co
Description: Land at the east end of Blountville; being one half of a piece
of a land conveyed by John Tipton to Jacob Hartman by indenture dated
July 29, 1811, being Lot No. 46
Wit: William Anderson

Acknowledged: By Jacob Hartman, Sullivan Co, TN, 1814
Test: Mattw. Rhea, C.S.C, by his deputy
Regst: Nov. 29, 1814

(Page)
(455) JOSHUA MILLER   :
            TO   :   DEED OF CONVEYANCE
       MATTHEW RHEA   :

Date: Nov. 1, 1814
Consideration: $85.00
Amt of land: 1 qrtr of an acre
Location: Town of Blountville, Sullivan Co
Description: One lot, No. 27, in Blountville, containing 1/4 acre
Wit: J. Gitt, Joseph N. Len, Cyris R. Humphreys
Acknowledged: By Joshua Miller, Sullivan Co, TN, Nov, 1814
Test: Mattw. Rhea, C.S.C, by his deputy
Regst: Nov. 29, 1814

----

(456) JAMES CHASTIAN   :
            TO   :   DEED OF WARRANTY
       DAVID BRAGG   :

Date: Oct. 25, 1814
Consideration: $100.00
Amt of land: 300 acres
Location: Sullivan Co
Description: Land on Indian Camp Creek, in Sullivan Co
Wit: Howel Sullivan, Mesheck Hail, Charles Hail
Proven: By Mesheck and Charles Hail, Sullivan Co, TN, Nov, 1814
Test: Mattw. Rhea, C.S.C, by his deputy
Regst: Nov. 30, 1814

----

(457) GEORGE BROWN   :
            TO   :   DEED OF WARRANTY
       THOMAS WHITE   :

Date: Sept. 2, 1814
Consideration: $1100.00
Amt of land: 234 acres
Location: Sullivan Co, TN
Description: Land on the waters of Beaver Creek
Wit: George Burkhart, James I. George, Jacob Booker
Proven: By Jacob Booker, George Burkhart, Sullivan Co, TN, Nov, 1814
Test: Mattw. Rhea, C.S.C, by his deputy
Regst: Nov. 30, 1814

----

(458) AARON BACON   :
            TO   :   DEED OF CONVEYANCE
       WILLIAM BASKETT   :

Date: Nov. 5, 1814

Consideration: $700.00
Amt of land: 200 acres
Location: Sullivan Co
Description: Land containing 200 acres in county aforesaid
Wit: John Carbury, John A. Owens
Proven: By Jacob White and John Owens, Sullivan Co, Tn, Nov, 1814
Test: Mattw. Rhea, C.S.C, by his deputy
Regst: Nov. 30, 1814

(Page)
(459)

PETER BRECKHILL	:	
TO	:	DEED OF WARRANTY
JACOB THOMAS	:	

Date: Aug. 13, 1814
Consideration: $10.00
Amt of land: 1 qrtr of an acre
Location: Sullivan co, Town of Greenfield
Description: A lot in town of Greenfield in Sullivan Co, near the bank of
Sinking Creek containing 1 qrtr of an acre
Wit: Thomas Majors, John Thomas
Proven: By Thomas Majors, John Thomas, Sullivan Co, Tn, Aug, 1814
Test: Mattw. Rhea, C.S.C, by his deputy
Regst: Nov. 30, 1814

----

(459)

WALLER KING	:	
TO	:	DEED OF CONVEYANCE
BENJAMIN & JOHN BRITT	:	

Date: Sept. 22, 1813
Consideration: $120.00
Amt of land: 92 acres
Location: Sullivan Co, TN
Description: Land on south side of Holston River
Wit: William Baskett, John Owens, Elisha Embree
Proven: By William Baskett, John Owen, Sullivan Co, TN, Nov, 1814
Test: Mattw. Rhea, C.S.C, by his deputy
Regst: Nov. 30, 1814

----

(460)

WILLIAM WALLACE	:	
TO	:	DEED OF WARRANTY
HENRY PECTOL	:	

Date: Aug. 22, 1814
Consideration: a valuable consideration
Amt of land: 100 acres
Location: Sullivan Co
Description: Land on the waters of Reedy
Wit: John Anderson, John Carrithers
(Proven): Sullivan Co, TN, Nov, 1814
Test: Mattw. Rhea, C.S.C, by his deputy
Regst: Nov. 30, 1814

162

```
STATE OF NORTH CAROLINA        :
RICHARD DOBBS SPAIGHT, GOV     :    LAND GRANT
        TO                     :    NO. 582
HENRY HUGHES                   :
```

Date: June 27, 1793
Consideraton: Not stated
Amt of land: 150 acres
Location: Sullivan Co
Description: 150 acres on the waters of Reedy Creek
Richard Dobbs Spaight, J. Glasgow, Sec. A true copy of a grant the
records of a grant given Sept. 12, 1814
Wm Hill, Sec. of NC
Regst: Nov. 30, 1814

----

(461)   JOHN SHARP of Roane Co   :
              to   :   DEED OF WARRANTY
         ROBERT RHEA   :

Date: June 6, 1812
Consideration: A valuable consideration
Amt of land: Not stated
Location: Sullivan Co
Description: William Anderson, dec'd, did by his last will and testament in
writing devise unto Sarah Sharp formerly Sarah Anderson, daughter of
William Anderson, now wife of John Sharp an equal divide with his children
of his person and real estae as in and by the sd last will and testament
may now fully appear do give unto Robert Rhea dna to his heirs and
assigns forever all the estate title which he the sd John Sharp now hath
or may or in any wise ought to have in the sd equal part of sd real
estate before mentioned which sd part is an equal divide with the
surviving children of William Anderson of the plantation where he formerly
lives
Wit: John Anderson, Wm scott
Proven: By John Anderson, William Soctt, Sullivan Co, TN, Nov, 1812
Test: Mattw. Rhea, C.S.C
Regst: Nov. 30, 1814

----

(461)   JAMES ANDERSON   :
              TO   :   DEED OF WARRANTY
         ROBERT RHEA   :

Date: June 12, 1812
Consideration: A valuable consideration
Amt of land: Not stated
Location: Sullivan Co
Description: William Anderson, dec'd, did by his last will and testament in
writing devise unto James Anderson, an equal divide with his other children
of his personal and real estate as in by the last will and testament
Do give and grant to Robert Rhea and heirs all the estate right title
which James Anderson now hath or may have to the equal part of estate
Wit: Wm Scott, John Anderson
Proven: By John Anderson, William Scott, Sullivan Co, Tn, Nov, 1812
Test: Mattw. Rhea, C.S.C.
Regst: Dec. 1, 1814

163

GEORGE DECKARD :
         TO : DEED OF WARRANTY
ROBERT RHEA :

Date: June 12, 1812
Consideration: A valuable consideration
Amt of land: Not stated
Location: Sullivan Co
Description: William Anderson, dec'd, of Sullivan Co by his last will and
testament in writing devise unto Mary Anderson, daughter of Wm Anderson
and wife of George Deckard, an equal divide with his other children of his
personal and real estate as by his last will and testament, may more fully
appear. Grant over unto Robert Rhea and his heirs all right in which he
the sd dec'd has in the equal part of the sd real estate before mentioned
which part is an equal divide with the surviving children of Wm of the
plantation where he formerly lived. To hold the same in as simple manner
the Deckard may have
Wit: John Anderson, Wm Scott
Proven: By John Anderson, William Scott, Sullivan Co, TN, Nov, 1812
Test: Mattw. Rhea, C.S.C.
Regst: Dec. 1, 1814

----

(463) MATTHEW RHEA :
         TO : QUIT CLAIMED DEED
JOHN ANDERSON :

Date: Nov. 8, 1814
Consideration: $463.00
Amt of land: 119 acres
Location: Sullivan Co, TN
Description: Land containing 119 acres in aforesaid county and state
Wit: Jacob Goad, Zachariah Wicks
Proven: By Jacob Goad, Zachariah Wicks, Sullivan Co, TN, Nov, 1814
Test: Mattw. Rhea, C.S.C, by his deputy
Regst: Dec. 1, 1814

----

(464) STATE OF TENNESSEE :
REG OF EAST TN : LAND GRANT
         TO : NO. 2756
WILLIAM TATHAM :

Date: March 12, 1811
Consideration: An entry made in the surveyor's office of the 6th District
of No. 676, dated March 12, 1811, founded on a ceertificate of No. 183.
Issued by the Reg of E TN to William Tatham for 100 acres dated Jan. 8,
1811. 79 acres of which is assigned to Matthew Rhea, the enterer.
Description: Granted by Matthew Rhea and to his heirs a parcel of land
containing 15 acres in the Washington District on the waters of Reedy
Creek
To be affixed at Nashville, May 5, 1813, by Gov. Willie Blount, W.G.
Blount, Sec, Recorded Feb. 4, 1814
         Edw. Scott, Reg. of E TN

Dec. 12, 1814, rec'd tax on within grant
Test: Mattw. Rhea, C.S.C, by his deputy
Regst: Dec. 12, 1814

(Page)
(464)

WILLIAM HUGHES   :
      TO   :   DEED OF CONVEYANCE
SAMUEL MOORE   :

Date: Oct. 24, 1811
Consideration: $1200.00
Amt of land: 242 acres
Location: Sullivan Co, TN
Description: Land containing 243 acres on both sides of Reedy Creek; being part of a tract known by the name of Pendleton's and Taylor's Grant. The sd tract of land belonging or appertaining with the reversion, rents, issues, there of and all the estate right title, interest, property claim and demand of him the sd Wm Hughes of his heirs and of in and to the same and every sd and parcel there of either in law or equity to have and to hold the sd 242 acres of land with the sd Samuel Moore his heirs and assigns forever
Wit: Ambrose Gaines, Jacob Bealer, Wm Cruts
Proven: By Ambrose Gaines, Jacob Bealer, Sullivan Co, TN, Feb, 1811
Test: Mattw. Rhea, C.S.C, by his deputy
Regst: Dec. 13, 1814

----

(465)   STATE OF TENNESSEE :
        ARCHIBALD ROANE   :   LAND GRANT
           TO   :   NO. 2310
        JOB KEY   :

Date: Jan. 24, 1810
Consideration: An entry made in the surveyor's office of the 6th District of No. 392, dated Jan. 24, 1810, founded on a warrant of No. 495, issued by Archibald Roane to Job Key for 640 acres of land dated Feb. 9, 1808, 56 acres of which is assigned to Jacob Drake, the enterer
Description: There is granted by the state of TN to Jacob Drake land containing 4 acres in the Washington District on the waters of Reedy Creek
To be affixed at Knoxville, June 15, 1812, by Gov. Willie Blount, W.G. Blount Sec, Recorded June 15, 1812
                       Edw Scott, Reg of E TN
Dec. 13, 1814, rec'd tax on within grant
Test: Mattw. Rhea, C.S.C, by his deputy
Regst: Dec. 13, 1814

----

(466)   JOHN ROLLER   :
           TO   :   QUIT CLAIMED DEED
WILLIAM BARNS   :

Date: Oct. 10, 1812
Consideration: A valuable consideration
Amt of land: 3 acres

Location: Sullivan Co
Description: John Roller have released and forever quit-claimed unto William
Barns and to his heirs a tract of land containing 3 acres
Wit: John Anderson, John Barns
Proven: By John Anderson, John Barns, sullivan Co, TN, Nov, 1812
Test: Mattw. Rhea, C.S.C
Regst: Dec. 14, 1814

(Page)
(467)   JACOB PEARLER   :
                    TO   :   DEED OF WARRANTY
               SAMUEL MOORE   :

Date: June 5, 1813
Consideration: $300.00
Amt of land: 124 acres
Location: Sullivan Co, TN
Description: Land containing 124 acres excepting 1 acre that the Marling
Howe is conveyed by Martin Waddle on the top of Eaton's Ridge
Wit: Ambrose Gaines, Thomas Ruggles, Peter Waddle, Thomas Rye, George
Mullis
Proven: By Ambrose Gaines, Thomas Ruggles, Sullivan Co, TN, Nov, 1813
Test: Mattw. Rhea, C.S.C
Regst: Dec. 14, 1814

----

(468)   STATE OF TENNESSEE   :
               ARCHIBALD ROANE   :   LAND GRANT
                    TO   :   NO. 3219
               JOHN CARTER Heirs   :

Date: July 13, 1812
Consideration: An entry made in the surveyor's office of the 6th District
of No. 1369, dated July 13, 1812, founded on warrant No. 2855, issued by
Archibald Roane to John Carter heirs 640 acres of land dated Nov. 20,
1810; 70 acres of which is assigned to Robert Rhea, the enterer
Description: There is granted by the state of TN to Robert Rhea and his
heirs land containing 70 acres on the north side of Holston River
To be affixed at Nashville, Nov. 5, 1814, by Gov. Willie Blount, W.G.
Blount, Sec, Recorded Nov. 5, 1814
                              Edw Scott, Reg. of E TN
Jan. 14, 1815*, tax rec'd on within grant
Test: Mattw. Rhea, C.S.C, by his deputy
Regst: Jan. 14, 1815*

(*Note: Both years given)

(468)   STATE OF TENNESSEE   :
               REG. OF WEST TN   :   LAND GRANT
                    TO   :   NO. 3292
               NATHANIEL TAYLOR   :

Date: Sept. 4, 1812

166

Consideration: An entry made in the surveyor's office of the 6th District of No. 1448, dated Sept. 4, 1812, founded on a certificate of No. 895, issued by the Reg. of W. TN to Nathaniel Taylor for 214 acres dated Feb. 19, 1812; 100 acres of which are assigned to Lawrence Snapp, the enterer
Description: There is granted by state of TN to Lawrence Snapp, a tract of land containing 15 acres
To be affixed at Nashville, Nov. 21, 1814, by Gov. Willie Blount, W.G. Blount, Sec, Recorded in my office
                              Edw Scott, Reg of E TN
Jan. 14, 1815, tax paid on within grant
Test: Mattw. Rhea, C.S.C.
Regst: Jan. 14, 1815

(Page)
  (469)

THOMAS ANDERSON   :
      TO   :   DEED OF CONVEYANCE
JOSHUA RUSSELL   :

Date: Aug. 21, 1809
Consideration: A valuable consideration
Amt of land: 1 qrtr acre
Location: Town of Blountville, Sullivan Co
Description: A lot, No. 32, in the town of Blountville containing 1/4 acres
Wit: John Anderson, J. Isaack
Acknowledged: By Thomas Anderson, Sullivan Co, TN, Aug, 1809
Test: Mattw. Rhea, C.S.C, by his deputy
Regst: (No date given)

----

(470)

JOSHUA COX   :
      TO   :   DEED OF CONVEYANCE
EDWARD COX   :

Date: July 25, 1814
Consideration: $5,000.00 lawful money
Amt of land: 292 acres
Location: Sullivan Co
Description: Land containing 292 acres on the north side of Holston River
Wit: (No names given)
Acknowledged: By Joshua Cox, Sullivan Co, TN, Aug, 1814
Test: Mattw. Rhea, C.S.C, by his deputy
Regst: Feb. 20, 1815

----

(471)

WILLIAM SITZLER, SR. :
      TO   :   DEED OF WARRANTY
JOHN SAUNDERS   :

Date: Aug. 30, 1814
Consideration: $625.00
Amt of land: 194 acres
Location: Sullivan Co, TN
Description: Land on the south side of Holston River

Wit: James Gregg, John Sanders
Acknowledged: By William Sitzler, Sullivan Co, TN, Feb, 1815
Test: Mattw. Rhea, C.S.C, by his deputy
Regst: Feb. 21, 1815

(Page)
(472)

SOLOMON SMITH :
    TO :   BILL OF SALE
STEPHEN HIX, SR. :

Date: Dec. 7, 1814
Consideration: $420.00
Description: Solomon Smith have sold to Stephen Hix, Sr, a negro woman
named Chlne(?) aged 20 yrs
Wit: Matthew Rhea, Jr., William Dury
Proven: By Mattw. Rhea, Jr, William Dury, Sullivan Co, TN, Feb, 1815
Test: Mattw. Rhea, C.S.C, by his deputy
Regst: Feb. 21, 1815

----

(472)

JOHN TIPTON :
    TO :   DEED OF WARRANTY
BENJAMIN KELLY :

Date: Nov. 22, 1814
Consideration: $25.00
Amt of land: 1 qrtr acre
Location: Town of Blountville, Sullivan Co
Description: A lot, No. 36, containing 1/4 acre in Blountville
Wit: N. Lane, George Gammon
Acknowledged: By John Tipton, Sullivan Co, Tn, Nov, 1814
Test: Mattw. Rhea, C.S.C, by his deputy
Regst: Feb. 21, 1815

----

(472)

JOHN PRYOR :
    TO :   DEED OF WARRANTY
JERAMIAH CLOUD :

Date: Sept. 9, 1814
Consideration: $600.00
Amt of land: 135 acres
Location: Sullivan Co
Description: A tract of land on the south side of the Holston River
Wit: Jno M. Vaughan, Benjamin Cloud
Proven: By Benjamin Cloud, Sullivan Co, TN, Nov, 1814
Test: Mattw. Rhea, C.S.C, by his deputy
Regst: Feb. 21, 1815

----

(473)

JAMES KING, JR. :
    TO :   BILL OF SALE
JAMES WARE :

Date: Nov. 19, 1814

Consideration: $350.00
Description: I hereby sell to James Ware a negro girl named Letty aged between 12 and 14 yrs
Wit: Daniel Rogar, Ezekiel Key
Acknowledged: By James King, Sullivan Co, TN, Feb, 1815
Test: Mattw. Rhea, C.S.C, by his deputy
Regst: Feb. 21, 1815

(Page)
(474)

ABRAHAM COX   :
        TO   :   DEED OF WARRANTY
JOHN BROWN   :

Date: May 18, 1813
Consideration: $300.00
Location: Sullivan Co
Description: Land on the waters of Kinderick's Creek incl. the place where Cox did live
wit: Charles Jones, James P. Hulse
Proven: By Charles Jones, James P. Hulse, Sullivan Co, TN, May, 1813
Test: Mattw. Rhea, C.S.C, by his deputy
Regst: Feb. 22, 1814

----

(474)

JAMES KING   :
        TO   :   BILL OF SALE
JAMES WEAR   :

Date: Nov. 19, 1814
Consideration: $600.00
Description: One negro man named Dick aged between 20 & 25 yrs
Wit: Ezekiel Key, Daniel Rogar
Acknowledged: By James King, Sullivan Co, TN, Feb, 1815
Test: Mattw. Rhea, C.S.C, by his deputy
Regst: Feb. 21, 1815

----

(475)

STATE OF TENNESSEE   :
COMMISSIONERS OF E TN   :   LAND GRANT
        TO   :   NO. (Not given)
EDWARD LEVEADEN   :

Date: March 8, 1809
Consideration: An entry made in the surveyor's office of the 6th District of No. 249, founded on a warrant of No. 2917, issued by the commissioners of E TN to Edward Leveaden for 100 acres dated Jan. 13, 1809. Entry dated March 8, 1809, which is assigned by Leveaden to John Kennedy and by Kennedy to Joseph Elder, the enterer
Description: Granted by state of TN to Joseph Elder a parcel of land containing 100 acres in the Washington District on the waters of Reedy Creek; beginning surveyed May 27, 1809
To be affixed at Knoxville, Oct. 29, 1811, by Gov. Willie Blount, R. Houston, Sec, Recorded in my office Oct. 29, 1811
                    Edw. Scott, Reg. of E TN

Aug. 26, 1814, tax paid on with land grant
Test: Mattw. Rhea, C.S.C, by his deputy
Regst: Feb. 22, 1815

(Page)
    (476)   STATE OF TENNESSEE   :
          JOHN CARTER   :   LAND GRANT
                TO   :   NO. (Not given)
          JOHN COCKRAN   :

Date: March 8, 1809
Consideration: An entry made of No. 248, dated March 8, 1809, founded on
a warranty of No. 1825 issued by John Carter to John Cockran for 100
acres of land dated Feb. 3, 1780, and adjudged valid May 2, 1807, and
assigned by Cockran to Joseph Elder, the enterer
Description: Granted to Joseph Elder and his heirs a tract of land
containing 100 acres in Washington District on the waters of Reedy Creek,
surveyed May 27, 1809
To be affixed at Knoxville, July 2, 1810, by Gov. Willie Blount, R.
Houston, Sec, Recorded July 2, 1810
                              Edw Scott, Reg. of E TN
Aug. 20, 1814, tax paid on within grant
Test: Mattw. Rhea, C.S.C, by his deputy
Regst: Feb. 22, 1815

----

    (478)   WM N. GALE   :
                   TO   :   DEED OF WARRANTY
          GEORGE WOOLFORD   :

Date: Nov. 23, 1814
Consideration: $76.00
Amt of land: 19 acres
Location: Sullivan Co,TN
Description: Land containing 19 acres on the waters of Reedy Creek
Wit: (No names given)
Acknowledged: By william N. Gale, Sullivan Co, TN, Feb, 1815
Test: Mattw. Rhea, C.S.C, by his deputy
Regst: Feb. 22, 1815

----

    (479)   JOHN HAWKINS   :
                   TO   :   DEED OF CONVEYANCE
          PHILIP HOBAUGH   :

Date: Sept. 30, 1814
Consideration: A valuable consideration
Amt of land: 88 acres
Location: Sullivan Co, TN
Description: Land containing 88 acres
Wit: Samuel Hampton, Tatrick Hobaugh
Proven: By Samuel Hampton, Tatrick Hobaugh in open court
Test: Mattw. Rhea, C.S.C, by his deputy
Regst: Feb. 23, 1815

ISAAC SHELBY, Executor of   :
Evan Shelby, dec'd, and Susanna, :
His wife   :   DEED OF CONVEYANCE
     TO   :
JAMES KING, JR.   :

Date: Sept. 26, 1814
Consideration: $10,000 lawful money of the United States
Amt of land: 1600 acres
Location: Sullivan Co, TN
Description: Two tracts of land containing, in all, 1600 acres. One tract on
Beaver Creek, a branch of the Holston River, partly in Sullivan Co, TN,
and partly inf Washington Co, VA, conveyed to Isaac by John Preston,
Frances Preston, John Brickenridge, and John Brown, Executors of William
Preston, dec'd, who was executor of John Brickhannan, dec'd, on Nov. 2,
1799. As by reference to the deed signed by Frances and deed was
recorded in Washington Co will more fully appear. The same being one
marity(sic) of the Sapling Grove tract, beginning for the 1400 acres. And
one other tract supposed to contain 200 acres, adj. the before described
tract of 1400 acres on the south side there of and on both sides of
Beaver Creek, being one marity(sic) of a survey of 400 acres for Isaac
Shelby. Executors as aforesaid and extends down from the sapling grove
lines to the 200 acres conveyed by Isaac to John W. Brian*, the 200 acres
hereby conveyed is the residence of the said 400 acre tract out of which
Isaac conveyed to O'Brian* 200 acres.
Wit: Achilles Sneed, Clk of the County Court
    Do hereby certify that the forgoing deed was produced to me in my
office on Sept. 27, 1814, and acknowledged by Isaac Shelby, executor of
Evan Shelby, dec'd, and his wife Susanna
          Achilles Sneed
State of Kentucky: I, John Bayle, Chief Justice of the Commonwealth of
K Y and presiding Judge of the Court of Appeals of sd common, do certify
Achilles Sneed is Clerk of sd court and that is certificte above and within
and his attestation thereof are in due form - Sept. 29, 1814
          John Bayle
Virginia: At a court held for Washington Co, Nov. 15, 1814 - This
indenture of bargain and sale between Isaac Shelby and Susanna, his wife,
of the one part and James King, Jr. of the other part was exhibited into
court together with the certificate of acknowledgment
        Attest: D. Campbell, D.C.
Court of Pleas and Qrtr Session, Feb. 21, 1815 - This deed of conveyance
was exhibited in court and in virtue of the above certificate of the clerk
of the court of appeals of K Y and of the presiding judge of sd county is
is admitted to registration.
Test: Mattw. Rhea, C.S.C, by Mattw. Rhea, D.C.
Regst: Feb. 23, 1815

(*Note: Both names given)

(483)   ZECKARIAH WICKS   :
       TO   :   DEED OF WARRANTY
     GEORGE WALFORD   :

Date: Feb. 22, 1815
Consideration: A valuable consideration

Amt of land: 72 acres
Location: Sullivan Co, TN
Description: Land containing 72 acres on the waters of Reedy Creek
Wit: Wm N. Gale, William Nelson
(Proven): Sullivan Co, TN, Feb. 22, 1815
Test: Mattw. Rhea, C.S.C, by Mattw. Rhea, D.C.
(Regst): (No date given)

(Page)
(483)

```
STATE OF TENNESSEE    :
REGISTER OF E TN      :    LAND GRANT
        TO            :    NO. (Not given)
WILLIAM TATHAM        :
```

Date: June 12, 1811
Consideration: An Entry made in the Surveyor's office at the 6th District
of No. 721, June 12, 1811, founded on a certificate of No. 183, issued by
the Register of E TN to William Tatham for 100 acres, dated Jan. 8,
1811; 3 acres of which is assigned to Thomas Odd, the enterer
Description: Granted by state of TN to Thomas and his heirs, 3 acres
on the south side of Holston River
Surveyed: June 14, 1811
To be affixed at Nashville, Oct. 10, 1813, by Gov. Willie Blount, W.G.
Blount, Sec, Recorded Jan 3, 1814
                        Edw. Scott, Reg. of E TN
Feb. 20, 1815, rec'd tax on the within grant
Test: Mattw Rhea, C.S.C, by Mattw. Rhea, D.C.
Regst: Feb. 23, 1815

----

(484)

```
JAMES RHEA            :
        TO            :    DEED OF CONVEYANCE
WALTER JAMES          :
```

Date: Oct. 7, 1814
Consideration: $55.00
Amt of land: 73 poles
Location: Sullivan Co, TN
Description: Land adj. a back lot of ground belonging to Walter on the
north side of Blountville, containing 73 poles more or less
Wit: Joseph A. Brownlow, Amos Jones
Acknowledged: By James Rhea, Sullivan Co, Feb, 1815
Test: Mattw. Rhea, C.S.C, by Mattw. Rhea, D.C.
Regst: Feb. 23, 1815

(485

```
THOMAS ROCKHOLD       :
        TO            :    QUIT CLAIM DEED
MATTHEW RHEA, SR.     :
```

Date: Feb. 22, 1815
Consideration: A valuable consideration
Amt of land: 50 acres
Location: Sullivan Co

Description: Land containing 50 acres on the Fort Branch adj. Matthew
Rhea, John Miller and incl. the lines designated in the deed from John
Topp to Matthew
Wit: (No names given)
Acknowledged: By Thomas, Sullivan Co, TN, Feb, 1815
Test: Mattw. Rhea, C.S.C, by Mattw. Rhea, D.C.
Regst: Feb. 25, 1815

(Page)
486)

STATE OF TENNESSEE   :
REGISTER OF EAST TN   :   LAND GRANT
        TO   :   NO. (Not given)
WILLIAM KEY   :

Date: Aug. 5, 1811
Consideration: An entry made in the surveyor's office of the 6th District
of No. 739, dated Aug. 5, 1811, founded on a certificate of No. 201,
issued by the register of E TN, to the heirs of William Key for 100 acres,
dated, Jan. 11, 1811; 13 acres of which is assigned to William O'Del*, the
enterer.
Description: Granted by state of TN to William Odel* and his heirs, 13
acres
To be affixed at Nashville, Oct, 10, 1813, By Gov. Willie Blount, W.G.
Blount, Sec, Recorded Dec. 23, 1813
                              Edw. Scott, Reg of E TN
Feb. 20, 1815, rec'd tax on within grant
Test: Mattw. Rhea, C.S.C, by Mattw. Rhea, D.C.
Regst: Feb. 25, 1815

(*Note: Names spelled both ways)

(487)   ISSUED TO EVAN SHELBY   :
         BY STATE OF TENNESSEE   :   LAND GRANT
                 TO   :   NO. 2068
         LAWRENCE HARKLEROAD   :

Date: Jan. 15, 1780
Consideration: Entry made in Carter's office of No. 1717, founded on a
warranty of the same No. for 300 acres, issued to Evan Shelby, dated Jan.
15, 1780
Description: Granted by state of TN to Lawrence Harkleroad, who is
assigned of Isaac Shelby, executor of Evan Shelby, 300 acres
To be affixed at Knoxville, Oct. 29, 1811, by Gov. Willie Blount, R.
Houston, Sec, Recorded Oct. 29, 1815
                              Edw. Scott, Reg of E TN
Feb. 21, 1815, rec'd tax on within grant
Test: Mattw. Rhea, C.S.C, by Mattw. Rhea, D.C.
Regst: Feb. 26, 1815

----

(487)   JAMES PHAGAN, High Sheriff of   :
         Sullivan County   :
                 TO   :   DEED OF CONVEYANCE
         WILLIAM CARTER   :

Date: March 24, 1813

A wit of vendition exponas came unto the hands of Sheriff from Court of Pleas and Qrtr Session of Sullivan Co requiring him to expose to sale two tracts of land in Sullivan Co
Purpose: To satisfy a judgment of $33.13 which Samuel Smith had before that time obtained against William Scott, Administrator of George Webb, dec'd, and whereas afterwards on May 15, 1813.
Description: Two tracts of land in Sullivan Co; one containig 27 1/2 acres joining the Nicholas Matton and others; the other containing 25 acres joining Benjamin Webb as the property of George Webb. James Phagan, Sheriff, did after advertising according to law expose to public sale the 2 tracts and sold the 25 acres to William Carter for $1.00, that being the amt of his bid

I, James Phagan, High Sheriff, as aforesaid in consideration of the sale and purchase and payment of the money as aforesaid by William Carter this day have sold to William Carter and his heirs as for as I am authorized by sd vendition exponas all that right William Scott . administrator of George Webb, dec'd, had in 25 acres
Wit: (No names given)
Acknowledged: By James Phagan, Sullivan Co, Aug, 1814
Test: Mattw. Rhea, C.S.C, by Mattw. Rhea, D.C.
Regst: Feb. 26, 1815

(Page)
(489)

PETER CATRON   :
        TO   :   DEED OF CONVEYANCE
DANIEL DEVALT   :

Date: Oct. 3, 1814
Consideration: A valuable consideration
Amt of land: 102 acres
Location: Sullivan Co, TN
Description: 102 acres in state and county aforesaid
Wit: John Catron, Wisford Gulery
Acknowledged: By Peter Catron, Sullivan Co, TN, Nov. 1814
Test: Mattw. Rhea, C.S.C, by Mattw. Rhea, D.C.
Regst: Feb. 26, 1815

----

(489)

SAMUEL Z. BROWNLOW :
        TO   :   DEED OF CONVEYANCE
GEORGE WOLFORD   :

Date: Feb. 21, 1815
Purpose: Writ of fieri facias issued from Sullivan Co Court to me directed at the suit James Phagan against Zachariah Wicks which writ was levied on a tract of land in Sullivan Co. After being advertised according to law was exposed to public sale in Blountville, July 12. At which sale Jacob Sturm bid $96.25 and by virute of a written order from sd Sturm by me rec'd bearing date Nov. 28, 1814. And in the following wards(sic) Samuel Z. Brownlow. Sir please to make a title to the land I purchased at the sale of James Phagan vs Zachariah Wicks which title I wish made to George Wolford not binding on me no further than the claim of Wicks to the land when sold if his title was good my purchase was also, if not I wish to be accountable now neither will I be so signed Jacob Sturm now

174

therefore by virtue of the authority in me vested by law I do hereby sell
to George Wolford all right that Zachariah Wicks has in sd tract of land
above named containing 143 acres
To have and to hold the sd George Wolford and his heirs
Wit: (No names given)
Acknowledged: By Samuel Z. Brownlow, Sullivan Co, TN
Test: Mattw. Rhea, C.S.C, by Mattw. Rhea, D.C.
Regst: Feb. 26, 1915

(Page)
(491)

WILLIAM GODDARD   :
         TO   :   DEED OF WARRANTY
JACOB GOOD   :

Date: Jan. 3, 1815
Consideration: A valuable consideration
Amt of land: 70 acres
Location: Sullivan Co, TN
Description: 70 acres on the waters of Reedy Creek
Wit: John Anderson, William Hansher
Proven: By John Anderson, William Hansher, Sullivan Co, TN, Feb, 1815
Test: Mattw. Rhea, C.S.C, by Mattw. Rhea, D.C.
Regst: Feb. 28, 1815

----

(491)

WILLIAM GODDARD, SR. :
         TO   :   DEED OF WARRANTY
WILLIAM GODDARD, JR. :

Date: Dec. 31, 1814
Consideration: A valuable consideration
Amt of land: 95 acres
Location: Sullivan Co, TN
Description: 95 acres in county and state aforesaid
Wit: John Anderson, Jacob Good
Proven: By John Anderson, Jacob Good, Sullivan Co, TN, Feb, 1815
Test: Mattw. Rhea, C.S.C, by Mattw. Rhea, D.C.
Regst: Feb. 28, 1815

----

(492)

WILLIAM BASKET   :
         TO   :   DEED OF CONVEYANCE
ROBERT TRIBET   :

Date: Sept. 14, 1814
Consideration: $150.00
Amt of land: 40 acres
Location: Sullivan Co
Description: 40 acres on county and state aforesaid
Wit: Jacob Keer, Lot O. Gott, thomas Copass
Proven: By Lot O. Gott, Jacob Kerr, Sullivan Co, TN, Feb, 1815
Test: Mattw. Rhea, C.S.C, by Mattw. Rhea, D.C.
Regst: Feb. 28, 1815

----

(493)

```
WILLIAM DEERY        :
        TO           :      DEED OF CONVEYANCE
JAMES RHEA           :
```

Date: April 14, 1814
Consideration: A valuable consideration
Amt of land: 36 acres
Location: Sullivan Co, TN
Description: 36 acres in county and state aforesaid
Wit: Matthew Rhea, Jr, Joseph McLen
Proven: By Joseph McLen, Mattw. Rhea, Jr.
Test: Mattw. Rhea, C.S.C.
Regst: Feb. 28, 1815

----

(493)

```
ELIJAH CROSS         :
        TO           :      BILL OF SALE
ABRAHAM LOONEY       :
```

Date: nov. 14, 1814
Consideration: $450.00
Description: A negro man named Carter, aged 23 yrs
Wit: Joseph W. Looney, Felix Stephens
Acknowledged: By Elijah Cross, Sullivan Co, Nov, 1814
Test: Mattw. Rhea, C.S.C, by Mattw. Rhea, D.C.
Regst: Feb. 28, 1815

----

(494)

```
SOLOMON AND JOHN SMITH   :
        TO               :      DEED OF WARRANTY
HENRY HYSINGER           :
```

Date: Feb. 20, 1814
Consideration: A valuable consideration
Amt of land: 110 acres
Location: Sullivan Co, TN
Description: 110 acres in county and state aforesaid
Wit: (No names given)
Acknowledged: By Solomon Smith, John Smith, Sullivan Co, Tn, Feb, 1815
Test: Mattw. Rhea, C.S.C, by Mattw. Rhea, D.C.
Regst: Feb. 28, 1815

----

(495)

```
GEORGE LOWE          :
        TO           :      DEED OF CONVEYANCE
LEONARD KAIN         :
```

Date: Aug. 15, 1814
Consideration: $200.00
Amt of land: 100 acres
Location: Sullivan Co, Tn
Description: 100 acres on the waters of Reedy Creek
Wit: John Anderson
Acknowledged: By George Lowe, Sullivan Co, TN, Aug, 1814
Test: Mattw. Rhea, C.S.C, by Mattw. Rhea, D.C.
Regst: Feb. 28, 1815

STATE OF TENNESSEE :
REGISTER OF EAST TN :   LAND GRANT
        TO   :   NO. 3222
JAMES TAYLOR   :

Date: April 3, 1813
Consideration: An entry made in the surveyor's office of the 6th District
of No. 1679, April 3, 1813, founded on a certificate of No. 481, issued by
the Reg of E TN to James Taylor for 50 acres dated Nov. 25, 1812; 36
acres of which are assigned to John Thomas, the enterer
Description: Granted by TN to John Thomas 36 acres in Sullivan Co
To be affixed at Nashville, Nov. 8, 1814, by Gov. Willie Blount, W.G.
Blount, Sec, Recorded Nov. 8, 1814
                            Edw Scott, Reg of E TN
Feb. 28, 1815, rec'd tax on within grant
Test: Mattw. Rhea, C.S.C, by Mattw. Rhea, D.C.
Regst: Feb. 28, 1815

----

(496)   WILLIAM SCOTT   :
           TO   :   DEED OF CONVEYANCE
     NICHOLAS MATTON   :

Date: Aug. 21, 1813
Consideration: $30.00
Amt of land: 20 acres
Location: Sullivan Co
Description: 30 acres in Sullivan Co
Wit: (No names given)
Proven: By William Scott, Sullivan Co, TN, Feb, 1815
Test: Mattw. Rhea, C.S.C, by Mattw. Rhea, D.C.
Regst: March 1, 1815

----

(497)   ELISHA JAMES   :
           TO   :   DEED OF WARRANTY
     MARTIN BOOKER*   :

Date: Aug. 7, 1814
Consideration: A valuable consideration
Amt of land: 352 acres
Location: Sullivan Co
Description: 352 acres in aforesaid county
Wit: George Burkhart, Jacob Booker, Nathan Willely
Proven: By George Burkhart, Jacob Booker, Sullivan Co, TN, Nov, 1814
Test: Mattw. Rhea, C.S.C, by Mattw. Rhea, D.C.
Regst: March 1, 1815

(*Note: Name could possibly be Booher)

(498)   JONAS NICELY   :
           TO   :   DEED OF CONVEYANCE
     MARTIN HARKLEROAD :

Date: Nov. 12, 1814

Consideration: $150.00
Amt of land: 59 acres
Location: Sullivan Co
Description: Quit claim to Martin Harkleroad for 59 acres by virtur of a grant dated Sept. 26, 1809, and of No. 672
Wit: Henry Harkleroad, Lawrence Harkleroad, martin Godsey
Proven: By Lawrence Harkleroad, Martin Godsey, Sullivan Co, TN, Feb, 1815
Test: Mattw. Rhea, C.S.C, by Mattw. Rhea, D.C.
Regst: March 1, 1815

(Page)
(499)

```
SAMUEL L. STEPHENS    :
        TO            :        DEED OF WARRANTY
JOHN GIESLER          :
```

Date: Feb. 21, 1815
Consideration: $400.00
Amt of land: 100 acres
Location: Sullivan Co
Description: 100 acres, by estimation, on south side of Holston River
Wit: (No names given)
(Proven): By Samuel L. Stephens, Sullivan Co, TN, Feb, 1815
Test: Mattw. Rhea, C.S.C, by Mattw. Rhea, D.C.
Regst: March 1, 1815

----

(500)

```
JOHN SHARP            :
        TO            :        DEED OF CONVEYANCE
JOHN VANCE            :
```

Date: Feb. 8, 1815
Consideration: $1600.00
Amt of land: 413 3/4 acres
Location: Sullivan Co, TN
Description: 413 3/4 acres being part of a large tract of 717 acres granted to John Sharp by patent
Wit: Ireson Longacre, William King
Proven: By Ireson Longacre, William King, Sullivan Co, TN, Feb, 1815
Test: Mattw. Rhea, C.S.C, by Mattw. Rhea, D.C.
Regst: March 1, 1815

----

(501)

```
ABRAHAM COX           :
        TO            :        DEED OF WARRANTY
JOHN BOWER            :
```

Date: May 18, 1814
Consideration: $300.00
Amt of land: 93 acres
Location: Sullivan Co
Description: 93 acres on a branch of Kindricks Creek Young the plantation where Cox did live
Wit: Charles Jones, James P. Hulse

Proven: By Charles Jones, James P. Hulse, Sullivan Co, TN, May, 1813
Test: Mattw. Rhea, C.S.C, by Mattw. Rhea, D.C.
Regst: March 2, 1815

(Page)
(502)

JAMES RHEA   :
      TO   :   DEED OF WARRANTY
WILLIAM DEERY   :

Date: April 15, 1814
Consideration: A valuable consideration
Amt of land: 36 acres
Location: Sullivan Co
Description: Quit claimed to William Deery 36 acres, more or less
Wit: John Anderson, Matthew Rhea, Jr.
Proven: By John Anderson, Matthew Rhea, Jr, Sullivan Co, Tn, Feb, 1815
Test: Mattw. Rhea, C.S.C, by Mattw. Rhea, D.C.
Regst: March 2, 1815

----

(503)

JAMES KAINE   :
      TO   :   DEED OF CONVEYANCE
ELIJAH TAYLOR   :

Date: Feb. 22, 1814
Consideration: $600.00
Amt of land: 118 1/2 acres
Location: Sullivan Co, TN
Description: 118 1/2 acres incl. the plantation where Elijah Cross now lives
Wit: John Jennings, Henry Pecktol
Acknowledged: By James Kaine, Sullivan Co, TN, Feb, 1814
Test: Mattw. Rhea, C.S.C, by Mattw. Rhea, D.C.
Regst: March 22, 1815

----

(504)

THOMAS TOWER and His wife, :
MARY TOWER   :
      TO   :   DEED OF WARRANTY
GEORGE LYDICAY*   :

Date: Feb. 20, 1815
Consideration: $700.00
Amt of land: 167 acres
Location: Sullivan Co, TN
Description: 167 acres adj. George Lydicay, Sr, and Frances Hainley
Wit: John S. Gaines, Sam Moore
Proven: By John S. Gaines, Samuel Moore, Sullivan Co,TN, Feb, 1815
Test: Mattw. Rhea, C.S.C, by Mattw. Rhea, D.C.
Regst: March 22, 1815

(*Note: Name could possible be Ledick)

(505)

THOMAS ROCKHOLD   :
      TO   :   DEED OF WARRANTY
ANDREW RYLEY   :

Date: April 13, 18th(sic)
Consideration: A valuable consideration
Amt of land: 60 acres
Location: Sullivan Co
Description: 60 acres more or less in Sullivan Co
Wit: Benjamin Stone
Acknowledged: By Thomas Rockhold, Sullivan Co, Feb, 1815
Test: Mattw. Rhea, C.S.C, by Mattw. Rhea, D.C.
Regst: March 3, 1815

(Page)
(505)

ROBERT TRIBET   :
        TO   :   DEED OF CONVEYANCE
WILLIAM BASKET   :

Date: Aug. 2, 1814
Consideration: $300.00
Amt of land: 100 acres
Location: Sullivan Co
Description: 100 acres on the south side of Holston River
Wit: Thomas Copass, Lot O. Gott, Henry Hartman
Acknowledged: By Robert Tribett, Sullivan Co, TN, Aug, 1814
Test: Mattw. Rhea,C.S.C, by Mattw. Rhea, D.C.
Regst: March 2, 1815

----

(506)

STATE OF TENNESSEE   :
COMMISSIONERS OF EAST TN :   LAND GRANT
        TO   :   NO. 3118
JOHN KEY   :

Date: June 4, 1809
Consideration: An entry made in the surveyor's office of the 6th District
of No. 284, dated June 4, 1809, founded on a warranty of no. 495, dated
Feb. 9, 1808, issued by the Commissioners of E TN to Job Key for 640
acres; 19 acres are assigned to Henry Shrite, the enterer
Description: Granted by TN to Henry Shrite 19 acres on the north side of
Holston River
Surveyed Sept. 4, 1809, seal affixed at Nashville, June 13, 1814 by Gov.
Willie Blount, W.G. Blount, Sec, Recorded Jan. 5, 1815
                              Edw Scott, Reg of E TN
Regst: March 23, 1815

----

(507)

STATE OF TENNESSEE   :
COMMISSIONERS OF EAST TN :   LAND GRANT
        TO   :   NO. 3226
GEORGE DAVIS   :

Date: Sept. 7, 1812
Consideration: An entry made in the surveyor's office of the 6th District
of No. 1446, dated Sept. 7, 1812, founded on a certificate of No. 24
issued by the Commissioners of E TN to George Davis for 12 1/2 acres
dated Aug. 14, 1807, (of which 5 1/2 acres are) assigned to Jacob
Slaughter, the enterer

Description: Granted by TN to Jacob Slaughter 5 1/2 acres on Holston
River
Surveyed May 8, 1813, seal affixed at Nashville Nov. 8, 1814, by Gov.
Willie Blount, W.G. Blount, Sec, Recorded Nov. 8, 1814
                              Edw Scott, Reg. of E TN
Jan. 14, 1815, rec'd tax on within grant
Test: Mattw. Rhea, C.S.C, by Mattw. Rhea, D.C.
Regst: March 23, 1815

(Page)
   (508)

STATE OF TENNESSEE   :
ARCHIBALD ROANE   :   LAND GRANT
         TO   :   NO. 3325
LANON CARTER   :

Date: Aug. 29, 1812
Consideration: An entry made in the surveyor's office of the 6th District
of No. 1430, dated Aug. 29, 1812, founded on a certificate of No. 80,
issued by Archibald Roane to Landon Carter for 640 acres; of which (100
acres) are assigned to Jacob Slaughter, the enterer
Description: Granted by Tn to Jacob Slaughter 100 acres on the road from
Blountville to Greenville
Surveyed May 8, 1813, seal affixed at Nashville, Nov. 8, 1814, by Gov.
Willie Blount, W.G. Blount, Sec, Recorded Nov. 8, 1814
                              Edw Scott, Reg of E TN
Jan 14, 1815, rec'd tax on within grant
Test: Mattw. Rhea, C.S.C, by Mattw. Rhea, D.C.
Regst: March 24, 1815

----

(509)   SAMUEL HAMPTON   :
             TO   :   DEED OF CONVEYANCE
        WILLIAM KING   :

Date: Aug. 16, 1814
Consideration: A valuable consideration
Amt of land: 23 acres
Location: Sullivan Co, TN
Description: 23 acres in Sullivan Co
Wit: John Anderson
Acknowledged: By Samuel Hampton, Sullivan Co, TN, Aug, 1814
Test: Mattw. Rhea, C.S.C, by Mattw. Rhea, D.C.
Regst: March 24, 1815

----

(510)   BENJAMIN HARDIN   :
             TO   :   DEED OF GRANT
        JAMES PICKENS   :

Date: June 5, 1784
Consideration: 150 lbs. species current money of NC
Amt of land: 200 acres
Location: Sullivan Co
Description: 200 acres on both sides of Kindrick; being part of land
granted by NC to Henry Clark by deed of grant No. 291, dated at

181

Fairfield, Oct. 24, 1782
Wit: Nile Lainken, Thomas Hardin, benjamin Hardin
(Proven): Sullivan Co, July, 1785
Test: Mattw. Rhea, C.S.C, by Mattw. Rhea, D.C.
Regst: March 29, 1815

(Page)
(512)

CATHARINE MACKY*	:	
TO	:	MORTGAGE
JOHN BORLAND* and Merchant of	:	
City of Baltimore, MD, and JOSEPH	:	
BIDDLE	:	

Date: May 19, 1814
Purpose: Catharine Mackey* to secure the debts hereafter mentioned hath
and by these presents doth sell to John Barland* and Joseph Riddle the
following lots in Middle Town in Sullivan Co, TN; Lot. No. 6 containing 1
qrtr of an acre adj. Robert Preston in sd town

I, Catharine Mackey, do agree with John Barland and Joseph Riddle,
their heirs and assigns. Shall enjoy the lot and improvement free from the
claim of all persons whatsoever provided, nevertheless, if Mackey shall pay
to Barland the sum of $166.74, with interest from Aug. 20, 1812, until
paid and also pay to Riddle $503.52 with interest from May 27, 1808, until
paid for which 2 sums of money Borland and Riddle hold the single bills
of Mackey for the payment of sd sums of money then the above deed
to be void, otherwise to remain in full force
Wit: John Kennedy, Jno. Mackey
Proven: By John Kennedy, John Mackey, Sullivan Co, TN, May, 1814
Test: Mattw. Rhea, C.S.C, by Mattw. Rhea, D.C.
Regst: April 3, 1815

(*Note: Names spelled both ways)

(513)

JACOB AND GEORGE GRASS	:	
TO	:	DEED OF CONVEYANCE
HENRY SMITH	:	

Date: Nov. 21, 1814
Consideration: A valuable consideration
Amt of land: Not stated
Location: Town of Blountville, Sullivan Co
Description: One lot, No. 47, in Blountville, near the east end of town
Wit: (No names given)
Acknowledged: By Jacob Grass, Sullivan Co, TN, Nov, 1814
Test: Mattw. Rhea, C.S.C, by Mattw. Rhea, D.C.
Regst: April 5, 1815

----

(513)

ELIPHALET BARBER	:	
TO	:	DEED OF WARRANTY
HENRY SMITH	:	

Date: Nov. 18, 1798
Consideration: 140 lbs
Amt of land: 100 acres

Location: A tract of land being part of a deed for 640 acres and judged to be 100 acres more or less
Wit: Jas Smith
Acknowledged: By Eliphalet Barber, Sullivan, Nov, 1798
Test: Mattw. Rhea, C.S.C
Regst: April 4, 1815

(Page)
(514)   STATE OF NORTH CAROLINA :
ALEXANDER MARTIN, GOV.   :   LAND GRANT
            TO   :   NO. 150

SURVEY: Date: Aug. 29, 1781, for James McClarving 300 acres in Sullivan Co, NC, on Muddy Creek on the north side of Holston River
(Wit): Stickley Dovelson, D.S; David Shelby, C.S.
Date: Oct. 23, 1782
Consideration: 50 shillings for every hundred acres
Amt of land: 300 acres
Location: Sullivan Co
Description: 300 acres on Muddy Creek on the north side of Holston River
By his Excellency Com'd J. Glasgow, Sec, Recorded June 8, 1786, rec'd in Register office the same day
                        Alex Martin
Reg. in Liver C. Page 161
George Vincen Rec
Regst: April 7, 1815

----

(515)   JOHN TIPTON   :
            TO   :   DEED OF CONVEYANCE
LAWRENCE SNAPP, JR. :

Date: Sept. 16, 1813
Consideration: Of a bond given by John Tipton on Sept. 14, 1798, and in compliance with sd bond and $1.00 in hand paid have given and granted to Lawrence Snapp, Jr. and his heirs forever
Amt of land: 70 acres
Location: Sullivan Co
Description: 70 acres on the waters of Muddy Creek
Wit: Jacob K. Snapp, John Snapp, Lawrence Snapp
Acknowledged: By John Tipton, Sullivan Co, Tn, Feb, 1815
Test: Mattw. Rhea, C.S.C, by Mattw. Rhea, D.C.
Regst: April 8, 1815

----

(516)   JOHN TIPTON   :
            TO   :   DEED OF CONVEYANCE
LAWRENCE SNAPP, JR. :

Date: Sept. 16, 1813
Consideration: Of a bond given by John Tipton on Nov. 13, 1798, $1.00 in hand paid
Amt of land: 49 acres
Location: Sullivan Co

Description: Granted to Lawrence Snapp 49 acres
Wit: Jacob K. Snapp, John Snapp, Lawrence Snapp
Acknowledged: By John Tipton, Sullivan Co, TN, Feb, 1815
Test: Mattw. Rhea, C.S.C, by Mattw. Rhea, D.C.
Regst: April 7, 1815

(Page)
(517)

JAMES ERWIN   :
        TO   :   DEED OF CONVEYANCE
DAVID ROLLIN   :

Date: Nov. 26, 1814
Consideration: $400.00
Amt of land: 540 acres
Location: Sullivan Co
Description: 1/6 part of 2 tracts of land both containing 540 acres more
or less in Sullivan Co on the north side of Holston River; one tract
containing 100 acres adj. John Erwin, Seth Porterfield, James Kerr, and
the old survey which David Erwin, dec'd, was possess of immediately before
his death, the old tract being 440 acres
Wit: Patrick Neil, William Hanley, John Jennings
Proven: By John Jennings, Patrick Neil, Sullivan Co, TN, Feb, 1815
Test: Mattw. Rhea, C.S.C, by Mattw. Rhea, D.C.
Regst: April 10, 1815

----

(519)   JOHN BIRCH   :
             TO   :   DEED OF CONVEYANCE
           DAVID GUIRE   :

Date: April 19, 1813
Consideration: $400.00 lawful money of this Commonwealth
Amt of land: 100 acres
Location: Sullivan Co
Description: 100 acres on the north side of the big Holston on a branch of
Reade(sic) Creek convinces to sd birch by John Kingston
Wit: thomas Hopkins, Michael Dickard, John Thompson
Proven: By John Thompson, Sullivan Co, TN, May, 1814
Test: Mattw. Rhea, C.S.C, by Mattw. Rhea, D.C.
Regst: April 11, 1815

----

(520)   GEORGE WEBB & DAVID LOONEY   :
             TO   :   DEED OF CONVEYANCE
           ELIJAH CROSS   :

Date: Nov. 14, 1814
Consideration: A valuable consideration
Amt of land: 600 acres
Location: Sullivan Co
Description: Bargain and sell unto Elijah Cross, his heirs and assigns their
undivided mority 2/3 or 1/3 each of certain tract of land in Sullivan Co
containing 400 acres; also one other tract of land adj. the above or ther
undivided mority there of 1/3 each, containing by estimation 200 acres
more or less

184

Wit: Abraham Looney, Elijah Cross, Joseph Wm Looney
Proven: By Elijah Cross, Joseph W. Looney, Sullivan Co, TN, Nov, 1814
Test: Mattw. Rhea, C.S.C, by Mattw. Rhea, D.C.
Regst: April 12, 1815

(Page)
(521)

ELISHA JAMES   :
      TO   :   DEED OF WARRANTY
JAMES HOGARD   :

Date: Feb. 16, 1813
Consideration: A valuable consideration
Amt of land: 100 acres
Location: Sullivan Co, TN
Description: 100 acres, except 1 1/2 of which within the bounds of tract
and hath been made use of as a place of religious worship
Wit: John Anderson
Acknowledged: By Elisha James, Sullivan Co, TN, Feb, 1813
Test: Mattw. Rhea, C.S.C
Regst: April 18, 1815

----

(522)

THOMAS HOPKINS   :
      TO   :   DEED OF WARRANTY
CHRISTOPHER JENNINGS :

Date: May 14, 1813
Consideration: $270.00
Amt of land: 33 acres
Location: Sullivan Co
Description: 33 acres on the south side of Holston River incl. the first
bottom below the mouth of Horse Creek and bounded by Boys Mountain and
the river
Wit: Jno. W. Vaughan, David Geyer
Proven: By John W. Vaughan, David Geyer, Sullivan Co, Tn, Nov, 1814
Test: Mattw. Rhea, C.S.C, by Mattw. Rhea, D.C
Regst: April 22, 1815

----

(523)

JACOB GRUBB   :
      TO   :   QUIT CLAIM DEED
ABRAHAM GRUBB   :

Date: Jan. 6, 1814
Consideration: A valuable consideration
Amt of land: 134 acres
Location: Sullivan Co, TN
Description: Quit claim to Abraham Grubb 134 acres incl. the plantation
where Abraham Grubb now lives
Wit: John Anderson, George Burkhart, John Thomas
Proven: By John Anderson, John Thomas, Sullivan Co,TN, May, 1814
Test: Mattw. Rhea, C.S.C, by Mattw. Rhea, D.C.
Regst: April 24, 1815

----

(523)

```
ABRAHAM GRUBB        :
        TO           :      QUIT CLAIM DEED
JACOB GRUBB          :
```

Date: Jan. 6, 1814
Consideration: A valuable consideration
Amt of land: 134 acres
Location: Sullivan Co, TN
Description: Quit claim to Jacob Grubb a tract of land containing 134 acres incl the plantation where Grubb now lives
Wit: John Andrson, George Burkhart, John Thomas
Proven: By John Anderson, John Thomas, Sullivan Co, Tn, May, 1814
Test: Mattw. Rhea, C.S.C, by Mattw. Rhea, D.C.
Regst: April 25, 1815

----

(524)

```
JAMES PHAGAN, Sheriff of    :
Sullivan County             :
        TO                  :      DEED OF CONVEYANCE
WILLIAM ROCKHOLD            :
```

Date: Nov. 19, 1808
        A writ of vendition exponas isued from the Court of Pleas and Qrtr Session for county aforesaid directing sd sheriff to expose to public auction 104 acres levied by the directions of John Buckles, guardian of Polly, Anne, & John McGinney, heirs of Andrew McGinney, dec'd, in the hands of John Buckles. In order that sheriff should cause to be made out of tract the sum of $121.772 mills purpose to satisfy judgment obtained by John Buckles against the sd Polly, Ane and John McGinney
Description: The aforesaid tract on the south side of Holston River adj. William Morrel and others, being duly executed by Sheriff and exposed to public auction to highest bidder; William Rockhold appeared at sd auction and bid $20.00 for land.
        I, James Phagan, Sheriff of Sullivan Co have sold and set over without any recover to me for performance in my office and assigns all claim to Rockhold
Acknowledged: By James Phagan, Sullivan Co, TN, Aug, 1814
Test: Mattw. Rhea, C.S.C, by Mattw. Rhea, D.C.
Regst: April 26, 1815

----

(525)

```
STATE OF TENNESSEE   :
ARCHIBALD ROANE      :      LAND GRANT
        TO           :      NO. 3216
JOHN CARTER Heirs    :
```

Date: July 13, 1812
Consideration: An entry made in the surveyor's office of the 6th District of No. 1370, dated July 13, 1812, founded on a warranty of No. 2855, issued by Archibald Roane to John Carter, heirs for 640 acres of land dated Nov. 20, 1810; 10 acres of which are assigned to Wallace Willoughby and the survey by Willoughby to George Burkhart and Jacob Booker
Description: Granted by TN to George Burkhart and Jacob Booker 10 acres on both sides of Sinking Creek

Seal affixed at Nashville Nov, 5, 1814, By Gov. Willie Blount, W.G. Blount,
Sec, Recorded Nov. 5, 1814

Edw. Scott, Reg of E TN

May 5, 1815, rec'd tax on within grant
Test: Mattw. Rhea, C.S.C, by Mattw. Rhea, D.C.
Regst: May 5, 1815

(Page)
(525)   STATE OF TENNESSEE   :
         ARCHIBALD ROANE   :   LAND GRANT
                TO   :   NO. 3217
         JOHN CARTER, Heirs   :

Date: July 13, 1812
Consideration: An entry made in the surveyor's office of the 6th District
of No. 1368, dated July 13, 1812, founded on a warranty of No. 2855,
issued by Archibald Roane to John Carter, heirs for 640 acres dated Nov.
20, 1810; 50 acres of which are assigned to Beorge Burkhart, the enterer
Description: Granted by TN to George Burkhart 50 acres on the waters of
Sinking Creek
Seal to be affixed at Nashville, Nov. 5, 1814, by Gov. Willie Blount, W.G.
Blount, Sec, Recorded Nov. 5, 1814

Edw. Scott, Reg of E TN

May 5, 1815, rec'd tax on within grant
Test: Mattw. Rhea, C.S.C, by Mattw. Rhea, D.C.
Regst: May 5, 1815

----

(526)   JOHN WALTER*   :
                TO   :   DEED OF WARRANTY
         WALTER JAMES   :

Date: Aug. 8, 1814
Consideration: $100.00
Amt of land: 23 acres
Location: Sullivan Co, TN
Description: 23 acres being part of a tract where Waller* now lives
Wit: Robert Easley, John Isley
Proven: By Robert Easley, Sullivan Co, TN, Aug, 1814
Test: Mattw. Rhea, C.S.C, by Mattw. Rhea, D.C.
Regst: May 9, 1815

(*Note: Name spelled both ways)

(527)   JOHN HITE   :
                TO   :   DEED OF WARRANTY
         SAMUEL STUCKLER   :

Date: Feb. 15, 1813
Consideration: $225.00
Amt of land: 43 acres
Location: Sullivan Co
Description: (43 acres) on south side of Holston River originally granted to
Daniel Allen

Wit: Jacob Slaughter, Frederick Brandstaller, Samuel Code
Proven: By Frederick Brandstaller, Samuel Code, Sullivan Co, TN, Feb, 1813
Test: Mattw. Rhea, C.S.C
Regst: May 9, 1815

(Page)
(528)   JOHN HITE   :
                      TO   :   DEED OF WARRANTY
               SAMUEL STRICKLER   :

               Date: Feb. 15, 1813
               Consideration: $225.00
               Amt of land: 50 acres
               Location: Sullivan Co, TN
               Description: 50 acres on south side of HolstonRiver part of the Sugar Tree
               Valley
               Wit: Jacob Slaughter, Frederick Brandstaller, Samuel Code
               Proven: Frederick Brandstaller, Samuel Code, Sullivan Co, TN, Feb, 1813
               Test: Mattw. Rhea, C.S.C.
               Regst: May 10, 1815

               ----

(528)   HENRY MAUCK*   :
                      TO   :   DEED OF WRRANTY
               GEORGE WILLYERAD   :

               Date: May 15, 1815
               Consideration: $66.66
               Amt of land: 27 acres
               Location: Sullivan Co, TN
               Description: 27 acres in Sullivan Co, TN
               Wit: Samuel Looney, John Childress
               Proven: By Henry Mauk*, Sullivan Co, TN, May, 1815
               Test: Mattw. Rhea, C.S.C, by Mattw. Rhea, D.C.
               Regst: May 15, 1815

(*Note: Name spelled both ways)

(529)   JAMES KEER   :
                      TO   :   DEED OF WARRANTY
               WILLIAM SNODGRASS   :

               Date: May 16, 1815
               Consideration: $800.00
               Amt of land: 202 acres
               Location: Sullivan Co
               Description: A tract of land in county aforesaid
               (Proven): Sullivan Co, Tn May, 1815
               Test: Mattw. Rhea, C.S.C, by Mattw. Rhea, D.C.
               Regst: May 18, 1815

               ----

(530)   JOHN TIPTON   :
                      TO   :   DEED OF WARRANTY
               ELIJAH GREENWAY   :

Date: June 29, 1813
Consideration: A valuable consideration
Amt of land: 1/2 acre
Location: Town of Blountville, Sullivan Co
Description: A lot of land, No. 37, in Blountville containing 1/2 acre
Wit: Henry Pecktol, John Anderson
Acknowledged: By John Tipton, Sullivan Co, TN, Nov, 1814
Test: Mattw. Rhea, C.S.C, by Mattw. Rhea, D.C.
Regst: May 19, 1815

(Page)
(531)   JOHN ISLEY   :
               TO   :   DEED OF WARRANTY
           JACOB DUK*   :

Date: April 15, 1815
Consideration: $32.00 good and lawful money of the U.S.
Amt of land: Not stated
Location: Sullivan Co, TN
Description: A tract of land adj. Duk*, William Canale
Wit: Wm Snodgrass, Robert Johnson
Proven: By William Snodgrass, Robert Johnson, Sullivan Co, TN, May, 1815
Test: Mattw. Rhea, C.S.C, by Mattw. Rhea, D.C.
Regst: May 22, 1815

(*Note: Name could possible be Duke)

(531)   JOHN COLLINS   :
               TO   :   DEED OF CONVEYANCE
           JACOB DUK*   :

Date: April 15, 1815
Consideration: $32.00 good and lawful money of the U.S.
Amt of land: Not stated
Location: Sullivan Co, TN
Description: A tract of land adj. land of sd Duk* and others
Wit: George Willhelen, Jacob Duk*
Proven: By George Willhelen, Jacob Duk*, Sullivan Co, TN, May, 1815
Test: Mattw. Rhea, C.S.C, by Mattw. Rhea, D.C.
Regst: May 22, 1815

(*Note: Name could possible be Duke)

(532)   ELIZABETH ISLEY   :
               TO   :   DEED OF CONVEYANCE
           JACOB DUK*   :

Date: April 15, 1815
Consideration: $32.00 good and lawful money of the U.S.
Amt of land: Not stated
Location: Sullivan Co, TN
Description: A tract of land adj. Duk*, William Canale, and others
Wit: George Willhelen, Jacob Duk*

199

Proven: By George Willhelen, Jacob Duk*, Sullivan Co, TN, May, 1815
Test: Mattw. Rhea, C.S.C, by Mattw. Rhea, D.C.
Regst: May 22, 1815

(Page)
(532)

STATE OF TENNESSEE	:	
ARCHIBALD ROANE	:	LAND GRANT
TO	:	NO. 3215
JOHN CARTER, Heirs	:	

Date: July 1, 1813
Consideration: An entry made in the surveyor's office of the 6th District
of No. 1753, dated July 1, 1813, founded on a warrant of No. 2855, issued
by Archibald Roane to John Carter, heirs for 640 acres dated Nov. 20,
1810; 20* acres of which are assigned to Francis Hanely, the enterer
Description: Granted by TN to Francis Hanley 3* acres in Sullivan Co
Seal affixed at Nashville, Nov, 5, 1814, by Gov. Willie Blount, W.G. Blount,
Sec, Recorded Nov. 5, 1814

Edw. Scott, Reg of E TN
May 23, 1815, rec'd tax on within grant
Test: Mattw. Rhea, C.S.C, by Mattw. Rhea, D.C.
Regst: May 23, 1815

(*Note: Both amounts given)

(533)

BENJAMIN KELLY	:	
TO	:	DEED OF WARRANTY
JOHN GIBSON	:	

Date: Jan. 4, 1815
Consideration: $200.00
Amt of land: 1/4 acre
Location: Sullivan Co, Blountville
Description: A lot, No. 36, containing 1/4 acre in Blountville on the south
side of the main street, where Kelly now lives
Wit: W. Rockhold, Matthew Rhea
Proven: By William Rockhold, Matthew Rhea, Sullivan Co, Tn, May, 1815
Test: Mattw. Rhea, C.S.C, by Mattw. Rhea, D.C.
Regst: May 23, 1815

----

(534)

NICHOLAS FAIN	:	
TO	:	BILL OF SALE
MARY NICELY	:	

Date: Feb. 17, 1815
Consideration: $450.00
Description: A male slave named Joshua abt 30 yrs of age
Wit: George Keys, Joseph McLin
Proven: By George Keys, Joseph McLin
Test: Mattw. Rhea, C.S.C, by Mattw. Rhea, D.C.
Regst: May 24, 1815

190

JOHN TIPTON   :
        TO   :   DEED OF WARRANTY
JOHN GIFFORD   :

Date: March 10, 1815
Consideration: $300.00
Amt of land: 1/4 acre
Location: Sullivan Co, TN
Description: A lot in Blountville, containing 1/4 acre
Acknowledged: By John Tipton, Sullivan Co, Tn, May, 1815
Test: Mattw. Rhea, C.S.C, by Mattw Rhea, D.C.
Regst: May 25, 1815

----

(535)   JAMES PHAGAN, High Sheriff :
          of Sullivan County   :
                  TO   :   (No Deed given)
          WILLIAM SNODGRASS, by   :
          His agent, David Yearsley   :

Date: May 18, 1810
Consideration: $500.00
Amt of land: 92 acres
Purpose: Andrew Campbell assignes(sic) recovered a judgment before Elisha
Harbor, J.P. against John Richardson for $100 with cost of $3.90. Harbor
places the same in the hands of John Pryor, acting constable commanding
Pryor to make the sum of $100 with interest thereon by levying on
tenaments and lands of John Richardson. In obedience to which Pryor
levied on property of Richardson, Aug. 28, 1811. Sd execution returned to
the Court of Pleas and Qrtr Session of Sullivan Co, ordered Sheriff to
sale lands and tenaments of Richardson - Sold Feb. 15, 1812
Signed: James Phagan, High Sheriff of Sullivan Co
Acknowledged: By James Phagan, Sullivan Co, TN, May, 1815
Test: Mattw. Rhea, C.S.C, by Mattw. Rhea, D.C.
Regst: May 23, 1815

----

(536)   GEORGE WEAVER   :
                TO   :   DEED OF WARRANTY
          FRANCES HANLEY   :

Date: Sept. 20, 1814
Consideration: $250.00
Amt of land: 83 acres
Location: Sullivan Co, TN
Description: 83 acres in Sullivan Co
Wit: James Phagan, Sam L. Brownlow, Mike Hickman
Proven: By James Phagan, Samuel L. Brownlow, Sullivan Co, TN, Nov, 1814
Test: Mattw. Rhea, C.S.C, by Mattw. Rhea, D.C.
Regst: May 24, 1815

----

(536)   ANDREW CROCKET   :
                TO   :   DEED OF WARRANTY
          GEORGE GREENWAY   :

Date: Nov. 9, 1814
Consideration: $150.00 current money of TN
Amt of land: 1 house and lot and 1/4 acre
Location: Sullivan Co
Description: One house and lot, No. 281, in Middle Town being part of the tract Samuel McCorkle lived on
Wit: James Crockett, Elizabeth Crockett
Acknowledged: By Andrew Crockett, Sullivan Co, TN, Nov, 1814
Test: Mattw. Rhea, C.S.C, by Mattw. Rhea, D.C.
Regst: May 25, 1815

(Page)
(537)

THOMAS McCHESNEY	:	
TO	:	DEED OF WARRANTY
JOHN SHARP	:	

Date: Feb. 8, 1815
Consideration: $833.00
Amt of land: 197 acres
Location: Sullivan Co
Description: 197 acres together with another tract adj the same containing 43 acres more or less
Wit: Jonathan King, Ireson Longacre, William King
Proven: By Ireson Longacre, William King, Sullivan Co, TN, May, 1815
Test: Mattw. Rhea, C.S.C, by Mattw. Rhea, D.C.
Regt: May 25, 1815

----

(538)

DAVID PROFFIT, Executor of	:	
James Proffit, Dec'd.	:	
TO	:	DEED OF WARRANTY
DANIEL SIMMERMON	:	

Date: May 16, 1815
Consideration: A valuable consideration
Amt of land: 97 acres
Location: Sullivan Co
Description: 97 acres on the south side of Holston River
Wit: John Anderson
Acknowledged: By David Proffit, Sullivan Co, TN, May, 1815
Test: Mattw. Rhea, C.S.C, by Mattw. Rhea, D.C.
Regt: (No date given)

----

(539)

JOHN TIPTON	:	
TO	:	DEED OF WARRANTY
JOSEPH CARPER	:	

Date: May 19, 1815
Consideration: $20.00
Amt of land: 3/4 acres, 15* sq poles
Location: Sullivan Co, TN
Description: 3/4 acres and 1* sq pole in Sullivan Co
(Wit): (No names given)

192

Acknowledged: By John Tipton, Sullivan Co, TN, May, 1815
Test: Mattw. Rhea, C.S.C, by Mattw. Rhea, D.C.
Regst: May 25, 1815

(Page)
(539) JACOB LADY   :
          TO   :   DEED OF WARRANTY
JOHN & WILLIAM LADY :

Date: Feb. 22, 1814
Consideration: A valuable consideration
Amt of land: 74 acres
Location: Sullivan Co, TN
Description: 74 acres in Sullivan Co, TN
Wit: John Andrson, Ambrose Gaines, Thomas Cox, Joseph M. Brownlow
Proven: By John Anderson, Thomas Cox, Sullivan Co, TN, May, 1814
Test: Mattw. Rhea, C.S.C, by Mattw. Rhea, D.C.
Regst: May 30, 1815

----

(540)   JAMES HUGHES   :
          TO   :   DEED OF WARRANTY
ABRAHAM McCLELLAN   :

Date: May 16, 1815
Consideration: $300.00
Amt of land: 100 acres
Location: Sullivan Co
Description: 100 acres on White Top Creek in Sullivan Co
(Proven): Sullivan Co, TN, May, 1815
Test: Mattw. Rhea, C.S.C, by Mattw. Rhea, D.C.
Regt: May 30, 1815

----

(541)   DAVID STEEL   :
          TO   :   DEED OF CONVEYANCE
WILLIAM COWAN   :

Date: April 8, 1815
Consideration: $50.00
Amt of land: 28 acres
Location: Sullivan Co
Description: 28 acres in the county aforesaid
Wit: Simmon Roberts, John Anderson
Proven: By Simmon Roberts, John Anderson
Test: Mattw. Rhea, C.S.C, by Mattw. Rhea, D.C.
Regst: June 8, 1815

----

(541)   ANDREW GREER   :
          TO   :   DEED OF WARRANTY
HENRY HARKLEROAD, JR. & :
JACOB SENK(sic)   :

Date: April 29, 1815

193

Consideration: $250.00
Amt of land: 50 acres
Location: Sullivan Co, TN
Description: 50 acres in Sullivan Co, TN
Wit: Hen Harkleroad, Martin Harkleroad, John Garrett
Proven: By Henry and Martin Harkleroad, Sullivan Co, TN, May, 1815
Test: Mattw. Rhea, C.S.C, by Mattw. Rhea, D.C.
Regst: June 8, 1815

(Page)
(542)

JAMES HUGHES	:	
TO	:	DEED OF WARRANTY
JAMES GREGG	:	

Date: March 20, 1815
Consideration: $333.00
Amt of land: 100 acres
Location: Sullivan Co
Description: 100 acres between Holston and Watauga Rivers, being part of
a tract granted to James Gregg
Wit: Michael Owen, Abrhama McClellan
Acknowledged: By James Hughes, Sullivan Co, TN, May, 1815
Test: Mattw. Rhea, C.S.C, by Mattw. Rhea, D.C.
Regst: June 8, 1815

----

(543)

ROBERT RHEA	:	
TO	:	QUIT CLAIM DEED
JOHN ANDRSON	:	

Date: Jan. 5, 1814
Consideration: A valuable consideration
Amt of land: 250 acres
Location: Sullivan Co, TN
Description: Quit claimed to John Anderson 250 acres in county and state
aforesaid; being the same tract where William Anderson, dec'd, formerly
lived on the Island Road
Wit: Joseph Rhea, Lawrence Sanpp
Acknowledged: By Robert Rhea, Sullivan Co, TN, May, 1815
Test: Mattw. Rhea, C.S.C, by Mattw. Rhea, D.C.
Regst: June 8, 1815

----

(544)

JOHN TIPTON	:	
TO	:	DEED OF CONVEYANCE
MATTHEW RHEA, JR.	:	

Date: May 16, 1815
Consideration: A valuable consideration
Amt of land: Not stated
Location: Town of Blountville, Sullivan Co
Description: A lot, No. (not given), of land in Blountville
(Wit): (No names given)

Acknowledged: By John Tipton, Sullivan Co, Tn, May, 1815
Test: Mattw. Rhea, C.S.C
Regst: June 9, 1815

BENJAMIN WHITE   :
                TO   :   DEED OF WARRNTY
      JACOB AKERT   :

Date: Jan. 2, 1815
Consideration: $1,333.33
Amt of land: 230 acres
Location: Sullivan Co, TN
Description: Two tracts on the waters of Beaver Creek; one containing 150
acres which was conveyed to White by indenture dated March 27, 1802; the
other containing 80 acres conveyed to White dated same as above
Wit: George Burkhart, Jacob Booker, Nathan Willett
Proven: By George Burkhart, Jacob Booker, Sullivan Co, TN, May, 1815
Test: Mattw. Rhea, C.S.C, by Mattw. Rhea, D.C.
Regst: June 9, 1815

197

204